PAVILIONS OF PLENTY

PAVILIONS OF PLENTY

Exhibiting American Culture Abroad in the 1950s

ROBERT H. HADDOW

Smithsonian Institution Press
Washington and London

Copy editor: Joanne S. Ainsworth
Production editor: Duke Johns
Designer: Linda McKnight

Library of Congress Cataloging-in-Publication Data
Haddow, Robert H.
Pavilions of plenty : exhibiting American culture abroad in the 1950s / Robert H. Haddow.
p. cm.
Includes bibliographical references and index.
ISBN 1-56098-705-7 (alk. paper)
1. Trade shows—United States—History—20th century. 2. United States—Cultural policy. 3. United States—Relations—Foreign countries. I. Title.
T395.5.U6H33 1997
306'.0973'09045—dc20 96-43926

British Library Cataloguing-in-Publication Data is available

Manufactured in the United States of America
04 03 02 01 00 99 98 97 5 4 3 2 1

∞ The paper used in this publication meets the minimum requirements of the American National Standard for Information Sciences—Permanence of Paper for Printed Library Materials ANSI Z39.48-1984.

To Moe and Sadie Rose Clio

Contents

Acknowledgments

Much of this book is derived from primary sources in public libraries and archives, so first of all I would like to thank the librarians and archivists who make these sources comprehensible. Dwight E. Strandberg at the Dwight D. Eisenhower Library and Martin Manning at the United States Information Agency, Historical Collections, worked especially hard on my behalf. A few scholars allowed me to read their unpublished manuscripts bearing upon crucial topics: Robert Rydell, professor of history at Montana State University, sent me a rough draft of his study on the 1958 Brussels World's Fair long before it appeared in print, which indicated where the most important records of that fair were located. Daniel Horowitz sent me his manuscript on David Potter, and Charles McGovern urged me to investigate the Advertising Council to see if there was any relationship between that organization, trade fairs, and the Eisenhower administration.

Charles McGovern served as my principal adviser during a year as a Smithsonian predoctoral fellow at the National Museum of American History. He read early drafts of nearly every chapter and offered critical, time-consuming commentary. Many of his colleagues at the museum also contributed their time and expertise to this project, notably William Bird Jr., Shelly Foote, Rodris Roth, and Priscilla Wood. Shelly Foote and Priscilla Wood allowed me to peruse their back issues of *Vogue* and tried to explain some of the finer points of the fashion industry to me; I hope I haven't disappointed them too much.

Many people at the Smithsonian took time to read drafts of my chapters, listen to my questions, and offer advice. I would especially like to thank Margaret Cogswell, from the National Museum of American Art, a staff member at the American Pavilion at the 1958 Brussels World's Fair, for her patience and guidance. Although she often disagreed with my conclusions she offered insightful commentary on the personalities of the 1950s and helped me to locate crucial documents relating to the art exhibition in the 1958 American Pavilion, the most important of which was her own correspondence with many of the principal administrators. I would also like to thank Lois Fink for inviting me to deliver a paper at the National Museum of American Art on the Children's Creative Center and for pointing out the influence of John Dewey on American education.

Many scholars, museum curators, exhibit designers and former participants in the fairs mentioned in this project took an interest in my work, and some of them provided me with primary documents from their own collections. Charles H. Clarke, George Gardner, Lois Lord, Arthur Pulos, and Richard Sullivan were especially generous in this regard. I would also like to thank Frances F. Davant and Jack Masey for their insights and opinions and Ernie Jacks, professor emeritus of architecture at the University of Arkansas and a former colleague of Edward Durell Stone, who read my chapter on the construction of the 1958 American Pavilion and offered critical comments. Jacks tirelessly assisted my attempts to describe the first important suspension structures, helped me obtain photographs and blueprints of the American Pavilion, and provided me with the addresses of his former co-workers in the Stone office.

Mark Hirsch helped structure the manuscript, and Joanne S. Ainsworth provided superb editorial assistance. My friends and family in Minneapolis have graciously contributed their talents: Carter Meland read drafts of the concluding chapter, and Jim Berg provided me with photographs. Finally, none of this work would have been possible without the generous support of Dr. Susan Haddow, who has been a friend on research trips as well as a hardworking and generous spouse.

Abbreviations

AAA	Archives of American Art
AFA	American Federation of Arts
AFL-CIO	American Federation of Labor–Congress of Industrial Organizations
AIA	American Institute of Architects
CED	Committee for Economic Development
CENIS	Center for International Studies, Massachusetts Institute of Technology
CIA	Central Intelligence Agency
DDE	Dwight D. Eisenhower Library, Abilene, Kansas
ECA	Economic Cooperation Administration
IBEC	International Basic Economy Corporation
IBM	International Business Machines Corporation
ICA	International Cooperation Agency
MIT	Massachusetts Institute of Technology
MOMA	Museum of Modern Art, New York
NATO	North Atlantic Treaty Organization
OEEC	Organization of European Economic Cooperation
OFB	Office of Foreign Buildings Operations, U.S. Department of State
RCA	Radio Corporation of America
UN	United Nations
USIA	United States Information Agency
USIS	United States Information Service
VOA	Voice of America
WPA	Works Progress Administration

Introduction

The new military and trade alliances that the United States entered into after World War II made American culture into a vastly more exotic and far-flung network of cultural contacts than it had been at any other time in the past. Containing the Soviets required military bases in strategic locations and encouraged trade with all the nations bordering the USSR.

Internationalism was promoted by the interests of large corporations and, more generally, the allure of a world becoming smaller through trade, travel, and the new communication technologies. Americans did not just try to bring the world home—they also attempted to Americanize other nations. At times the administration of President Dwight D. Eisenhower seemed convinced that the United States would not survive unless the domestic ideal then in force in the nation could be successfully exported to the rest of the world, especially to those countries that teetered on the edge of becoming Soviet satellites. Foreign-policy makers developed a two-pronged approach that used both economics (or *culture* in the broadest sense of the term) and military power. In strategic countries such as Germany and Japan the economic front sustained war-weakened industry, rebuilt infrastructure, and then focused on getting cheap, mass-produced goods into the hands of the people. There were disagreements among politicians and corporate leaders, between activists and conservatives, as to which approach worked best—developmental aid and corporate expansion or just containment—but the notion that the United States had a sacred mission, or at least an obligation, to export freedom, democracy, and capitalism was rarely questioned during the Eisenhower years.[1]

Trade fairs, international exhibitions, and the American Pavilion at the 1958 Brussels World's Fair showcased an international liberal capitalist economy dominated by Americans. These exhibitions provided opportunities to place consumer products into narratives of larger import, helped create a dazzling image of the consumer, and fueled the desire for modern products. U.S. administrators and corporate donors hoped that their ideal of progress and material abundance would encourage people of other nations to adopt American business methods and open their economies to American companies.

At international trade fairs and world's fairs during the cold war, an aggressive group of volunteers and contractors advanced the notion that a global consumer economy on the U.S. model was the only effective way of preserving civilization from the clutches of Communist tyranny. This group was drawn from the corporate community, the art world, the industrial design profession, the advertising world, and their counterparts in government—the Department of Commerce, the United States Information Agency (USIA), and the office of the presidency.

Free trade and international corporations are hardly an American invention. Expansion-minded merchants from the world's industrial nations formed their very own "businessmen's league of nations" in the years just before World War I: the International Chamber of Commerce. These self-styled "merchants of peace" were followers of Adam Smith and his belief that the forces of industry and trade should be free to operate in accordance with the "natural" economic law of supply and demand. They believed that economic expansion, if not allowed to proceed in a rational manner, inevitably took the form of colonialism, or worse, war. In his history of the International Chamber of Commerce, George L. Ridgeway notes, "The First World War proved to be a catastrophic demonstration of the need to develop world-wide responsibility in political, economic, and social fields. Leading businessmen from the five Allied countries who believed in the basic concept of international trade sought to meet this challenge in the sphere of business by establishing a new world institution free of government control."[2] But the Great

Depression taught business leaders, in the United States at least, that even if they despised government they would have to try to influence it. By necessity, members of the National Association of Manufacturers, Rotary clubs, the International Chamber of Commerce, and newly formed groups such as the Business Council—an assembly of sixty or so CEOs formed in 1933 to lobby Congress and the Roosevelt administration on matters relating to labor policies—became activists during the New Deal.[3] And businessmen did not limit their efforts to Capitol Hill. The world's fairs of the interwar years in Chicago, New York, and San Francisco proved powerful methods of getting the opinions and visions of corporate leadership out in front of the public, as did advertisements, Hollywood movies, museums, and department stores.[4]

International exhibitions provided excellent opportunities for businessmen to popularize their gospel of free trade, one-worldism, and the benevolent guidance of corporate leadership. The historian Robert Rydell writes of an "exhibition culture" that had become full blown by the turn of the century, with leadership sharing acquired skills and themes across national and economic boundaries, promoting an ever-widening consensus of support for business culture and the culture of material abundance. At Paris (1867, 1889, 1925, 1931, and 1937); Buffalo (1901); New Orleans (1915); Chicago (1893, 1933); and New York (1939–40) power brokers displayed their wealth within narratives of progress and in educational displays promising the masses universal prosperity. During the depression this message was a powerful counterweight to the New Deal claim that good government and social planning were the only routes to prosperity. At world's fairs, corporations were able to exhibit private versions of benevolent control and development, keeping before the public dramatic visions of utopian cities developed by enlightened self-interest—socially responsible corporate leadership that rendered excessive regulation obsolete. Corporate exhibits, such as General Motors's *Futurama* at the 1939–40 New York World's Fair, put before the people tangible examples of a prosperous, responsible capitalism—in this case a planned city with superhighways—in the belief that popular support would follow glamorous design and visionary planning.[5]

As World War II came to an end, fraternal business organizations pulled together in order to ensure a renewed prosperity and to counter the perceived threat to business posed by both domestic New Deal programs and Soviet competition. Certain individuals and associations worked especially hard to form a rapprochement between government and industry outside of the existing New Deal model. Paul G. Hoffman of the Studebaker Company, vice chairman of the Business Council, formed the Committee for Economic Development (CED) with William Benton of the Benton and Bowles advertising agency, among others, in order to help advise business and government regarding reconversion to peacetime. The CED was closely allied with the Business Council and the Department of Commerce under W. Averell Harriman, establishing "a national network of volunteers dedicated to the twin principles of decentralization and voluntarism." If a group of businessmen, for example, in a local chamber of commerce, Kiwanis Club, Rotary organization, or chapter of the National Association of Manufacturers attempted to shape the postwar economy in their particular area, the CED's regional and national offices "publicized their efforts, provided advice, and applauded heartily when problems were seriously addressed." The two thousand-plus members of the CED assisted postwar planning groups scattered throughout the American heartland who were motivated by the concern that depression would follow the war, destroying "the marketplace capitalist system."[6] The Advertising Council, a trade group formed during World War II to help sell war bonds and promote victory gardens, salvage campaigns, and perform similarly patriotic activities, provided crucial publicity for the business community. The historian Robert Griffith explains that whereas the CED was concerned with the *manufacture* of information in the public interest, the Advertising Council, which never demobilized after the war, deciding to help fight communism and sponsor public service campaigns, was concerned with its mass distribution.[7]

Hope of reestablishing an international economic system after World War II was threatened primarily by the power of the American economy in relation to the rest of the world and by the Soviet Union's growing competition for resources and markets. Corporate leaders who had learned how to work with the U.S. government during the New Deal, despite their dislike of regulation, entered into partnership with government in order to "maintain American economic, military, and political interests in strategic parts of the globe."[8] When Truman needed support for the Marshall Plan, for example, he asked the former Business Council chairman, W. Averell Harriman, to help expedite government-industry collaboration among conservative businessmen. Harriman later became the foreign representative of the Economic Cooperation Administration (ECA), the economic and technical arm of the Marshall Plan, and Paul Hoffman became the head of the ECA's domestic office.

The U.S. economic system emerged from World War II a highly developed consumer society in which the style and glamour of objects were becoming as important as their availability. Glamour as symbolized by the streamlined look in the 1930s and 1940s was developed by the new industrial designers: Russel Wright, Raymond Loewy, Norman Bel Geddes, and Walter Dorwin Teague. In the United States this superficial modernism was enlivened by the ethics of the Bauhaus refugees, notably Walter Gropius and László Moholy-Nagy, part of the emigration of artistic and architectural talent from fascist Europe. Walter Gropius had established the Bauhaus in Germany "to create cultural integration—more that just industrial design—a blend of arts and humanities." For Moholy-Nagy, who was the driving force behind the transplantation of the Bauhaus to Chicago, design and architecture were a method of cultural reform, a way of creating "the total man."[9] In the 1950s, streamlined glamour and irrepressible bursts of American-style opulence would be accompanied by the holistic, organic modernism that was a blend of Bauhaus moralizing and the necessarily stripped-down look of inexpensive, mass-produced housing and consumer products. Whatever its virtues, modernism's so-called democratic spirit and progressive, antitraditional aesthetic made it the favorite design choice at international exhibitions during the cold war.

The cultural reform movement inspired by the Bauhaus might not have taken hold in the United States except that it meshed with a tradition of philanthropy carried on by tycoons like Nelson Rockefeller of Standard Oil, and Chicago's Walter Paepke, CEO of the Container Corporation of America. More important, the idea that moral reform could be the core project of a business enterprise appealed to businessmen like Henry Luce, CEO of Time Inc., who had been reared with the social gospel. Luce's parents were missionaries; he was born while the family was winning souls in China. These businessmen were attracted to the idea of improving their commercial empires while simultaneously improving social welfare through a benevolent, global capitalism. To these ends Rockefeller supported fledgling industries in the Third World; Luce used his publishing empire to help reform business culture and celebrate consumerism; Walter Paepke helped Moholy-Nagy revive the Bauhaus in Chicago in order to unite the humanities with commerce.

Paepke launched his crusade of international cultural reform by sponsoring a Goethe bicentennial celebration in 1947. As the historian James Sloan Allen explains in *The Romance of Commerce and Culture,* Paepke and Robert M. Hutchins from the University of Chicago became the nucleus of a midwestern movement intent on expanding the humanist values of Goethe into a "celebration of the universal man."[10] Albert Schweitzer was invited to be the keynote speaker of the Goethe festival, and Paepke hoped the conference would help "reunite a shattered Western culture."[11] The Voice of America broadcast the proceedings of the festival around the world, in six languages, providing a contrast, or counter, to a similar festival in East Germany celebrating Goethe as an early exponent of "world communism." The Chicago speakers were aware of the fact that their festival played a role in the global struggle between democracy and communism. One of the guest speakers fired off the opening salvos in what the historian Christopher Lasch has called the "cultural cold war" by asserting that "free men in a free meeting will . . . refute the Red line."[12]

The Goethe festival was a success, inspiring an annual conference on Paepke's land in Colorado. Paepke called his retreat the "Aspen Institute" and invited CEOs, industrial designers, and cultural figures to find common ground in the idyllic conference setting. At Aspen, businessmen were encouraged to put their troubles aside and focus on the "universal" truths presented by guest speakers. Aspen was both unique and typical of its time. A similar retreat was created by Eisenhower while he was president of Columbia University in the late 1940s. Eisenhower was alarmed by the lack of respect for what he considered to be the sterling virtues of the American way of life. His was a Norman Rockwell America, a moral nation with recognizable, three-dimensional heroes, and the academic "fuzziness" of Columbia vexed him.[13] Guided by his friends Philip Reed, chairman of General Electric; Philip Young, dean of the Columbia Business School; and the wide assortment of corporate leaders he was introduced to after leaving the military, Eisenhower planned the American Assembly as a way of encouraging within the corporate and academic spheres the kind of practical thinking and esprit de corps that made the armed forces effective. The historian Blanche Wiesen Cook writes that Eisenhower was concerned about the businessman's limited horizons: "Most businessmen are so busy meeting payrolls and paying taxes that they have little chance for study and contemplation."[14] In November 1950, Paepke contacted Eisenhower to compare notes on their respective retreats.[15] Indeed, both men were trying to accomplish essentially the same thing: a merging of cultural, academic, and corporate concerns into a crusade for international peace and prosperity. The Aspen Institute and the American Assembly retreats were aimed at reconciling American foreign policy with a feel-good humanism. Aspen promulgated the fuzzy "universals," whereas the American Assembly focused upon strategy, facts, and figures. The retreats had the additional benefit of providing a pool of corporate and aesthetic talent for the kind of public-private cooperation that Eisenhower would use during his presidency.

After his stint at Columbia, Eisenhower became the supreme commander of the North Atlantic Treaty Organization (NATO) forces and as such challenged isolationist opposition to Truman's foreign policy. American isolationists, led by the Republican Robert A. Taft, attacked the "traps, the costs, and the haggling associated with a complicated alliance system that involved impoverished, reluctant, and unstable nations."[16] But Eisenhower also had to tackle the protectionists and isolationists of Europe; his task was to guide West Germany into the Atlantic alliance while simultaneously persuading the former enemies of Germany that the return of American troops was solely to guarantee the economic restoration and stability of

Europe." Eisenhower's internationalist reputation and his intentions for Europe, at least, were clearly defined long before he became the chief executive. It was Eisenhower's skill as an internationalist that led liberal businessmen such as Paul Hoffman, Henry Luce, and Nelson Rockefeller to campaign vigorously in his behalf.

Nelson Rockefeller, whose efforts to help create "a world economic policy based on government-business cooperation" had also been supported by President Franklin D. Roosevelt and Truman, was one of the more influential businessmen willing to assist Eisenhower (especially up through 1955).[17] Rockefeller helped create the Department of Health, Education, and Welfare, which consolidated programs like social security into a new cabinet post. After resigning from the department in 1954, Rockefeller moved into offices in the White House and became the special assistant to the president for foreign affairs. He immediately formed a planning group to advise Eisenhower on the integration of economic and psychological factors in foreign policy.[18] Rockefeller was a model of the activist-businessman that Ike used to advantage, especially within the trade fair program and the technical-assistance programs, which needed strong involvement from the private sector in order to be successful.

In 1942 Rockefeller had been appointed by Roosevelt to run the State Department's Office of Inter-American Affairs, and through that office he constructed links between industry and government with Paul Hoffman and other liberal businessmen. Their aim was to sustain Latin America during World War II and help replace former economic ties between Latin America and Germany with new alliances controlled by the United States. After World War II, in 1946, Rockefeller created the privately held International Basic Economy Corporation (IBEC) to carry out extensive economic reforms in Latin America with the hope that U.S. government support would follow. Only the authority of the U.S. government could maintain stable international relations; only stability ensured prosperity and a return on long-term investment. Members of the U.S. section of the International Chamber of Commerce, the National Association of Manufacturers, and the Advertising Council hoped for a similar partnership with government. Essentially, businessmen wanted to "use the government's resources and services" but remain free from government regulations.[19]

Nelson Rockefeller learned how to cultivate popular support in Latin America while on assignment for Standard Oil (the family business) and its subsidiaries. Through Standard Oil and IBEC he built schools, health facilities, new roads, supermarkets, and related infrastructure projects near the oil company's holdings. IBEC extended the simple reform of company towns to include national economic planning in Venezuela and Brazil. Rockefeller's efforts were publicized as part of the new "enlightened capitalism" being adopted by U.S. entrepreneurs. The financial magazine *Barron's* quipped that Rockefeller had created his own "Point Four Program," referring to the technical-assistance program announced by President Truman in his inaugural address.[20]

IBEC pioneered social engineering in Mexico, Brazil, Venezuela, the Caribbean, and Italy, and through its new method of mass-producing concrete houses, became one of the largest low-cost home builders in Puerto Rico and Florida. In 1949 the corporation introduced modern retailing into Venezuela with a self-service supermarket called Todos (Everything), featuring canned and frozen foods, neon lighting, and pushcarts. Todos was staffed by the U.S.-born wives of Standard Oil and IBEC employees, who showed local women how to use imported products. By 1960, IBEC supermarkets in Venezuela were doing about $28 million a year in business. When they first opened, these markets had to import about 80 percent of their goods, but the new merchandising techniques and products quickly became part of the local economy. By 1959, 70 percent of the goods in Todos stores were produced locally. Trade fairs introduced the supermarket into Italy, and by 1960, four stores jointly owned by IBEC and Italian investors were operating in Milan.[21]

A variety of methods were used by American and European internationalists in the post–World War II era to bind nations into the emerging global economy: international currency reform, trade agreements, international law reforms, and various schemes designed to alleviate the dollar gap, such as the use of counterpart funds. Counterpart funds enabled foreign countries to buy and sell products to the United States while maintaining a stable currency. But there was a gritty dimension to foreign policy, too, exemplified by IBEC in the private sector and U.S. technical-assistance programs under Truman and Eisenhower, which were partly inspired by IBEC's success.

In an address before the American Assembly in 1956, John Lindeman, a consulting economist working for the U.S. government in Burma, reported that the number of contractors working on economic strategy for the U.S. government was the largest number by far engaged in "any single civilian activity abroad." By the mid-1950s, members of the U.S. International Cooperation Administration were designing and building dams, organizing agricultural extension systems, staffing public health services, and assisting foreign manufacturers to find their niche in the American marketplace. In effect, they were emulating Rockefeller's success in Latin America, preparing the ground for long-term corporate investment by improving infrastructure and reforming fiscal policy. Foreign-assistance programs took some of the risk out of international investment at a time when the strength of the American market made foreign expansion unnecessary for many U.S. companies.[22]

Economic reforms were accompanied by psychological strategists who had learned their trade in the advertising profession, or during World War II under Nelson Rockefeller in the Office of the Coordinator of Inter-American Affairs, in the Office of Strategic Services, and in the Office of War Information. Industrial designers, economists, and advertising professionals offered their talent to the U.S. government through organizations like the Advertising Council, corporations like the Container Corporation of American, or Time Inc.'s *Time, Life, Fortune,* and *Architectural Forum.*

C. D. Jackson, for example, the publisher of *Fortune,* had worked closely with the Eisenhower campaign in North Africa and Italy in the Office of War Information. Later, he supported NATO policies as president of the National Committee for a Free Europe—an organization that included the diplomat Allen Dulles and Eisenhower as well as liberal businessmen such as Jackson's associate Henry Luce and the Hollywood figures Cecil B. DeMille and Darryl Zanuck. The committee was formed to counteract Soviet ideology through so-called information campaigns and the support of dissident exiles from Eastern Europe. Radio Free Europe was the committee's most important operation, broadcasting to Czechoslovakia and later to Hungary and Poland from Munich, beginning on May Day 1951. The broadcasts accompanied trade fair exhibits as "the psychological front line of counterrevolution through seduction," contrasting the virtues of American material culture with the prospect of an "enslaving, death-dealing communism."[23]

Working through the private sector, C. D. Jackson and his colleagues were able to wage a propaganda war that disguised the support and collusion of the U.S. government. The facade of independence gave a degree of authenticity to the programs sponsored by the National Committee for a Free Europe, but more important, it allowed the State Department to disavow any and all U.S. responsibility for such events as the 1956 popular revolt in Hungary, which invited speedy, and bloody, Soviet repression. The Eisenhower administration avoided military confrontations whenever propaganda, cultural, and economic programs would suffice. President Eisenhower was willing to make the long haul and win the cold war with subversive tactics rather than risk nuclear conflagration.

Bureaucratic reform within the agencies responsible for U.S. information and cultural programs was one of the first tasks of the new Eisenhower administration. The USIA, created in 1953, inherited the tasks pioneered by the Office of War Information during World War II: the dissemination and interpretation of information. So-called disinformation, or propaganda campaigns, which had been the job of the Office of Strategic Services during World War II, became the concern of the CIA. The State Department retained the cultural programs, which sent artists, scholars, and athletes abroad on goodwill missions. This bureaucratic division of tasks made it appear that the USIA, the Commerce Department, and the State Department were free of propaganda activities, but foreigners soon came to suspect, with good reason, that all U.S. cultural programs were fronts for the CIA and covert action. At least one contemporary American scholar, Robert Rydell, has expressed the same point of view in *World of Fairs,* in which he compares CIA shenanigans within the American Pavilion at the 1958 Brussels World's Fair (a State Department responsibility) to the spy-versus-spy cartoons of *Mad* magazine.[24]

The Eisenhower administration employed corporations, artists, intellectuals, architects, and industrial designers to accomplish its goal of spreading liberal capitalism because artistic and consumer products easily crossed ethnic and political borders and because they represented the uncoerced expressions of free individuals. Artists and intellectuals, for their part, were usually eager to take government money. CIA money supported, in part, magazines such as *Der Monat* in Germany and *Encounter* in England, cultural broadcasts over Radio Free Europe, and the humanist debates of the Congress for Cultural Freedom, an affiliation of writers, artists, and intellectuals who met in annual conferences to debate the relative merits of "free expression" and other topics. When it was discovered during the Vietnam era that these cultural and "information" programs were, to some extent, the creatures of the CIA, the brutal reputation of that organization made it appear that some intellectuals may have betrayed a sacred trust. Writing about the Congress for Cultural Freedom during the late 1960s, Christopher Lasch railed against the monstrosity of such a hoax. The idea that intellectuals such as Arthur Schlesinger Jr. and John Kenneth Galbraith could pretend to be champions of intellectual freedom, on the one hand, and serve as mouthpieces of the "war machine" on the other, seemed to Lasch an unforgivable crime.[25]

Lasch may have erred on the side of melodrama, but his warning that the state requires not "paid propagandists or state-censored time-servers" but free, objective supporters to uphold its policies and promote its goals is an embarrassing truth and a keen indictment of the entire era.[26] Still, intellectuals were not as effective in advertising the American way of life as the consumer products that IBEC and the Commerce Department sent to Asia, Latin America, and Europe. Nylon stockings were far more influential than the CIA-funded debates of the Congress for Cultural Freedom, the jazz programs sent out over the Voice of America, and the exhibitions of abstract art underwritten by MOMA, which were aimed at a narrow range of intellectuals. Consumer products—from refrigerators on up to prefabricated homes—and the installment plans and other selling strategies that accompanied them, were the heart and soul of Eisenhower's "globalism." The gadgets that now threaten to bury the world knee-deep in banality have proven to have been the most effective weapon of the cold war.

In 1954 President Eisenhower launched the government's consumer-oriented offensive when he allocated a portion of his Special Emergency Fund, a fund earmarked by Congress expressly for cultural programs, for the new trade fair program that Sinclair Weeks was developing in the Department of Commerce. In the mid-1950s, U.S. exports vastly outnumbered imports. The Eisenhower administration argued that trade fairs were an important way of building a balance of trade between the United States, Europe, and strategic nations around the world. The Commerce Department used its allocation as seed money; the real substance of the trade fair program came from corporate donations in the form of manpower, equipment, and financial support. The Commerce Department promised corporations that it would ship their products to the foreign fairs, set up exhibition booths for them, provide translators for their business representatives, and prepare the ground with trade "missionaries"—businessmen sent abroad ahead of the fairs to explain what American products could do, how they could be purchased, and how foreign manufacturers could sell their own products to U.S. importers.[27]

Supporting American companies abroad and presenting American commercial products at international exhibitions had distinct advantages over traditional cultural exchanges and expensive developmental aid, which drew the scorn of isolationist and populist critics. As Frank Ninkovitch has pointed out in his study of cultural exchanges *The Diplomacy of Ideas,* many people—both intellectuals and philistines—were repelled by the mating of government and culture. Any hint of a government subsidy for the arts, especially by an intelligence agency, usually offended intellectuals, who cherished the belief that intellectual integrity was at odds with official commands of any stripe. For their part, philistines were offended by the thought that their tax dollars were supporting obscure, unintelligible artistic expression, or worse, a decadent, subversive, even communistic aesthetic. The definition of freedom in the arts was particularly embattled during the 1950s, when abstract expressionism seemed to be the quintessential expression of American freedom simply because it stood in dramatic contrast to Soviet socialist realism. It was nearly impossible for the State Department to support the arts without suffering intense criticism from populists, on the one hand, or ridicule from the avant-garde on the other. Commercial products, by contrast, which were as much a part of American culture as the arts, if not more so, were difficult to criticize on aesthetic grounds. By the late 1950s the industrial-design profession had integrated aesthetic principles and mass-production technology so successfully that a careful selection of consumer products could be exhibited abroad in lieu of the traditional arts with comparable prestige but only a fraction of the controversy.[28]

Criticism regarding the way American culture was presented overseas reached an early peak when Senator McCarthy's minions Roy Cohn and G. David Schine, in April 1953, made a quick tour of U.S. information centers in Europe and discovered books that, they maintained, had been written by Communist agitators. Authors such as Erskine Caldwell and Dashiell Hammett were indeed easy targets for the isolationist wing of the Republican party. But while the isolationists were making spectacles out of themselves, raging about the nefarious influence of bad literature, Eisenhower and his advisers were devising foolproof methods of disseminating American culture through the promotion of free trade and consumer goods.

Eisenhower had important allies within the Advertising Council, and when he decided to plunge into the trade fair game the council developed the conservative, McCarthy-proof "People's Capitalism" campaign to provide ideological unity for the trade fair exhibitions of the 1950s. The People's Capitalism campaign provided the Republican party with a positive ideology, as opposed to the negative, fanatical campaigns launched by McCarthyites. Eisenhower may have been wary of the New Deal–style foreign aid proposed by left-wing Republicans like Nelson Rockefeller, but he was just as leery, usually more so, of isolationism and fanatical conservatives.

The Advertising Council was a powerful consensus-building organization, like Time Inc., the American Assembly, and the Aspen retreats, only with a more practical working relationship with the White House. Some of the council's post–World War II campaigns were launched on behalf of the Marshall Plan, the armed forces, CARE (the relief organization), and Radio Free Europe. In 1953 the council developed the "Future of America" campaign, coordinated by Robert Gray of Esso Standard Oil and produced with some $10 million in corporate donations, which helped end an economic downturn threatening Eisenhower's popularity. The Advertising Council was like a voluntary wing of the government that supported and sustained Eisenhower administration policies.[29] Not only did the council dream up promotional campaigns for the White House, it held round-table discussions on crucial issues of public interest, which drew a wide circle of influential business leaders, publishers, and intellectuals into the political process. It was this broadly based support within the corporate community that enabled the Eisenhower administration to pursue its internationalist policies whenever Congress tightened the purse strings, whenever a "chosen instrument" was needed, whenever covert action needed concealment from Congress.

The image of the United States in foreign countries changed dramatically when the USIA, the State Department, the Department of Commerce, and the technical-assistance agencies, such as the International Cooperation Administration (ICA), began hiring the artists and industrial designers whose work expressed the mythic freedoms that democracy was said to harbor. In the mid-1950s, the ICA sent the industrial designer Russel Wright to Vietnam, where he helped transform handicraft industries into mass-production factories aimed at the American market (a case of too little too late if there ever was one). Peter Müller-Munk went to Israel, and Walter Dorwin Teague to Greece. Jane Fiske Mitarachi described the patriotic work of designers in an aptly titled article: "Design as a Political Force."[30]

In 1955 the Commerce Department sponsored pavilions at a mere fifteen trade fairs. By 1960 the Office of International Trade Fairs, a division of the Commerce Department, would boast that there had been "97 official exhibits in 29 countries, participated in by over 5,000 American contributors—and seen by more than 60,000,000 people." The office estimated that more than 13,800,000 people visited American pavilions in 1960 alone, with 600,000 attending the exhibit on "testing for quality in mass-produced goods" in Milan, Italy, and more than 1 million stopping in at the exhibit *Tradeways to Peace and Prosperity* in Damascus, Syria.[31] At these fairs consumer products were presented as choices or votes, which enabled the individual to elect the items in the marketplace that best served them. Trade fair exhibits presented an America in which the government was almost nonexistent—where liberty was best expressed by selecting from among consumer products. Exhibits transformed political rhetoric and democratic principles into tangible, three-dimensional objects (a strategy with obvious appeal to corporate underwriters).

Robert Griffith has noted that as early as 1952 there had been so many pro-business campaigns in the United States that "the detritus . . . lay scattered about America's cultural landscape in books, articles and pamphlets, in motion pictures, on billboards and posters, on radio and television, on car cards in buses, trains, and trolleys," varying in quality from "the sophisticated articles of the Committee for Economic Development to the hard sell comic books of the National Association of Manufacturers." The campaigns all had the same purpose: "to arrest the momentum of New Deal liberalism and create a political culture conducive to the autonomous expansion of corporate enterprise." Trade fairs and exhibitions helped to carry this pro-business message abroad.[32]

In later years the conservative approach won out, creating a "global marketplace" instead of a universal "great society." It must be noted, however, that the goals of both the activists and conservatives during the 1950s were much the same: Most moderate politicians and liberal business leaders advocated something like a global version of the United States. There was little awareness, at least in the 1950s, of the cultural and ecological devastation implicit within the renewed American mission. "The Soviets can only be met and bested by American businessmen," wrote one of Eisenhower's advisers, Clarence B. Randall, in his primer for U.S. trade missionaries, *The Communist Challenge to American Business.* Randall asked his private-sector colleagues to set themselves "individually and collectively, to the task of winning a glorious victory on the new battleground.[33] Randall urged his friends to participate in Eisenhower's new trade fair and trade mission programs; to spread the message of People's Capitalism; to head for the developing world with their rolled-up back issues of *Life* magazines as missionaries once did with their Bibles. And that is exactly what thousands of U.S. artists, industrial designers, intellectuals, and businessmen did. They traveled from Leipzig to Bangkok like old fashioned door-to-door salesmen, harvesting sales contracts as if they were souls and shepherding converts to capitalism out of the darkness of socialism, communism, and inefficient, tradition-bound economies toward the absolutely guaranteed promised land of skyscrapers, supermarkets, and shopping malls.

1 The Chicago Fairs of 1950

During the 1950s the U.S. Commerce Department used its pavilions at international trade fairs to explain tariff controls and manufacturing processes, and private corporations erected their own exhibits nearby. American businessmen forged networks through a program of trade "missions" that sent volunteers from the U.S. business community to fairs around the globe, where they explained to foreign people how the American system worked.[1] This alliance between government and industry was typical of the fairs after 1954, which were given an added boost by the enthusiastic financial support offered by the Eisenhower administration.[2] In the early 1950s, however, there was little U.S. corporate participation in international fairs. This participation increased as Marshall Plan administrators—often businessmen themselves—exhorted the private sector to support the government initiative abroad, and as propaganda organizations like the "Crusade for Freedom" familiarized Americans with the precarious health of democracies in Europe and the consequences to U.S. prosperity if Soviet ideological and economic expansion were allowed to grow apace.[3]

The U.S. Department of Commerce was reorganized following World War II and a new Office of International Trade was established in 1946. In the words of Arthur Paul, its director, the intention was to

> encourage and facilitate the expansion and balanced growth of international trade; promote stability of international economic relations; cooperate with other nations in the solving of trade and exchange problems through international organizations and con-

> ferences; assist other nations toward higher economic development . . . facilitate United States participation in peacetime trade with former enemy and other areas in which normal channels of trade do not exist; and reduce obstacles to and restrictions upon international trade.[4]

It was crucial that foreign nations receive hard currency and thus essential that the American market be open to their products and raw materials. But American manufacturers were understandably nervous about a foreign policy that sought to turn Europe and Asia into competitors for U.S. consumer dollars.[5] In its overtures to the American business community, the Commerce Department stressed the patriotic nature of establishing international trade relations. Ideally, the United States would import cheap raw materials (and thus retain factory jobs) while providing developing nations with enough currency to buy agricultural surpluses, machine tools, sewing machines, and the many other products that the United States manufactured.[6] In the grand scheme of things it was hoped that American corporations could eventually turn developing countries into consumer markets for strategically important Western Europe and Japan, too. But until a global economy was established, the United States would have to subsidize production abroad and consumption at home through favorable import tariffs and foreign aid.[7]

American victories in World War II did not guarantee that the rest of the globe would accept American-style capitalism, especially with the Communist alternative constantly eroding U.S. hegemony: The Soviets offered a compelling alternative model of rapid industrialization, development, and scientific achievement, forcing U.S. administrators to help rebuild Western Europe, Greece, and Japan into prosperous, stable democracies and close allies.[8] The Truman administration began the process by supporting supranational defense organizations, such as NATO, and financial institutions, such as the World Bank and the International Monetary Fund, in order to forge an anti-Soviet coalition. Economic productivity shored up with military strength was the key to building stable democracies on the eastern and western flanks of the democratic perimeter and of asserting the "superiority of American values: individual liberty, representative government, free enterprise, private property, and a marketplace economy."[9]

President Truman encouraged international responsibility in his 1949 inaugural address when he put forward a "Fair Deal" solution to the poverty and misery of the developing world, a solution that appeared to be both humanitarian and politically necessary. The Fair Deal appealed to those who believed that Americans had an obligation to export prosperity as well as to those who worried that the "rising expectations" of the Third World might result in the Soviet takeover of the resource-rich areas of Africa, Southeast Asia, and even South and Central America. Truman's initiative resulted in a combined effort on the part of the United States, the United Nations, the Organization of American States, Britain, France, Norway, and other relatively prosperous nations to send technical-assistance teams and volunteers from the business community on a worldwide mission to develop economic alliances.[10] The Fair Deal aspired to be something like an international version of the old New Deal.

The first practical steps in creating trade and aid policy after World War II were made by the Economic Cooperation Administration (ECA), established in connection with the Marshall Plan in 1948 and staffed with businessmen in order to "create new sorts of linkages between the public and private sectors."[11] The ECA dispensed propaganda as well as financial aid; its object was to explain "the nature and motives of American economic assistance" and counter the "distortions widely broadcast by Soviet propaganda."[12] The ECA and Marshall Plan ensured that idealistic phrases such as "one world" and "international understanding," which had become popular after the establishment of the United Nations, were expressed concretely in standardized weights and measures, lower trade barriers, and stabilized currencies.

The ECA helped the Marshall Plan by creating links between business groups and government administrators, offering technical assistance, and experimenting with promotional campaigns that explained the American way of life. From the American point of view, at least, the program was a great success. It was not surprising that Paul Hoffman, a "prominent automobile executive and progressive businessman" and head of the domestic office of the ECA, proposed

Paul G. Hoffman, administrator of the Economic Cooperation Administration, visits the Portuguese exhibit at the International Trade Exhibit, held for a week in May 1949, at the U.S. Department of Commerce. National Archives.

that the lessons learned in Europe be put to use in Asia and wherever else the Soviets threatened.[13] Written in the shadow of the Korean War, Hoffman's book, *Peace Can Be Won*, provided a blueprint for U.S. government action. It reveals something of the atmosphere from which programs for trade fairs and exhibitions during the early 1950s would emerge.[14]

Hoffman identified four "fronts" of the cold war. To win the peace America needed to fight militarily, economically, politically, and psychologically.[15] America had failed to win the peace so far because the Soviets had been allowed to walk out of the Marshall Plan and create an antithetical program of expansion and confrontation without serious challenge. The Marshall Plan was a success, he believed, but should be followed with an aggressive propaganda war in which U.S. intelligence anticipated Soviet initiatives, thwarted them at every turn, and eradicated the "social, political, and economic conditions on which Communism thrives." He wanted to implement a global form of the Marshall Plan in which "hydroelectric plants, housing developments, tractors and seed," were put up against communism: "Set the Marshall Plan's bread and butter," up against "the hollow cake of the Big Lie."[16] These notions became popular in cold war America, especially after the Communist invasion of South Korea in June 1950.[17]

The ECA administrators emphasized productivity in Europe to keep inflation down and to build up surpluses of essential commodities—copper, cobalt, chrome, rubber, and manganese—which could be stockpiled in case of war with the Soviets.[18] And these strategies helped to keep Communists in Europe from convincing their fellow citizens that the Soviets offered a better way of achieving a middle-class lifestyle. Along with NATO, productivity helped to turn Western Europe into a fortress of democracy. Economic strength, according to Hoffman, was the key to Europe's military defense. He agreed with one of Stalin's favorite maxims: "Production wins wars." The real battle today, he said, "is between the American assembly line and the Communist party line."[19]

The ECA also set up exchange programs. Hoffman enlisted Philip Reed of General Electric and the labor leader Victor Reuther to demonstrate American management and labor relations in an Anglo-American exchange. Their job was to encourage the idea that workers and management shared in the benefits of increased productivity and overall prosperity. By 1951 the ECA had brought some three thousand European technicians, mostly from Britain, to U.S. factories, farms, and businesses. It was hoped that they would learn how to "break tradition" in their home factories and replace inefficient methods of production with American methods of management and organization.[20] But Hoffman understood that by bringing foreign technicians and officials to the United States they would learn much more than technical information. It was crucial that foreign managers be exposed to the bulging shelves of supermarkets and shops crammed with inexpensive, mass-produced goods that provided material evidence of the results that the ECA was aiming at in Europe.

Hoffman developed a "free world doctrine," which was intended to accompany his program of economic rejuvenation. This had four points: "Freedom of religion and the brotherhood of man; the civil liberties inherent within the U.S. Constitution; a new, socially conscious capitalism based on widespread ownership, diffusion of initiative, decision, enterprise, and the ever-widening distribution of benefits; and a new humanism that emphasizes the expansion of equal opportunity."[21] Winning the peace, or building what the media mogul Henry Luce called the "American Century," and saving the world for democracy required more than just international prosperity. It meant nurturing and disseminating a secular, commercial culture that cut across cultural differences and forged a unity of common interests. Hoffman assumed that despite cultural variants everyone in the world wanted a higher standard of living, and so his "one-worldism" focused on promoting mass production and the consumer society. These ideas were similar to those promoted by the "round table" discussions of *Life* and the "American Round Table Forum," sponsored by the Advertising Council (Hoffman was the moderator of an Advertising Council Forum in 1951).[22]

The ECA and U.S. voluntary organizations recruited talent from top American newspapers, magazines, radio networks, and movie concerns to promote the new economic and cultural programs. In Western Europe, mobile exhibits operating on a shoestring budget featured puppet shows and movies in several languages that dramatized European political unification as the wave of the future. There were publicity stunts to garner attention, along with dramatic broadcasts over the airwaves of Radio Free Europe, which was sponsored by the Crusade for Freedom. In 1950 a traveling exhibit called the "Marshall Plan Caravan" released about seventy thousand balloons in Denmark, bearing the message: "This balloon is a symbol of the hopes for peace and prosperity entertained by the free, democratic citizens of the 18 Marshall Plan countries. It is a symbol of the free exchange of goods and ideas that all of us attempt to realize. . . . The Marshall Plan—a plan for democratic peace."[23] These crude propaganda tactics were aimed at people in the Soviet satellite countries, where Hoffman hoped to find a sympathetic audience. "The best thing that could happen," he concluded in *Peace Can Be Won*, "would be a revolution inside the USSR that would turn it toward democracy and then provide a solid basis for enduring peace."[24]

In the late 1940s, Arthur M. Schlesinger Jr., who had been in the Office of War Information and Strategic Services during World War

Mrs. Eugenie Anderson (center), U.S. ambassador to Denmark, watches the launching of message-bearing balloons at a Marshall Plan mobile trade exhibit (1950). National Archives.

II, assessed the global strategy of the postwar era as a consultant for the ECA. The experience helped him to write his influential *The Vital Center: The Politics of Freedom,* which appeared in 1949 (a year after he began teaching at Harvard). Like Hoffman, Schlesinger was trying to encourage the process of democratization in areas of the world controlled by communism, but instead of the goal-oriented propaganda campaigns more characteristic of wartime, he advised "exporting technology rather than commodities" and opening the United States to foreign goods.[25] He attributed the acceptance of totalitarianism to a misdirected search for community, and his call to "restore the center" was a warning that Americans needed to "reunite the individual and the community" both at home and abroad if there was ever going to be a form of world government on the democratic model.[26] Trade fairs and exhibitions were natural seedbeds for the kind of community ideals Schlesinger wished to encourage because they promoted an aggressive liberal capitalism, they helped the export trade in capital goods and technology, they taught foreign exporters how to sell in the U.S. market, and they helped to goad neutral nations toward the West.

Not all Americans were entranced by the prospect of global prosperity on the American model. David Riesman, principal author of *The Lonely Crowd* (a sociological study on the deleterious effects of the production economy), lampooned "productivity" and American propaganda in his satirical essay "The Nylon War," which described the fictional bombing of the USSR with American consumer goods. Although it was intended as a send-up of America's economic war, many people saw no humor in it. Indeed, the craze for consumer products had so gripped the American public that by 1951, when his essay was first published, many people were unable to grasp Riesman's satire. According to "The Nylon War," the U.S. Air Force had recently begun dropping modern appliances—instead of bombs—inside the USSR, creating panic among Soviet housewives. Soviet women, eager to keep up with their neighbors, pestered their local stores for more and more consumer products—thereby disrupting the political system. American refrigerators created demands "not only for electricity, but also for many foods which can now be stored (and hoarded)."[27]

Riesman wrote "The Nylon War" while on the faculty of the University of Chicago, and it appeared in the February 1951 issue of the journal *Common Cause,* published by the Committee to Frame a World Constitution. The article was probably intended to appeal to those readers who believed that the slavish pursuit of materialism was no substitute for the traditional humanities, that the unlettered masses were just as much a threat now as they had been in the thirties, when charismatic leaders such as Mussolini and Hitler swept crowds along with similarly fantastic promises. It was just this belief that American productivity, unleavened by the humanizing influence of culture, would be another dead end that led Robert M. Hutchins, the president of the University of Chicago and one of the founders of the Committee to Frame a World Constitution, to work with the businessman Walter Paepke in his efforts to reform commercial culture. Paepke's annual retreat for businessmen, cultural figures, and industrial designers in Aspen, Colorado, became a favorite rendezvous for tastemakers and CEOs throughout the 1950s.[28] Mass-produced abundance was not enough. Paepke, Riesman, Luce, and other reformers believed that the new U.S. prosperity should be accompanied by a renewal of (an as yet undefined) humanism.

Henry Luce, the founder of Time Inc., was probably the best-known crusader of the cold war era. Luce had dedicated a full issue of *Fortune* to Mussolini in 1934, praising him as a decisive leader. Later, after the full horror of that "decisiveness" was unveiled, Luce turned to the new humanism, which would be popularized by Hutchins and Paepke during the first decades of the cold war. Luce was especially moved by *The Revolt of the Masses*—José Ortega y Gasset's critique of "mass man"—which may have helped him decide that "a failed press was the prelude to barbarism and tyranny."[29] In 1940 Luce presented a paper, "The American Century," to a meeting in Pasadena, California, of the Association of American Colleges. Obviously influenced by the events in Europe, Luce warned his audience that America's "morality, freedom, democracy, and free enterprise" would either triumph across the globe or be crowded out by its opposite. Luce's "The American Century" appeared in the February 17, 1941, issue of *Life,* dominating that issue and becoming a popular manifesto of U.S. internationalism for the next two decades (at least).[30]

During the post–World War II era, the Time corporation's *Life* and *Fortune* would relentlessly promote the promise of abundance and the spread of liberal capitalism in the hope that consumer demand would fuel the growth of democracy. *Life* reporters followed the American exhibits at international trade fairs, popularizing the notion that consumerism could become more than just a crass pacifier of the mob—that consumer products could be forms of artistic expression and that consumer choices could actually amount to a creative act. It was this conflation of consumerism, humanism, and political ideology—coupled with the fear of Communist expansion—that launched the real-life version of the nylon war at trade fairs and exhibitions. As the Soviets and Americans became eager contributors to the material wealth of Third World nations, Riesman's scenario became a commonplace. Indeed, both of the superpowers promised neutral nations that they would enjoy material abundance as the reward for political and economic cooperation. As the economic war escalated, trade fairs and cultural exhibitions became competitive events, taxing the ingenuity of American and Soviet designers to outdo one another in the battle for the hearts and minds of men.

The first trade fair to assert the global positioning of the United States in the cold war—to persuade Americans that a global economy was desirable while impressing upon foreigners that the abundant society could be best achieved through a mix of U.S. technical wizardry and liberal economic reforms—came in the summer of 1950 on Chicago's Navy Pier. The First United States International Trade Fair had some of the ideological characteristics associated with Marshall Plan balloon "offensives" but went much further in the direction of the community-building called for by Schlesinger. It was lacking only in drama, in entertainments that would bring the social implications of international trade to the fore. This crucial task was undertaken by another fair held simultaneously, nearby: the Chicago Fair of 1950. The First United States International Trade Fair (August 7–19, 1950) was smaller and shorter than the Chicago Fair (June 24–September 4, 1950), but the two events were geographically close enough and governed by so many of the same individuals that they can be regarded as part of the same social matrix.

The First United States International Trade Fair was held on Chicago's Navy Pier (with industrial exhibits at the Chicago Amphitheater). The promotional announcements included testimonials from the U.S. secretary of commerce, Chicago's mayor Martin H. Kennelly, President Truman, and Paul Hoffman. Truman sent word that "the interchange of goods among nations is an important means of improving political and economic relationships throughout the world" and the "establishing of a fair peace." Hoffman stated, "[I]t is my belief that an international trade fair is one of the best methods of bringing buyers and sellers together from all parts of the world and is an important means of enabling Marshall Plan countries to earn more dollars."[31] The First United States International Trade Fair was very much a part of the U.S. effort to construct an international economy.

Catalog cover for the United States International Trade Fair, 1950. Chicago Historical Society, F38MZ, 1950, U6A1.

Helping Western European nations enter the American economy was the primary purpose of the trade fair (just as foreign fairs helped American companies get a foothold abroad). Jacques Kunstenaar, chief of the Fairs and Exhibitions branch of the Commerce Department's Office of International Trade, was sent to Europe late in 1949 in order to open offices in numerous foreign countries and accommodate foreign manufacturers desiring to enter the American market. Kunstenaar had been the U.S. representative of the ECA in 1949 and thus had an intimate knowledge of Hoffman's goals. He managed to bring companies from eighteen Marshall Plan nations to Chicago by promising them that the fair would help expand productive forces, help reduce trade barriers, and stabilize the world economy.[32] Chicago, fair promoters said, was "the center of the nation's economy" and therefore one of the most important trading centers in the world.[33]

The First United States International Trade Fair was a model of private and public cooperation, with the Department of Commerce, the ECA, the Organization of European Economic Cooperation (OEEC), and the International Chamber of Commerce "hovering over it like mother hens."[34] Government information booths, tourism booths, and consumer goods were housed together at Navy Pier. Products were arranged up and down the north and south halls, and a "Hall of Nations" and the foreign government exhibits rounded out the tip. Western European nations gave out information on shipping facilities, ports, and marketing possibilities. The OEEC had a special exhibit, *Europe Today and Tomorrow,* showing the progress toward an integrated European recovery. Visitors could study the main export products of each European country on an illuminated map and register their opinions on European recovery at polling machines.

Forty-seven countries were represented at the trade fair. Traditional U.S. multinational companies like International Harvester, International Business Machines (IBM), National Cash Register, and Singer Sewing Machines represented traditional U.S. expertise in the international marketplace. The inauguration ceremonies included an address by Lucien Cooremans, vice president of the Union of International Fairs and managing director of the Brussels International Trade Fair (an annual event on the outskirts of Brussels). Mayor Kennelly cut the ribbon to open the fair and led a formal inspection of the eight miles of displays. In his opening address the mayor was careful to trace a line of development from the 1893 World's Columbian Exposition through the 1933 Century of Progress Exposition and the more recent Railroad Fair of 1948–49 to this current exposition, which demonstrated "the spirit of achievement on the part of Chicago's business leaders," and "America's great modern achievements in science, agriculture, commerce, and industry."[35]

Adlai E. Stevenson, the governor of Illinois, added to the promotional effort. Speaking to nervous local businessmen, who were feeling threatened by the influx of competition from abroad, Stevenson soothed their worries by explaining:

> Most of our imports are raw materials and semi-manufactured foods, all of which require U.S. employment before they are transformed into finished products. . . . The U.S.—and particularly the Midwest—needs export markets for surplus industrial and farm products . . . so every dollar Americans spend for imports comes back home to us in the form of orders, placed with our manufacturers and farmers.[36]

The goals were balanced trade, an end to foreign-aid programs, and a strengthening of international financial networks.

At least one journal noted that the tremendous foreign interest in the fair was generated by the incipient end of the Marshall Plan: "Overseas exhibitors see the Fair as a proving ground for their ability to snag U.S. department stores and industrial buyers," as a place to "crack the American markets," said the trade journal *Modern Industry,* which also reported that the Department of Commerce, the ECA, and the International Chamber of Commerce were using "every effort to make selling and buying as painless as possible." Indeed, so eager were Hoffman and his colleagues to bring Marshall Plan countries into the domestic market that they pressured foreign governments into sending companies that had little hope of selling anything in the short term.[37]

The First United States International Trade Fair revealed that creating a global marketplace would not be painless. Nobody bought durable goods and heavy machinery just because the ECA said it was a vote for world peace, or because the Commerce Department had redoubled its efforts to engage private corporations in the flow of money to beleaguered nations in the hope of achieving a balanced trade. As part of the Truman administration's Fair Deal policies, the First United States International Trade Fair was a positive step toward managing the new geopolitics, but trade fairs had certain failings as markets.

Department stores and specialized trade centers like the Chicago Merchandise Mart had made traditional fairs obsolete for actual business purposes. Retailers could visit the Merchandise Mart all year round, and contemporary travel networks made foreign buying trips comparatively simple. In Europe and in the Third World, trade fairs would satisfy practical needs for some time to come, but the International Trade Fair held in Chicago was primarily an educational event, part of the one-world idealism prevalent among civic leaders. It only came about through the urging of government planners who wanted to publicize foreign products and regulate the type of imports sent to the United States. The focus on handicrafts, for example, was a way of bringing foreign produce into the U.S. market without threatening domestic industry. The next international fair, also held in Chicago, would not be held until 1959, by which time foreign products were of a much better quality and had become fashionable symbols of U.S. global hegemony.

The post–World War II American shopper was attracted by specialized home shows and shopping centers, places where goods and services were placed within domestic narratives that taught consumers to associate commercial products with carefree excitement and a promising future. Above all, the new consumer wanted spectacle of the sort provided by the Chicago Fair of 1950, which was held on a sixty-acre site that was ten minutes from downtown, the same site once occupied by the Century of Progress Exposition (1933) and the Railroad Fair (1948–49). Exhibits depicted "not only the merits of the items displayed but also their importance in the American political and economic system under which they are produced." Instead of anti-Communist tracts or dreary Commerce Department lectures on the circulation of capital, which the International Trade Fair featured, the Chicago Fair had model homes, folk dancing, and demonstrations of atomic power that promised glamorous domesticity and international goodwill—abundance for all in a global, multicultural, Americanized future.[38]

Opening the day before the invasion of South Korea by the Communist north, the Chicago Fair was conceived to "dramatize achievements of agriculture, commerce, industry and science, which under our pioneer heritage promise new, ever higher standards of American living." Narratives of history as economic progress were portrayed in the stories of atomic energy, telephone communications, electricity and its application to rural living and farm productivity, and in the stories of oil, food processing and distribution, television, city recreation, health and hygiene. The fair trumpeted American superiority with its displays of new technologies and their ability to transform age-old problems into a modern utopia.[39]

In keeping with its world-class pretensions the Chicago Fair of 1950 had its own design consultants—Walter Dorwin Teague and Raymond Loewy Associates—and its own symbolic theme sculpture, the chalk-white "Spiramid," designed by the local artist Charles Bracken. The Spiramid was "part pyramid and part spiral, a symbol of the solid base of freedom and enterprise which has keynoted American progress."[40] The spiral of the Spiramid rose from a slightly rounded base like the unwinding peel of an orange or a curl of smoke. It suggested the growth of the U.S. economy by combining purity of form and color with the suggestion of infinite potential. It was sleek and modern, but unlike the absolute geometric forms of the Trylon and Perisphere, symbols of modernity at the 1939 New York World's Fair, it was more illustrational—the very shape of progress.

The Chicago Fair boasted a variety of entertaining exhibits—a circus and an ice-skating rink, for example—but few exhibits compared with the Theater of the Atom, a prototype of the Atoms for Peace exhibits popularized by President Eisenhower at fairs after 1953. Westinghouse built this pavilion in order to demonstrate "the power of atomic energy for constructive purposes." The Theater of the Atom featured a simulated atomic chain reaction: "Gasp at the 200,000 volt model atom smasher," urged the guide book. "See world recognized scientists" and "atomic exploding mousetraps. . . . Learn how atomic power may someday cure cancer, discover long-hidden polar mineral deposits, drive ocean liners and, perhaps, carry rockets to the moon."[41] These exhibits endeavored to mask the atom's destructive potential by demonstrating beneficial uses of atomic energy. Novelty shows made atomic power look harmless while exhibits emphasizing space travel dramatized the promise of cheap, abundant energy for domestic use.

Other exhibits simply updated corporate exhibits from older world's fairs. Elsie, the Borden Milk Company's cow, billed as the "Beautiful Lactress," made her first personal appearance since the New York World's Fair of 1939, with a redesigned "bovine boudoir," which included plenty of room for her new line of "cowsmetics." Appointments were so lavish in Elsie's ideal model home that it drew "the scorn of a Russian humor magazine" (the sure sign of success). Similarly, the Bell Telephone exhibit featured free demonstration calls: a 1939 public relations gimmick brought up to date with the display of electronic computing equipment that kept track of thousands of calls and "remembered" who made them, how long they talked, and what numbers were dialed.[42]

At the south entrance the fairgrounds were divided symbolically between past and future, the historical exhibits claiming a place nearest the city and the "Avenue of American Homes" presiding over the lakefront. Commuters could drive up and park next to the American Homes section and catch a bus to the entertainment exhibits at the other end of the grounds, take the narrow-gauge railroad past the Showboat Theater and Dixieland exhibits, or walk about at their leisure.

The model homes, some with futuristic materials and designer accents, some just marginally improved Cape Cod and ranch-style all-purpose suburban tract houses, were symbolic restatements of the fair's most crucial themes. The private home was the center of the American Dream.[43] To this lair someday would be dragged the exploding atomic mousetraps, the high-frequency cooking appliances (in the Wonder Worker electricity pavilion run by Commonwealth Edison and local utility companies), as well as the handmade lamp from Greece or the rattan chair from Asia displayed on Navy Pier. The fair's executive manager opined: "If any one thing may be taken as a symbol of what our nation has achieved it might very well be the American home. For embodied therein are the manpower and dreams of the country surrounded by examples of its creative and cultural accomplishments."[44] For those who could not afford to buy new homes, there were do-it-yourself tips, blueprints, and specifications. The fair was selling design trends, fashions, and ideals in order to fuel consumer demand. The exhibits provided entertainment and a conceptual framework for new technologies while pointing the way toward an ideal, corporate future in which Elsie would be more productive thanks to scientific breeding, atomic power would provide abundant energy, and electric appliances would transform drudgery into elegant gestures of control.

The benevolent intent of U.S. business culture was celebrated thrice daily in an hour-long pageant on a lakefront stage across from the television center, adjacent to the model homes. *Frontiers of Freedom* retold the history of the United States in terms of economic expansion. "This is the American story," the program explained in thunderous prose, "an epic tidal wave of freedom-loving men and women sweeping on to a new world rich with natural resources beyond the dreams of the ages . . . with their unquenchable spirit it was the pioneers and their successors who opened to all men the 'Frontiers of Freedom.'" The pageant told the American story by encapsulating history into theatrical units beginning with "The Red Man's Gift," in which the Indians gave their agricultural secrets to the Quakers. In this friendly deal, meant to sum up the entire colonial period, William Penn swapped a scroll entitled "The Great Treaty" for corn. The next scene found George Washington on Murray's Wharf, New York, which was "piled high with the industry of Yankee craftsmen and merchants." Washington was the "People's Choice" and his appearance was meant to illustrate to any foreigners in the audience how Americans had thrown off the yoke of oppressive aristocracy in favor of representative government.

Scene three dramatized the story of transportation, westward expansion, the building of the Erie Canal, the arrival of the Tom Thumb steam engine, and the speedy Yankee clipper ships that began the assertion of American mercantile power abroad by carrying "the infant Stars and Stripes to the outermost corners of the seven seas." Picking up this thread, scene four celebrated Chicago, the "Inland Empire," the center of the western commodity trade. "The Trail Blazers of 1849" followed, pushing the mercantile frontier to the Pacific, and unifying the nation with telegraph and railroad. The Civil War was condensed into a narrative of dramatic rebirth in which divisions of race and class threatened to consume the nation until the flames were quenched by Illinois's native son Abraham Lincoln. Then came the age of industry, in which "research" and "mass production" combined to ensure the "scientific development" of America's "boundless natural resources."[45]

The pageant wound up with a spectacular "march of machines"; a "mechanized America on parade," in which antique covered wagons rolled on stage to be replaced by tractors, then trains, and finally a jet airplane. "Here they come," the program announced, "titans of

Cover of the guide book for the Chicago Fair, 1950. Chicago Historical Society, F38MZ, 1950, C3.

industry . . . products of coal, steel and oil, born of the white heat of the blast furnace and shaped from molten metal. Farming, lumbering, road-building, ditch-digging, pipe-laying . . . they continue the quest and the conquest of ever new frontiers." The pageant director, Helen Tieken Garaghty, who had also masterminded the *Wings of a Century* pageant for the 1933 Century of Progress Exposition and directed the *Wheels a-Rolling* pageant for the Chicago Railroad Fair of 1948–49, thus updated the progressive spirit for her internationally minded audience by asserting that each new type of machine had enabled the pioneer to exploit a new resource. Technology created new possibilities, and Americans, "as a pioneer people," were bound by destiny to "go forward, to surmount obstacles, to keep the faith."[46]

Appearing in between performances of the pageant was a folk festival that dramatized the cooperative effort among different races and cultures living in the Chicago area. As at the International Trade Fair, promoters urged Chicagoans to overlook racial differences and strive for cultural and economic unity. The fair proclaimed to any visiting businessmen, to newly arrived immigrants, and to visiting dignitaries that America was a place where foreigners could feel free to dress in their native fashion, speak their own tongue, eat their native food. The United States was portrayed as a giant, multinational marketplace, a crossroads of the world, where the only thing that really mattered was technological progress and the attainment of economic abundance.

The freedom that Americans would have the world enjoy was also a fragile ideal. To acknowledge the gravity of the nation's entry into the Korean crisis, for example, uniformed members of the armed services were allowed into the Chicago Fair free of charge and encouraged to see the pageant that, in the words of the fair's president, "shows what we are fighting for" and reveals "how our natural blessings, liberties . . . and national progress have made us the truest example of democratic life and civilization's most privileged people." A "uniformed Goddess of Liberty" followed the jet plane on stage to lead the audience in a rousing version of the "Star-Spangled Banner."[47]

In essence, the Chicago fairs of 1950 combined a linear history of mercantile progress characterized by friendly exchanges, with a future in which the pioneer spirit would reach new frontiers through science, industry, consumer empowerment, and martial vigor. This was a conservative version of the one-worldism promulgated nearby at the University of Chicago, in Henry Luce's magazines, and at Walter Paepke's Aspen retreats. The civic leaders behind the Chicago Fair of 1950 would have probably agreed with the aforementioned cultural reformers and liberal ECA administrators that U.S. expansion was benevolent, that U.S.-style democracy had to expand or be overwhelmed by communism, but they would have ridiculed the notion that the public needed a dose of humanism with their consumerism. Still, although the liberals and the conservatives quibbled over whether or not the world should be "conquered" by free enterprise or "unified" by liberal capitalism, they did agree on fundamentals. Isolationism, in the old-fashioned sense of the term, was dead.

As the United States carried its doctrine of abundance, gadgetry, and home-centered democracy abroad to new consumer frontiers, the crude exhibition techniques of the Marshall Plan days would give way to the type of displays seen at the two Chicago fairs of 1950. Appliance exhibits, model homes, modern kitchens, television, hi-fi, and movie demonstrations were sent abroad to dazzle audiences and win friends for the American way. Uniting the "free world" against the Communists meant teaching consumerism and family values. People of the Third World and Soviet satellite nations would be entertained with fashion shows, jazz bands, and blender demonstrations in order to show that in the United States the extremes of wealth and poverty were leveling out into a "people's capitalism," characterized by a huge, all-inclusive middle class. In the Third World, folk dancing, fashion shows, and Cinerama spectacles would demonstrate a democratic culture that could be understood without an upper-class education; in sophisticated Western Europe, jazz bands, *Porgy and Bess,* and the Philadelphia Orchestra would argue that democracy did not mean a descent into mobocracy.

2 From Union Station to Yugoslavia

International Trade Fairs and the People's Capitalism Campaign

After Chicago's First United States International Trade Fair of 1950, the Department of Commerce continued to promote foreign participation in domestic trade fairs, such as the Washington State International Trade Fairs of 1951, 1954, and 1955, and to cooperate with other government agencies in operating U.S. pavilions at European fairs. The American section of the Berlin International Trade Fair (September 19–October 5, 1952), for example, was designed by the Commerce Department in cooperation with the Department of State, the National Association of Manufacturers, and prominent American businessmen. The U.S. display featured a fully equipped "dream home" with an automobile in the carport, an electric kitchen, laundry, television, radio-phonograph units, a hobby shop with do-it-yourself tools, and an information booth where visitors could view Sears, Roebuck catalogs. Specialists in American marketing techniques and in the export trade were available for individual consultation. Approximately 395,000 Germans viewed the exhibit over seventeen days, and as a result of this show of interest, the U.S. display was kept open a full month after the fair had closed. The exhibits at the 1952 Berlin fair demonstrated how products were part of a family-centered culture and not just a manifestation of greedy materialism; they provided a more convincing display of the American way of life than a simple window display of luxury goods.[1]

Fair themes were developed according to local conditions and the advice of local Foreign Service personnel. At the 1952 İzmir Trade Fair, for example, the theme "Turkey and America—Free World Partners Working for Peace" advertised how Turkey and the United States could profit from mutually beneficial business deals. An

American cigarette machine churned out cigarettes from a Turkish and American blend, alongside chrome-plated products made in the United States with Turkish chromium.[2] Coaxed by the Department of Commerce, American business groups took tours of Europe to visit these trade fairs, combining business with pleasure. Year after year, attendance at European fairs increased as countries recovered from World War II, making fairs into important vehicles of international cooperation. In order to augment American participation in foreign trade fairs, the house organ of the Department of Commerce, *Foreign Commerce Weekly*, was redesigned in July 1952 so that foreign exhibitions would have better coverage.[3]

The Soviets had a considerable head start in the "nylon war." The USSR participated in more than a hundred international fairs between 1950 and 1954, aiming their displays not only at the merchants who went to these events but also at the hundreds of impressionable people eager to see a free show.[4] The fact that trade fairs were key events for the Soviet propaganda effort convinced President Eisenhower that official participation by the U.S. government was imperative. The American propaganda program, operating through nominally private organizations such as the Crusade for Freedom and Radio Free Europe, was already a powerful advocate of Eisenhower's goals; but trade fairs provided tangible evidence of American achievements and, more important, encouraged the interpenetration of U.S. and foreign business concerns, drawing neutral or even Communist nations into the sphere of U.S. influence.

The trade fair program became part of Eisenhower's reevaluation of foreign economic policy that began with a special commission chaired by Clarence B. Randall, chairman of the board of Inland Steel and a trustee of the Aspen Institute, who was appointed by the president in August 1953 to study trade problems.[5] *Fortune*, in its never-ending effort to promote international trade, was glad to see the government taking this initiative but accused the Randall Commission of not going far enough in emphasizing self-interest. *Fortune* assembled an impressive array of facts to show that foreign markets were the most promising consumer frontier:

> The mere fact that 162 million Americans now absorb more than half the world's manufactured goods provides some measure of

> the consumption capacity that remains to be developed abroad. Consider that some 2.3 billion people now live outside the United States; make allowance for the fact that some 800 million are behind the Iron Curtain; admit that scores of obstacles to trade exist within the free world; and the potential of the world market is still staggering.[6]

Some corporations, as *Fortune* noted, had already carved out impressive international niches: Sears, Roebuck had more than twenty stores in Latin America, and General Motors was well on the way to becoming a billion-dollar overseas corporation. To assist these companies, the Eisenhower administration promised to make trading more profitable with tax concessions and tariff reductions. These new concessions to industry, coupled with the foreign-aid programs and military expenditures already funneling money into foreign economies, revealed the extent of Ike's resolve to nourish a steadily expanding world economy in his attempt to outflank the Soviets. Two powerful groups shaped the new American exhibits at international trade fairs: businessmen searching for markets and a government seeking international stability.

In August 1954 President Eisenhower appropriated $2 million from a discretionary fund and earmarked it for American participation at foreign trade fairs. This was used to attract American business to the trade fair circuit. The Commerce Department opened an information center on international trade fairs in Washington, D.C., and promised to establish a central exhibit at important fairs around which private business could organize company booths. It also stepped up its recruiting programs, enlisting volunteers to go abroad in advance of a given fair on trade "missions" in order to introduce the products and marketing techniques that the fair would showcase.[7] This new "industry-government" program even offered to ship and display samples for companies that could not afford the costs. Companies were told to ship their products collect to a given port, and the Commerce Department took care of unloading and setting up. American products could enter foreign trade fairs with a minimum of effort because President Eisenhower considered it essential that "we take immediate and vigorous action to demonstrate the superiority of the products and cultural values of our system of free enterprise."[8]

Depending on the size of the business community in a foreign country, a trade mission of four or five U.S. businessmen, led by a Department of Commerce official, could meet with between one and five thousand local business people and often the political leadership as well. In the words of a sales manager sent to Italy in 1955: "Our objective was selling; selling on many levels. We were selling our government's sincerity and interest in promoting two-way trade; selling our president's over-all interest and sincerity of purpose in bringing a closer rapprochement between countries; selling the American way of life and the democratic philosophy of our government."[9]

The missionaries were underpaid and had to endure a tough schedule. Fred Wittner, an advertising executive who participated in a mission to Yugoslavia in 1958, spent several days at the trade information centers inside the American pavilions at the Belgrade and Zagreb fairs, held group meetings in ten cities, visited eleven tourist resorts (to advise on methods of attracting Americans), and visited sixteen industrial plants. Along with "missionaries" the Department of Commerce sent a reference library consisting of more than a thousand business publications and directories, covering the spectrum of U.S. private enterprise. These miniature research departments were set up in the American pavilions at trade fairs, where the mission specialists could answer any questions the locals might have about the articles provided. Many of the U.S. businessmen who participated in the program confessed to having had an enriching experience, despite the grueling timetable. The mission program offered participants a little adventure and a chance to make a real contribution to international peace and prosperity.[10]

The first trade fair display influenced by the new government-industry program took place in Bangkok, Thailand, in December 1954. Earl J. Wilson handled ideological exhibits for the United States Information Service (USIS), the overseas division of the USIA, and Worthen Paxton, a former art editor at *Life*, was hired by the Department of Commerce to oversee products, fashion shows, and do-it-yourself demonstrations. Wilson suggested that Cinerama, a new type of wide-screen film projection, be used as an entertainment exhibit, and it proved to be an effective way of pulling people into the American section.

Cinerama had been developed in the 1940s by the American inventor Fred Waller. It began as a multiple-camera projector system that permitted the projection of color slides on five giant screens simultaneously. Time Inc. and Laurance S. Rockefeller formed the Cinerama Company in 1947 to produce motion pictures by a similar technique, and *Life* used the Cinerama process to create a promotional film, *The New America,* featuring "a series of remarkable panoramic pictures that showed not only the natural glories of the United States but . . . the new factories, the prosperous and exploding suburbs with their schools and shopping centers." *Life* showed the entertainment spectacle to potential advertisers, hoping to drum up business. The U.S. Army, recognizing the propaganda value of the process, had *The New America* translated and shown extensively in Germany, Japan, and Korea.[11] Cinerama movies that celebrated the dramatic natural wonders of the United States alongside the post–World War II economic miracle quickly became staples of the exhibition circuit—for obvious reasons.

Once in the American pavilion at Bangkok, visitors saw an anti-Communist exhibit, attributed to the local police. Wilson had instructed the Thai police to make a papier-mâché spider hanging from the ceiling, with a map of Asia on the walls around its web. Then he added a whip made of barbed wire, allegedly from a prison in Korea where it had been used to scourge prisoners, and a Korean flag covered with hundreds of signatures in the "blood of Korean soldiers" pledging to defend their country. "It was corny," he said. "But at least the place was crowded with people all the time."[12]

The USIA/Department of Commerce cooperation at Bangkok was commemorated by *Life* in a photograph that recorded representatives from both agencies receiving the first-prize award from a Thai official. *Life* described the fair in terms that made explicit the Communist-versus-capitalist rivalry and crooned over the hastily constructed but popular exhibits.[13] *Life*'s photographers put a rosy glow on the affair. Their still pictures showed an American model in a runway show wearing a striped bathing suit, and a crowd mesmerized by water-skiing beauties on the curved Cinerama screen.

Life described the exhibits as a "trail blazing effort" on the part of the U.S. government, overlooking the fact that such American products were not always relevant to Thai culture. This point was made in tragic fashion by the U.S. ambassador to Thailand, John E. Peurifoy, who bought the Thunderbird sports car exhibited at the fair and drove it head-on into a truck on a primitive one-way bridge shortly thereafter.[14]

The American pavilions at the 1955 spring and summer fairs in Europe were built around an "Industry in the Service of Mankind" theme, in order to integrate the hundreds of American products snugly within a narrative context. The Paris Trade Fair (May 14–30), overseen by Peter G. Harnden, the new chief of design and production in the Commerce Department's Office of International Trade Fairs,featured a photographic panorama of a Levittown-type community and scale-model homes. *House Beautiful* magazine furnished a living room and a fully equipped kitchen, and Harnden added a section from a supermarket to show how the kitchen was linked to an advanced food-distribution network. A kindergarten for the children from local military families, staffed by women from these families, demonstrated the value that Americans placed on education. This was an attempt to show that the U.S. system did more than just award profits to wealthy capitalists, that middle-class comforts also enhanced childhood development and public welfare. Closed-circuit TV, like Cinerama at other shows, provided the sensational buzz that drew the crowds.

Products were displayed to show the benefits of mass production for the average family. Patio chairs, barbecues, lawn mowers, and plastic containers did more than exhibit the aesthetic talents of industrial designers and the efficiency of factories—they revealed how leisure and labor-saving devices were part of the domestic sphere.[15] Joseph Barry, a *House Beautiful* reporter, described the success of Commerce Department exhibits in Milan, Paris, Barcelona, and the Italian city of Bari, at which *House Beautiful* set up "a life-size picture of how Americans live." He claimed that middle-class Europeans, when exposed to the new postwar model homes, were indeed surprised by the new "open spaciousness of their rooms, their views of pleasant gardens and neighbors."[16]

To create a sense of authenticity, *House Beautiful* furnished, decorated, and then photographed their model home exhibits before packing them off to Europe, where they were then reassembled. Interpretive captions assured visitors that these were representative homes of "American school teachers, office workers, carpenters, plumbers, bricklayers, mechanics," and that they represented the high standards toward which housing in America was tending, "not only for slightly-above-average income families, but for those below."[17]

The model homes were a little spartan in comparison to what *House Beautiful* tried to sell Americans; Barry explained that the higher standards of the domestic market had been achieved only gradually. "We at *House Beautiful,*" he wrote, "are convinced that the golden age of consumer culture in America has been brought about by a consumer who is distinctly not interested in being common. He doesn't want to live an average or minimum life and that is why, we believe, America is exploding with new ideas, new interests, new standards of living."[18] By presenting these average (and authentic-looking) homes to Europeans, *House Beautiful* aimed low, but hoped that foreign consumers would soon demand the same sort of products available to their American counterparts.

Model homes were effective in markets where the audience was suspicious of propaganda. "We think," said Barry, "that Europeans will understand the basic dignity of separate bathrooms, hot and cold running water, an abundance of sunlight and electric light, air, space, and green surroundings. And they'll understand, as some of our own intellectuals do not, the freedom offered by washing machines and dishwashers, vacuum cleaners, automobiles, and refrigerators."[19] *House Beautiful* researchers had determined that built-in features would be especially impressive because few homes abroad were constructed in this fashion. And by hiding clutter, built-in closets and shelves maintained the spacious look of these rather small, open-plan houses. Photographs in the exhibits showed families in the living room listening to music, gardening together and watching the agreeable neighbors next door.

As *House Beautiful* (a Hearst Corporation magazine), and Time Inc.'s *Life* and *Fortune* publicized the trade fairs, they welded together the notion of a domesticated capitalism with consumer products. A variety of accents helped to make the model homes into symbols of the American way of life. Linoleum kitchen floors in a "confetti" pattern hinted that the home was a reward for those who had married successfully. The home furnishings reinforced the illusion that the American economy was a kind of support system for the nuclear family. Labels assured visitors that "the most advanced technological tools of efficient homemaking" are made available to the common consumer at an affordable price and in a style that would credit the homes of the wealthy.[20] Reproductions of museum-quality sculpture, also made affordable through mass production, added a touch of sophistication, and Fostoria glass and Stangl pottery added warmth and elegance. Life was easy: the kitchen of the $14,000 model home had a table on wheels so that it was ready to roll into the living room in front of the television, or out onto the patio where a barbecue might be placed. Mass-produced but elegant "casual china" by the designer Russel Wright completed the aura of inexpensive but elegant functionalism. Even if Europeans totally rejected the trade fair exhibits, the publicity they generated for the abundant society provided great ad copy for the domestic market.

House Beautiful's displays suggested that creating a successful trade alliance between the United States and Europe required far more than exchanging products. And indeed, American homes and their appliances were part of a social and psychological framework that could be most effectively exported only as a complete package: big refrigerators need big kitchens; lawn mowers need lawns. *House Beautiful*'s displays were the most ambitious campaign thus far in the so-called nylon war.

The USIA, like the Department of Commerce, relied on the goodwill of the business community to transform U.S. ideals into meaningful deeds. Shortly after the USIA was created, in August 1953, its director, Theodore C. Streibert, attempted to mobilize the private sector to bring America's story to "the people of friendly nations."[21] The goal was to gain the support of the same business and voluntary associations that had come to the aid of the nation during World War II. Through a series of talks with influential business groups, Streibert encouraged international corporations to conduct

Cover of a guide to advertising in foreign countries, prepared by the Advertising Council and the United States Information Service. National Archives.

public relations campaigns for the U.S. government in order to mask the overt operations of his propaganda agency—which foreigners tended to discount. In his address on March 16, 1954, to the International Advertising Association and the Export Manager's Club of New York, for example, Streibert asked that the principal holders of overseas investments pool their resources in a single organization that could supervise a unified overseas public relations program. He hoped such an organization could "aim primarily at increasing understanding of our economic system and the beneficial results which can flow from private investment."[22]

Streibert emphasized the crucial relationship between public and private interests. "Latin America," he said, "is as important as all of Europe and more important than Asia, Africa, and Oceania combined. . . . [It] represents almost 30 percent of the total U.S. private long term investment abroad." As a consequence, American businessmen represented an intimidating power bloc when they appeared in southern capitals. To overcome the fear of Yankees,

Streibert recommended that companies help him "submit convincing evidence to the people of Latin America that private capital has actually become the servant of the community and serves as a responsible member of the community overseas. We must dispel the distorted picture of U.S. imperialism directed by Wall Street which the Communists portray in so much of their propaganda," he said.[23] The Radio Corporation of America (RCA), IBM, Eastman Kodak, and trade associations such as the Art Director's Club of New York and the Advertising Council promised to cooperate with the USIA.[24] The Advertising Council would, in fact, not only become the coordinating agency for international corporations that Streibert was searching for, but also a great influence on the USIA itself through the People's Capitalism campaign—which the Advertising Council developed for use as an ideological theme in advertisements and popular publications.

People's Capitalism was the invention of Ted Repplier, President of the Advertising Council—a powerful association made up of advertising industry executives formed during World War II to bolster the government's productivity drives and other public relations campaigns. The council was a pro-business group, eager to improve the image of the advertising industry and naturally careful to cement ties with important business concerns in the course of volunteer work; it was by no means a docile handmaiden of the government. During World War II, Elmer Davis, a writer, radio commentator, and head of the Office of War Information, had kept a wary eye on the council's ethical standards, but in the Eisenhower administration the lines between big business and government were often blurred by expedience; consequently, during the 1950s, suggestions from the Advertising Council received little opposition.[25]

In 1951–53 the Advertising Council sponsored a series of round-table discussions with some forty experts from various fields in an attempt to distill the American way of life into a formula that could be diffused through advertisements, economic programs, and the international exhibitions sponsored by the Department of Commerce and the USIA. The Advertising Council members governing the round-table discussions included Roy E. Larsen, president of Time Inc.; Evans Clark, executive director of the Twentieth Century Fund;

and Repplier, among others. Guest moderators included Henry M. Wriston, president of Brown University, who presided over the panels "The Moral and Religious Basis of the American Society" and the "Cultural Aspects of the American Society" in 1953; and Paul Hoffman, who was the moderator of the first panel, in 1951, "The Basic Elements of a Free Dynamic Society." This prestigious group of Advertising Council leaders and supporters was able to attract guest participants of equal prominence from the fields of publishing, academia, labor, and the arts. The 1953 panel on American culture, for example, featured the poet W. H. Auden; John Ely Burchard, dean of the School of Humanities and Social Studies, Massachusetts Institute of Technology; the British Broadcasting Company correspondent Alistair Cooke; and the television producer and writer Gilbert Seldes, to name only a few of the eminent individuals who figured into the formulation of what would eventually be called the People's Capitalism campaign.[26]

Repplier supplemented the information gleaned from the round-table discussions from 1951 to 1953 with some primary research. He was awarded an Eisenhower Exchange Fellowship to travel abroad in the first half of 1955, in order to compile a comprehensive review of the American propaganda effort. He traveled to strategically important areas in the Far East, Europe, and North Africa and compiled a report of his findings immediately upon return. Repplier concluded from his experiences abroad that American information policies had been doomed from the start because they aimed at giving "a full and fair picture" of the United States, a nation so diverse that to do justice to this aim would naturally lead to contradictions, confusion, incomprehensibility.[27] In some USIS offices, he had encountered a disturbing vagueness. Propaganda, he said, required two essentials: the selection of a few key truths that forward the chosen objectives, and the movement of these truths from paper to mind with the force and frequency to make them stick.[28]

Something of an alarmist, Repplier warned that communism was making headway throughout Europe, aided by obsolete Third World economic ideas that "obstruct the processes which would bring a higher standard of living to the masses, and hence hasten the end of Communism."[29] He discovered that progress had been made in implementing American ideals such as productivity, but little had been done to show how prosperity arises from the spread of productivity. As a result, labor everywhere seemed headed into the Communist camp, and intellectuals appeared to all be "either outright Communists" or fellow travelers.[30] "Why do we who know that right is with us, so often make no headway with our arguments?" he asked. "What does Communism have that we lack? If we can discover this lack and supply it, the whole Cold War might turn in our favor."[31]

Repplier determined that the USIA approach was hampered by a reactionary policy that continually harped on negatives, such as the Soviet prison camps. Likewise, in regard to foreign policy the United States had no key inspirational theme comparable to that of the Soviets—nothing that could shape national ideals into a crusade. "Communism promised relief for the oppressed, help for the helpless, self respect for the downtrodden," but the United States had failed to state its goals clearly.[32] Embellishing ideas already articulated by Paul Hoffman in *Peace Can Be Won,* Repplier believed a new campaign should be built around ideals long advanced through Marshall Plan and Point Four programs—a campaign that declared the goal of the United States to be the elimination of poverty everywhere.

As a traveling Eisenhower Fellow, Repplier discovered a cultural affinity with the USIA staff, who turned out to have backgrounds much like his own. The agency chief, Ted Streibert, was the former board chairman of the Mutual Broadcasting System, and his assistant, Abbott Washburn, had been a wartime employee of the Office of Strategic Services. Most of the overseas representatives of the USIA, he discovered, were former newspapermen and advertising people. During the fall of 1955, Repplier lectured influential business groups and wrote articles as an unofficial USIA representative, attempting to drum up support for his propaganda crusade, which he called the People's Capitalism campaign.[33] He was so influential within the relatively new USIA that in October 1955 Abbott Washburn sent a "General Justification Statement" of agency aims, heavily salted with Repplier's ideas, to area directors and media staffs.[34]

Washburn, Repplier, and Streibert hoped to show that the American way of life had already accomplished what communism

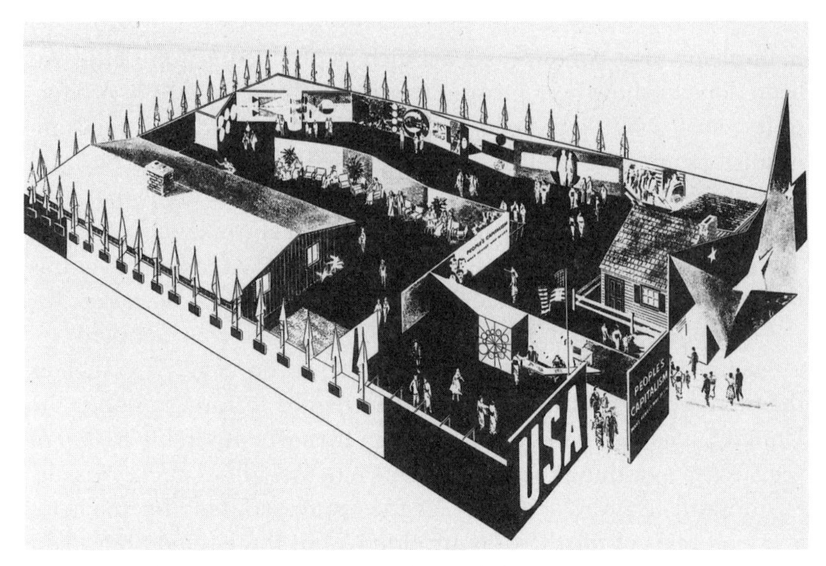

Illustration of the 1956 People's Capitalism *exhibit in Union Station, Washington, D.C., from the cover of the U.S. Information Agency brochure,* People's Capitalism—Man's Newest Way of Life. *Dwight D. Eisenhower Library, Abilene, Kansas.*

only promised. As a theme, this new concept seemed foolproof. But this seeming perfection, which admitted no faults, was the creation of like minds and sympathetic ears. Whether or not men and women in the street would believe these concepts was another matter. Wisely, Repplier and the USIA created a trial exhibition that opened in February 1956 at Union Station in Washington, D.C., so that the People's Capitalism campaign could be tested before it was sent abroad to international trade fairs and USIS posts.

Walking through the exhibit, the visitor was confronted with a series of symbols and statistics. Inside a large rectangular area the visitor traveled along a controlled path interrupted by a pioneer home, a DuPont film on nylon production, a nail-making machine, and finally, a contemporary model home stocked with labor-saving appliances. Ed Barnes, a millwright at U.S. Steel (the manufacturer of the prefabricated house), had allowed his family to be photographed in the house and during the exhibit those photographs were dis-

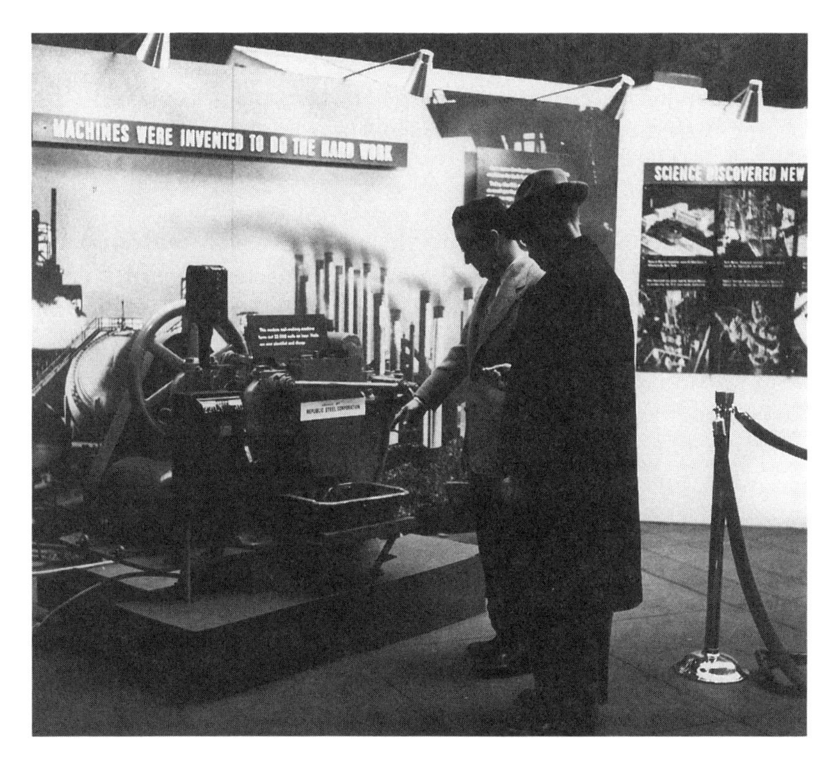

A nail-making machine demonstrates the benefits of automation in the People's Capitalism *exhibit in Union Station, Washington, D.C., 1956. National Archives.*

played outside the home with innocuous anecdotes about his family.

A log cabin near the entrance of the *People's Capitalism* exhibit symbolized the nation's origins, whereas the modern prefab near the exit with its family-centered leisure displays marked the distance between past and present. The idea was to show how the life of an average worker had dramatically improved in the modern era. Like the 1955 trade fair exhibits, the *People's Capitalism* exhibition portrayed "industry in the service of mankind." Publicity brochures explained that

> People's Capitalism is not only a new economic system but a new social system, too. The exhibit shows that the proportions of the

> very rich and the very poor have steadily diminished in America, in direct contradiction to the views of Karl Marx. It makes plain that this trend is continuing to the point where America is becoming classless. Already worker and boss have much the same comforts and recreations.[35]

The progressive theme was embellished by a blacksmith making nails juxtaposed with a modern nail-making machine that produced 16,000 nails an hour. Labels made the point that machines did the hard work. The U.S. worker produced five times as much per hour as his great-grandfather could 100 years ago. Today the people themselves were the capitalists: 70 million had savings accounts, 115 million owned life insurance, 7 million owned stocks, 27,000 companies and many Unions had pension funds.[36]

George Meany, president of the American Federation of Labor-Congress of Industrial Organizations (AFL-CIO), sent a representative with a prepared speech to introduce the exhibits at the opening ceremonies. His comments were mostly positive; after all, the labor movement had as much to gain from this crusade as their big-business counterparts—more—if the fantasy world envisioned by the exhibit ever came true. "Let us make no mistake," said the labor representative. "We are committed to the proposition that material abundance without political, social, and economic freedom is a sham, and we are equally committed to the proposition that there is no real freedom without a decent standard of living."[37] His cautious encouragement was offered because the campaign did indeed support big labor by turning a limited form of socialized capitalism into what I. F. Stone called a "kind of secular religion." But the campaign suffered from more than optimism. As I. F. Stone pointed out, a People's Capitalism was fine for those who belonged to unions or corporations, but it offered nothing to the disenfranchised, the underprivileged, and the free thinker. People's Capitalism portrayed an America in which everyone was gainfully employed, middle class, and a docile consumer. As an ideological crusade against communism it was effective, but as a propaganda program directed toward the domestic, as well as the international audience, its pinched view of U.S. culture bordered on the insidious.[38]

The USIA chief, Ted Streibert, used the unveiling ceremonies to reveal that a worldwide People's Capitalism campaign was under way. For Streibert, the participation of the Advertising Council represented his ideal of private-public cooperation. Through these exhibits the goals of his agency spoke in concrete terms, becoming more than just the disembodied opinions of the Voice of America.[39] USIA staff members solicited reactions from the crowd in order to determine whether or not their new image of the national life appeared convincing. The viewers were not all pleased. The furniture in the model home, for example, was criticized for being too new. "Show some shabby pieces," said one visitor. "Put some faces on the figures in the colonial house," said another. But the majority of the observers were sympathetic. Taking it for granted that reality was hardly the issue, one viewer commented that the exhibit "makes certain generalizations and omits some of the less satisfying features of American life, such as race relations, but these are both necessary and proper features of good propaganda."[40] A few people insisted that the lack of factual details made the exhibit a sham. Frank E. Klapthor, a curator from the Daughters of the American Revolution Museum, said he would like to know "exactly where they got the flannel wrapping for the baby on the floor of the pioneer house, which looked as if it came from a department store's basement counter." He added that 90 percent of the furnishings were a century too late: there were modern andirons, a Victorian cupboard, and a contemporary doorway leading into the cellar.[41]

Obviously, the exhibit had not been intended for the nearby museum community. Indeed, Repplier had little interest in the facts of daily life; the objects were props in a morality play, and it was assumed that visitors already knew and believed in the ideals put forward. Repplier hoped that people would ignore the limitations and shortcomings of exhibits and focus instead on the ideals of his crusade.

It required nerve to criticize People's Capitalism, which was essentially a conservative propaganda program masquerading as liberal, enlightened capitalism. Sen. Hubert H. Humphrey (D-Minn.), who called the Union Station exhibit a boastful and materialistic display, sounded the alarm in Congress.

Douglas Cornell, Executive Officer of the National Academy of Sciences in Washington, wrote a critical letter that Humphrey inserted into the *Congressional Record.* "What is the exhibit designed to do?" Cornell asked.

> If it is to show what America has accomplished economically and industrially, then it does a splendid job. But I cannot see the relevance of that to other people's problems in the world today except insofar as it shows the magnificent physical equipment that we have to help others. It fails to say how, or even whether, we propose to use our wealth, our resources, our great good fortune, our energies, and our hearts to help solve the world's problems.[42]

Cornell's discerning opinion was not disregarded. The exhibit was shut down amid controversy, placed in a warehouse, and redesigned before being sent off to South America.

The revised exhibit included more photographs and a few conceptual adjustments, such as a crowd picture featuring ethnic faces. And the 1776 cabin was transformed into a replica of Abraham Lincoln's mythic boyhood home. The Lincoln image was an expedient way of addressing the race issue: one of the contemporary problems that questionnaire respondents had identified as a glaring omission. This was not too outrageous at a time when Eisenhower himself was often compared to Lincoln, the Great Conciliator (not Lincoln as the Great Emancipator). While the Union Station *People's Capitalism* exhibit was still up, for instance, Sen. George D. Aiken (R-Vt.), in an address to a Ford Theater audience on Lincoln's Birthday, said:

> We should be eternally grateful that the man in the White House today, like Lincoln, is a great moderator, yielding to no extreme faction of the left or of the right—that he has given this country moderate ideas, moderate laws, moderate executive action. . . . Much as Lincoln hated slavery he was loath to take drastic action to achieve its end. Instead, he stressed reliance on time, discussion, and the ballot box.[43]

Lincoln provided a convenient way for the status quo to acknowledge racism without incurring the wrath of segregationists. Besides, the 1959–60 Lincoln Sesquicentennial was not far away. The introduction of Lincoln into the USIA's international exhibition program in 1956 was a prelude to the radio addresses and movies about Lincoln that were to be shown from Liberia to Korea; to the ceremonial busts of Abe presented by Eisenhower to other world leaders as symbols of peace and friendship; to the new replica of Lincoln's cabin that would be built by American soldiers stationed in Frankfurt, West Germany, in front of the American Cultural Center; and to the gigantic bust of Lincoln featured at the 1959 National Exhibition in Moscow.[44]

The contemporary home was altered very little. New captions admitted that Ed Barnes's salary was slightly above average, but Barnes still had an implausible history: Captions described him as a descendent of the first pioneer family to cross the Allegheny Mountains. He had been born in Uniontown, Pennsylvania (of all places), bought his home on the installment plan, and liked watching football games on television. His fondest desire was to give his children the finest education possible. A pie chart showing the family budget rounded out the picture. The ideal Barnes family was the most important display in the exhibit because it illustrated what the Advertising Council called "[t]he iron law of American capitalism: because industry needs more customers, it is happy if the worker can buy more; because workers can buy more, they are happy if industry can produce more—this condition of mutual reliance creates mutual understanding and cooperation instead of class struggle." The Barnes family lived in a home produced by Ed's employer (U.S. Steel). And while Mrs. Barnes played a strictly traditional role, the children would have the opportunity to rise through education.[45]

Further alterations were made by replacing a Du Pont film, which compared modern nylon production to the making of homespun, with an exhibit giving a broader view of science. The new exhibits tried to show that research in chemistry and physics were part of all segments of American life. Visitors also saw an animated model of a nuclear power plant, the purpose of which was explained by means of telephone-listening devices. And an investment display, added specifically for the trade fair circuit, revealed how America was, itself, developed by foreign capital. Photographs showed how Europeans came to the United States and financed railroads, mining, and petroleum refineries (exactly those industries U.S. companies wished to finance in the Third World). The revamped exhibit was no different in spirit from the original. The basic principles of the campaign—individualism, scientific progress, labor-management cooperation, the classless society, the increase of leisure time allowing for cultural and spiritual enrichment—were just refined and simplified. The *People's Capitalism* exhibit delivered a "few key truths" clearly and forcefully.

The debate concerning the exhibit soon extended beyond Capitol Hill. Edgar Kemler, writing in *The Nation,* asked, "When will our tycoons learn that they will never be as popular as movie stars on the world stage?" Kemler warned that President Eisenhower was being led by the nose by CEOs who regarded world politics as a private struggle between themselves and a handful of Soviet apparatchiks; he was afraid to think what Asians and other foreign people (especially the poverty-stricken and people of color) might make of this "lethal dose of conservatism."[46]

In May 1956 Theodore Streibert sent descriptions of the exhibits and details of the captions out to USIS posts throughout the world, and People's Capitalism became the official theme of the information program that year. Reduced versions of the exhibit were made for export, and the Union Station version was shipped off to the International Trade Fair in Bogotá, Colombia (November 23–December 9, 1956), its first stop on a Latin American tour. But the fact that the exhibit had been revised did not impress the critics who followed its progress in sketchy press releases. Eugene W. Castle, author of *The Great Giveaway,* warned that the *People's Capitalism* exhibition would only "create envy, rekindle animosities, aid homegrown Communist agitators and incite dictators to make new and added demands for foreign aid forever." Castle's assessment of Latin American reception was partly accurate. USIA employees discovered that whenever they touted private enterprise in Latin America, the public inevitably suspected that the real aim was to help American firms expand their markets at the expense of local people. To their chagrin, USIA officials eventually discovered that in Latin America the word *capitalism* inevitably condemned anything and everyone associated with it.[47]

When *People's Capitalism* left Bogotá it went to Mexico City.

Smaller versions were created and sent to USIS posts for use in European and Asian fairs, making the Barnes family international ambassadors for the American way of life. As the exhibit traveled, USIS staff interviewed important visitors, educators, and government officials and encouraged them to integrate the People's Capitalism doctrine into school curricula and public policies. After the exhibit was shown in Guatemala City, the government of that country initiated a conference on the theories and concepts of People's Capitalism. A similar triumph was reported in Bogotá, where one of Colombia's most distinguished economists relied upon People's Capitalism formulas "to illustrate and fortify his ideas about the need for the complete freedom of private enterprise" during his address to a government economic advisory group.[48]

The exhibit was accompanied by articles in local magazines and in the English-language press; traveling businessmen and dignitaries used People's Capitalism themes in their speeches. In the summer of 1957, for example, Clarence B. Randall, the president's special assistant for foreign economic policy, delivered a speech on the People's Capitalism theme in Stuttgart, Germany, to representatives from thirty countries. In turn, these testimonials met with vigorous Soviet rebuttals. The Moscow Radio's Home Service, in a broadcast report, said, "Is there anyone who does not know that this so-called 'people's capitalism,' as before, means all power to the big owners, merciless exploitation of the working people, a wild arms race, and the suppression of all types of struggle of the working people for their rights?"[49]

During a meeting in May 1956, the Advertising Council agreed to a request by President Eisenhower to conduct a domestic version of the People's Capitalism campaign. The first step in this direction for the People's Capitalism committee was to seek a legitimate facade. Just as the USIA recruited private corporations to carry its ideology abroad—in order to mask the bias of a propaganda agency—so the Advertising Council looked for academic authorities who would disseminate their theories domestically: "It was recognized that because the idea [People's Capitalism] is identified with the Advertising Council it is already regarded by some journalists and others as merely an advertising stunt."[50]

The Advertising Council began its search for credibility by looking for an author who could transform the round-table discussions of 1951–53 into a convincing treatise on U.S. culture. In order for those earlier discussions to be brought up to date it was decided to arrange another series of talks, to be held in the fall of 1956, either at Yale or Columbia University. The Advertising Council hoped to enlist both a cultural authority and an economist. If the authors could not develop a book out of the People's Capitalism principles, the Advertising Council hoped to place an article in a journal such as the *Harvard Business Review* that could then be reprinted and circulated "to newspapers, magazines, business and community leaders."[51]

By 1956 many influential members of the popular press were ensconced within the Advertising Council's hierarchy: Roy Larsen from Time Inc., Philip Graham from the *Washington Post and Times Herald*, and Ted Patrick from *Holiday*. *House Beautiful* published a special issue around the campaign in the fall of 1956, and sympathetic corporations began sponsoring ads that used aspects of the People's Capitalism theme. The campaign was infectious. Writers and advertisers could pick up one of the many threads—General Electric, for example, used the worker-as-shareholder, everyman-as-capitalist theme in its ads—and elaborate it to suit the occasion.

The big break came when Yale University agreed to lend its authority to the campaign by hosting a round-table symposium. After the sessions had been condensed by David M. Potter, a professor of American history, Repplier wrote to James M. Lambie Jr. at the White House, stating that at last they had achieved an "intellectual foundation."[52] Potter had only recently completed his *People of Plenty: Economic Abundance and the American Character*, in which he had revised concepts relating to the American sense of mission and redefined for much of mid-century America the key role of "abundance" in the history of American exceptionalism.[53]

The round tables at Yale in November 1956 and at the Yale Club in New York City in May 1957 were the eighth session of an ongoing Advertising Council symposium aimed at establishing an economic, political, and cultural consensus of opinion among elites. This was the first forum with a focus on the term *people's capitalism*, although previous sessions had discussed related issues. Distinguished panelists included Edmund W. Sinnott (moderator), dean emeritus of the Yale Graduate School; Henry C. Wallich and William J. Fellner from the Yale Economics Department; Walter H. Wheeler Jr. and Lee H. Bristol, representing the corporate community; Henry C. Fleisher and George T. Brown from the AFL-CIO; John Davenport of the board of editors, *Fortune* magazine; and of course David Potter. The panelists defined the term *People's Capitalism*—as distinct from other forms of capitalism—and then discussed how People's Capitalism had developed, how it could be exported to other nations, its shortcomings, and how it related to human values.

Potter and his colleagues (perhaps unwittingly) provided theoretical rejoinders to the criticisms leveled by Humphrey, Castle, and all those of little faith who insisted upon measuring the distance between the real and the ideal. The Advertising Council hoped that the Yale sessions would, in the words of Chairman Chester J. LaRoche, "create a consensus that could become the possession of the average man; fill a serious vacuum and meet a need made clamorous by the challenge of international Communism."[54] Potter's digest of the Yale Round Table was printed in pamphlet form and, as with the proceedings of the other round-table symposiums, mailed free of charge to influential editors, educators, and business leaders.

By the summer of 1956 all the pieces had fallen into place for the American trade fair program. Experts from the Advertising Council were assisting with exhibit narratives. The USIA had coordinated its libraries and cultural centers to accommodate the aims of the *People's Capitalism* exhibit and to help disseminate American goals through the foreign and domestic press. The Commerce Department was busier than ever, setting up central pavilions at trade fairs and soliciting donations from private industry. And by July 1956 the Trade Mission Program, which sent businessmen on people-to-people tours, announced that the U.S. volunteers ("apostles," as one reporter called them) had met with more than 78,000 businessmen in nineteen countries since 1954.[55] The fairs had become a serious issue, not only because of their frequency, but because they were becoming more like the influential world's fairs with their ability to generate tourism, their displays of new and experimental products, their specialized promotional campaigns, and their ideological statements.

The Commerce Department developed its own approach to trade fair exhibits, different from that of the USIA and the Advertising Council. Although they had to accommodate USIA specialists, the Commerce Department pavilions at European fairs during the 1956 season used the talents of top-notch industrial designers (as opposed to advertising experts). Ideal families appeared in photographs inside model homes, but Commerce Department exhibits were head and shoulders above the simple USIA exhibit that had debuted in Union Station. Essentially, the Commerce Department put objects before ideas, arranging displays so that objects illustrated ideals in a subliminal manner.

In Vienna, Austria, the Commerce Department theme committee decided to focus on new products. Exhibits were created by Peter G. Harnden, who was already the favorite design contractor for shows in sophisticated Western capitals. Harnden was familiar with the elements pioneered by earlier "good design" shows at the Museum of Modern Art, the Chicago Merchandise Mart, and the high-style Milan Triennials, which relied heavily on visual appeal. In the American Pavilion at Vienna, for example, the horizontal lines of American flags were extended and juxtaposed against walls made from vertical beams, emphasizing the plastic beauty of the stars and stripes while defusing any imperialist associations the flag might have for foreign guests. Wire chairs, designed by the sculptor Harry Bertoia, complemented the informal, circular kitchen table in the model home, where designer cutlery and a modern dinner service demonstrated that mass-produced consumer products need not suffer from a strictly functional appearance. A fashion show, in cooperation with the Department of Agriculture, advertised "What's New" in cotton fabrics and their use in everything from ball gowns to the latest ready-to-wear sporting attire. Color television was used in an exhibit concerning medical education. Other "advanced technical devices" on display included a hi-fi record player built into the dashboard of a car and solar-battery-powered radios. These high-tech gadgets for the playboy set were the very antithesis of the scary image that technology had acquired from its association with military hardware.[56]

At the St. Erik's Fair in Stockholm, Sweden, exhibits designed by the Swedish-American Reino Aarnio were arranged according to a do-it-yourself theme. Navajo Indians were hired to demonstrate their weaving and silversmith skills, and a fashion show of dresses produced on the spot by seamstresses demonstrated how technology helped everyone—especially women. A Swedish couple were enlisted to perform a dance routine based on home improvement. The pirouetting couple painted and decorated with equipment available in the department store exhibit nearby. Children made creative paintings and assembled prefabricated toys under the supervision of adults. The key to a successful exhibition, Commerce Department designers learned, was an activated, participatory show that brought material culture to life and revealed how technology benefited the average person. The do-it-yourself theme was used again in many fairs because it demonstrated how the consumer society empowered the individual. It enabled visitors to involve themselves in the "democratic" process in a hands-on manner.

Kabul, Afghanistan, witnessed one of the big successes of the 1956 season with the trade fair debut of Buckminster Fuller's geodesic dome. While some 200 Soviet technicians labored on a $2 million pavilion, the U.S. dome was flown in and erected in two days, using local labor. It was the largest dome Buckminster Fuller had ever designed (100 feet in diameter), and it expressed perfectly the ability of American technology to be "ingenious rather than lavish."[57] At a time when scientific innovation was increasingly relegated to the laboratory under the supervision of experts, Buckminster Fuller represented the backyard tinkerer. He was the apogee of the do-it-yourself American, an iconoclast unhampered by tradition. Best of all, the dome had an uncanny resemblance to primitive structures: yurts, circus tents, and ancient tombs. Putting the dome together demonstrated to locals that innovation need not be expensive, arcane, or threatening. Similarly, scientific agriculture was made comprehensible to the mostly rural audience with a robotic "talking cow and chicken," which had their sides cut away to show internal organs. Photomurals of the New York skyline presented an Oz-like vision of the United States, and a Cinerama show outside pulled in curious onlookers.[58]

At the 1956 fair in Salonika, Greece, Bernard Phriem designed exhibits containing a closed-circuit television display, a children's playground illustrating a psychological approach to child training, an auto-repair shop, metal and woodworking shops, and a home-dressmaking and fashion show. The fashion runway, suspended over a pool of water in one of the exhibition halls, was probably Phriem's most innovative design. The serpentine pathway curved around mannequins on tiny islands in the center of the pool, thus weaving together islands and water—symbols of the Greek landscape—with American ready-made cotton dresses. Phriem's space quietly suggested to visitors that although America was far away it was full of people much like themselves.[59]

By the end of 1956 the USIA and the Commerce Department had learned some valuable lessons. In Berlin, the Sears, Roebuck catalogs had been stolen by visitors, revealing that people wanted to study goods and compare prices in the privacy of their own homes. And a supermarket exhibit—a new type of spectacle—had been the popular hit at Paris and Vienna. Peter Harnden's graphic techniques placed visitors within visually stimulating fields and created a receptive atmosphere. In Kabul, similarly, the geodesic dome had enveloped visitors in an engineering marvel that was instantly perceived as an "American" space. At all the fairs, designers demonstrated the adaptability of U.S. technology: how machines could be put "at the service of mankind" despite cultural variants. Bad reactions had been observed only when products were exhibited that the local people had no hope of ever attaining.

A symbolic art of exhibit design that promoted the aims first articulated by Marshall Plan administrators had become relatively well developed by 1957. By hiring architects and industrial designers under a system of competitive bidding, the Commerce Department's Office of International Trade Fairs, and to a lesser extent the USIA, had begun to tap a resourceful new pool of design professionals who were years ahead of the Advertising Council in their ability to draw people into an exhibit and make them feel as if they were participating in an authentic cultural experience, not just a propaganda event. Formulaic People's Capitalism exhibits were increasingly ignored by designers in the field, who realized that every location required a different approach. To assume that foreign people would immediately drop all of their customs in favor of a *Leave-It-to-Beaver* domesticity, for example, was absurd.[60]

On June 28, 1956, Polish workers demonstrated against the Soviets at the Poznań International Trade Fair. The United States had not been able to get a pavilion into Poland that year and so missed a great propaganda opportunity. But American officials were probably glad they had missed it when Hungarian workers revolted in Budapest later that autumn and critics blamed the U.S. propaganda machine for the resulting violence. The *New York Times* correspondent John MacCormac, who had been in Budapest during the revolt, reported that many of the Hungarians appeared to have been convinced by Voice of America broadcasts that the United Nations would come to their assistance once the fighting commenced. The USIA was quick to point out that broadcasting the "truth" about the Soviets was different from advocating violent insurrection.[61]

The 1956 Polish strike was one of the events leading up to the pro-Western regime of Wladyslaw Gomulka, an eager host for the U.S. trade fair exhibit of 1957. The American Pavilion in Poznań (another of Buckminster Fuller's domes) followed a U.S. aid agreement that promised up to $95 million in loans and credits. The money was earmarked mostly for the type of machinery and agricultural commodities that the upcoming trade fair would display, but there was also a model home, ladies' hats, 1957 cars, and frozen-food stands, which demonstrated to the crowds in a hands-on fashion the fruits of a capitalist economy.[62] In the attempt to incite delirious consumerism, the Commerce Department unleashed all of its gadgetry. *Time* called the American exhibit a "nylon wonderland," and *Life* photographed men admiring lawn mowers, teenagers ogling a jukebox, and children hypnotized by their reflections in the glass of a candy machine.[63] *House and Home* sponsored a $17,000 glass-gabled, redwood-paneled prefab house with built-ins. The reporter Edgar Clark observed that "The women were like little girls looking at a Christmas tree—a Christmas tree they could not have, one that would disappear like the dream it was. They were goggle-eyed at the superduper kitchen, and they all cooed at the nursery."[64] Communist papers compared the concentration on consumer goods as "akin to a rich man's showing off in front of a poor man," but the daily American fashion show was jammed with eager onlookers. Clever Commerce Department planners, knowing the Soviets would be showing off furs, had arranged to show inexpensive fashions within the reach of ordinary people, such as an imitation fur coat priced at $36.[65]

The final American production of the 1957 season, in Zagreb, Yugoslavia, was the most spectacular, aimed at dazzling the independent-minded president of the republic, Marshal Tito. Using a supermarket to anchor the U.S. pavilion, designers created a sensational picture of the American way of life that focused on food and basic amenities. Smaller supermarket exhibits had been used before. It was the functioning supermarket at a trade fair in Rome, held in June 1956 during the twenty-fifth annual meeting of the International Association of Chain Stores, that inspired the displays in Zagreb. The "American-Way" supermarket in Rome had been equipped, stocked, and opened for exhibition within sixty days and had attracted some 5,000 foreign distributors from twenty-five nations, along with about 400,000 curious Romans. Lansing P. Shield, the president of the International Association of Chain Stores, explained that the success of the supermarket concept derived from its ability to lower the average food budget by 20 percent. This provided cash for "houses, clothes, medical care, education, and a general rise in the national standard of living." Shield could have been speaking for many of his contemporaries, and certainly most trade missionaries, when he added, "as standards of living rise, so will prospects of an enduring peace." The businessmen who sponsored the supermarket displays in Italy and Yugoslavia viewed themselves, first and foremost, as social reformers.[66]

A group of Italian businessmen purchased the supermarket equipment in Rome and started a chain of *supermercatos,* at which a wide variety of food was sold at 8 to 10 percent below local prices. This coincided with the entry into the European market of other forms of American packaging, merchandising, and distribution. By 1957 General Foods was marketing baby food in Europe, and International Standard Brands was doing well with desserts and baking powder. Procter and Gamble's Tide laundry detergent was popular, as were other nonfood items by that company, often manufactured locally but merchandised in U.S. packaging. As the European Economic Community began to form, these companies hurried to set up operations behind tariff walls, to hire local managers and labor, and to become local in all but ownership. In 1955 the advertising trade journal *Printer's Ink* estimated that there were almost 6,500 self-service stores in forty-seven countries outside the United States. By 1957 there were more than 15,000; for 1958, the journal predicted a 20 percent increase.[67] The supermarket, like the shopping mall, was an engine of the consumer economy because it provided for the lowest-cost distribution of the largest possible variety of goods.

John A. Logan, the president of the National Association of Food Chains, predicted that what had happened in Italy could almost certainly be repeated in Yugoslavia. Branko Novakovic, the director of the Yugoslav Information Center, who helped sponsor the exhibit, explained during a press conference at the Waldorf-Astoria, "The supermarket will show our Yugoslav cooperatives and enterprises the importance of packaging, presenting, preserving of foods, the system of distribution of products, as well as the display and sale of competitive products and competitive pricing."[68] More than 600 American companies helped make the Zagreb exhibit a reality by contributing fixtures, supplies, and merchandise. The Commerce Department asked Walter Dorwin Teague Associates to design the pavilion, which would include an appliance store, a model apartment, an area for farm machinery, and a fully equipped laundromat. It was a spectacular vision of some of the things that normally excited the working class, and it aimed to help push Tito, a shrewd neutralist, closer to the West by creating consumer demands the Soviets could not yet fulfill.

The *New York Times* ran a story on the Zagreb supermarket showing crowds of well-dressed Yugoslavians snatching boxes of corn flakes off the shelves, elderly women eyeing mirrored meat coolers with the judicious eyes of budget-disciplined housewives, and more children gathered around automatic vending machines with expectant faces. There was no need to articulate the ideals of the People's Capitalism campaign. Those ideals were so deeply embedded within commercial products that propaganda slogans were totally redundant.

The only overt ideological statement was the Eisenhower quote at the entranceway to the American Pavilion, next to a blowup of

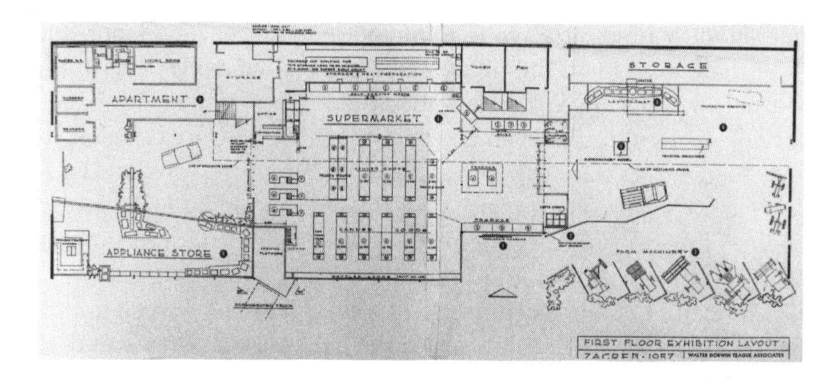

Exhibition layout in the American Pavilion, Zagreb Grand Fair, Zagreb, Yugoslavia, 1957, by Walter Dorwin Teague Associates. Collection of George S. Gardner.

Ike's full frontal portrait: "All countries today stand on the threshold of a more widely shared prosperity if they utilize wisely the knowledge of science and technology available to this age. International fairs help to spread this knowledge and to quicken man's imagination and ingenuity in the creation of a better life for all."[69] In Zagreb the marketing age and the advertising industry, which Potter believed to be the quintessential expressions of the abundant society, were everywhere in evidence.[70] The supermarket merged the new image of the abundant society with the old concept of amusement; like the shopping malls sprouting up all over the United States, the supermarket made consumerism into a raucous entertainment.

The doorway beneath President Eisenhower's message signaled the entrance into the world of prosperity. The visitor was guided past farm machinery: corn pickers and combines, tractors and plows, and, just around the corner of a partition, in the cool shade of an overhead mezzanine, a pick-up truck—the machine that symbolized the independent status of the small farmer and his command over the mechanical plantation. Beyond that, one encountered a fully automated laundromat—the first ever in Yugoslavia—and then, in the center of the complex, the supermarket, where a produce stand

Cover of a souvenir brochure of the supermarket at the Zagreb Grand Fair, Zagreb, Yugoslavia, 1957. Collection of the author.

stood squarely inside the glass doors, flanked by coolers of dairy products. Visitors discovered the ice cream and then the self-service meats, wrapped in cellophane by a butcher at the back of the room. Hamburger meat, spare ribs, and hot dogs (tasty ambassadors for the American way) were set out in tidy rows beneath their name tags. Commercial white bread, cake mixes, and canned goods with their enticing labels occupied the central rows. A self-service "drug-o-mat" stood in the back corner near the checkout stands.

University of Zagreb students were hired to push loaded shopping carts about the store while making small talk about pricing systems, shelving systems, distribution methods, and the mysterious cash register. On America Day, Sinclair Weeks, the U.S. secretary of commerce, entered into the spirit by posing for the camera while guiding a cart stocked with toilet paper past the checkout counter.

Another photographer found Clarence B. Randall, special assistant to President Eisenhower, chatting with the meat department manager over a produce counter heaped with preserves, grapes, bananas, peaches, and ripe apples.

Beyond the checkout counters was an appliance display and a model kitchen, where the frozen foods and other unfamiliar items were cooked and handed out to the crowd. There was a modest model apartment, where middle-class furnishings demonstrated how a typical worker's family enjoyed the television-centered life that the modern farm equipment, supermarkets, frozen and canned foods, and appliances provided. The Zagreb apartment had a nursery, two bedrooms, a modern bathroom, kitchen, and a living room with a dining area. The designers placed the apartment at the exit of the pavilion in order to illustrate that the family-centered home was the goal of the systems of production and consumption that went to make up this concise tour of a capitalist democracy.

At the close of the fair the consumer products and produce were donated to the local Red Cross. The supermarket itself was sold, as the one in Italy had been, ostensibly to save freight costs but also to help coax Zagreb into the international food distribution network. Shortly after the fair closed, the Yugoslav government announced plans to build a chain of sixty similar supermarkets throughout the country.[71]

The U.S. Commerce Department pavilions of 1956–57 taught exhibition planners the ideological power of consumer products and revealed how narrative themes like People's Capitalism could be integrated within subliminal, emotional, kinesthetic displays created by Peter G. Harnden, Bernard Phriem, or Walter Dorwin Teague Associates. Walking through an "American" (prefabricated) space, picking up and squeezing a pound of hamburger meat wrapped in cellophane, helping to build a geodesic dome, making the connection between corn pickers and the frozen TV dinners consumed by model families—these methods had the best chance of convincing foreign audiences that the United States was a benign, as well as a powerful, world leader.

When preparations began for the 1958 Brussels World's Fair, the biggest international exhibition of the post-World War II era, American planners were experienced enough to develop a highly sophisticated presentation. The U.S. architect Edward Durell Stone responded to the wealth of innovative ideas in the exhibition field by conceiving the largest circular pavilion ever built. It was an engineering marvel—like geodesic domes, an instantly recognizable symbol of American power and abundance. Peter G. Harnden was retained to design the exhibits because of his proven ability at trade fairs to translate American ideals into the sort of three-dimensional displays Western Europeans respected and admired. Ideological themes were hammered out under the guidance of the USIA and special consultants from the business community, the Advertising Council, and the Massachusetts Institute of Technology.

The American Pavilion at the Brussels World's Fair would be the largest U.S. international exhibition of culture during the 1950s. However, the ideological rivalries that emerged among liberal and conservative factions, each determined to have its own way at this highly visible interpretation of American mores, revealed that it was increasingly difficult, perhaps even impossible, to maintain an image of consensus for U.S. culture at any event larger than a trade fair.

3 Edward Durell Stone and the American Pavilion at the 1958 Brussels World's Fair

After the Kabul trade fair in 1955, Buckminster Fuller's geodesic domes became symbols of the U.S. trade fair program. They were simple to erect and impressive engineering marvels. A dome would have been an ideal choice for the American Pavilion at the 1958 Brussels World's Fair (as it was later at Expo '67 in Montreal). There is no evidence that Buckminster Fuller ever objected to how exhibition designers organized the displays within his domes, but Fuller was more of an engineer than an architect: although he was a pioneer in total systems—in synergism—his goal was to produce inexpensive, functional shelter. Modernists such as Frank Lloyd Wright, who were influenced by the Bauhaus ideal of an integrated design environment, by contrast, constructed their buildings from the inside out, attending to details of furniture, lighting, decoration, traffic flow: to the myriad things that enhanced their clients' lifestyles. Edward Durell Stone, the U.S. architect selected to build the American Pavilion at the 1958 Brussels World's Fair, was a modernist in the tradition of Frank Lloyd Wright. He should never have been asked to build a structure whose interior design was subject to committee decisions and the meddling of politicians. What the U.S. government needed was an empty shell—a big dome or a tent—within which they could organize things according to ideological schemes and the whims of powerful administrators. By hiring both Edward Durell Stone and a separate exhibition designer—Peter G. Harnden—the State Department invited an endless series of conflicts.

The Belgians wanted an exhibition of culture, not just commerce, and they asked the United States to respond accordingly. The emphasis on culture explains why the State Department was put in control of the U.S. program instead of the Department of Commerce or the USIA; however, the State Department was unprepared for an exhibition of this magnitude and did not proceed in a timely fashion. The invitation to participate in the fair was received on June 21, 1954, but it was not until January 1957 that the U.S. program was organized and functioning as a legal government entity under the authority of the secretary of state, John Foster Dulles. The intervening years had not been completely wasted—Edward Durell Stone, who was already building an embassy for the State Department in New Delhi, had been appointed sometime early in 1956. Howard Cullman was appointed the commissioner general on October 3, 1956, and he quickly assembled a staff from among his contacts in the private sector, the most important of whom was James S. Plaut, the director of the Boston Institute of Contemporary Art, who was appointed deputy commissioner general on November 24, 1956. Plaut would control many of the day-to-day details of exhibit design by hiring and supervising contractors, and overseeing the crucial arts, crafts, and vernacular culture exhibits. Headquarters were established in New York City, with liaison offices in Washington, D.C., and Brussels. After a basic management group with subordinate divisions was developed, immediate attention was directed toward theme planning and lobbying Congress for more funding (as late as March 1958, the commissioner general would still be fighting the U.S. Congress for supplemental funds).[1]

It was unfortunate that the State Department appointed Stone before Cullman. Foolishly, the State Department hired two individuals with radically different notions about how the U.S. program should be presented and then stepped back and ignored the inevitable squabbling. Stone assumed that he was responsible for the entire project—exhibition design included—and Cullman did not inform him otherwise until after his staff was hired and he had attended the theme-planning sessions organized by the State Department and the USIA in April 1957. By the time Cullman and Plaut had a moment to consider the type of pavilion they needed, Stone was already completing his designs and proposing to sweep the entire project in a direction of his own devising. Early in 1957 a power

Cover of the official U.S. guide book to the Brussels World's Fair, 1958. Collection of the University of Minnesota Libraries.

struggle ensued, during which the Peter G. Harnden design firm—a favorite with the Commerce Department and the USIA—was hired by Cullman to rework the interior of the pavilion so that it would accommodate the exhibits. The result was a mishmash of styles, a contrast between Stone's circular building, his airy simplicity, and Harnden's rectilinear, cluttered exhibit strategies. Stone's grand design for the pavilion complex was ignored, but in the end he received most of the glory. The American Pavilion, apart from everything within it, turned out to be the most celebrated aspect of the American participation at the Brussels World's Fair.

State Department officials had asked their American Institute of Architects (AIA) architectural advisory board (the same board that appointed architects to build embassies) to appoint a suitable architect early in 1956. Edward Durell Stone won the commission from a five-man panel of judges. Soon after the appointment, Stone and the advisory group went to Brussels to view the site as a team. They discovered that the Belgians had allotted the United States a choice triangular site with access from every side, adjacent to one of the main traffic arteries and flanked by the Soviet and Vatican pavilions. The Belgians had placed three of the world's great ideological powerhouses in the heart of the exhibition. Naturally, this would provide a dramatic confrontation.[2]

King Baudouin of Belgium had requested protection for eleven willow trees native to the site. The soggy plot was also transected by a tramway tunnel running underneath it, which would create certain difficulties when foundations were laid. A multistory building—any heavy structure—was out of the question. The advisory committee stopped short of dictating the final shape, but it did not want separate structures for the different aspects of science, commerce, and culture. Considering that the fair's theme emphasized humanism—a term that more and more people within the United States were using to mean an integration of business with the arts and sciences—a unified, circular structure seemed most appropriate. The AIA panel recommended that Stone get started immediately. Shortly thereafter, Stone asked Charles Middeleer to begin landscaping and the Belgian firm of Blanton-Aubert to handle engineering details and construction.[3]

Working as a team, the architects in the Stone office concluded that a large circular building with no internal supports other than the encircling wall would look best from the many different angles, cover the trees without crowding them, and provide a maximum amount of free space. It would also offer them the opportunity to experiment with lightweight modern materials and a sensational new type of ceiling. Emulating Frank Lloyd Wright, whose current project, the Guggenheim Museum in New York, aimed to redefine museum architecture, Stone wanted everything within his building to be part of the architectural experience.[4]

The complex eventually included a large modern attached theater, a small free-standing theater for the Walt Disney "Circarama" movie, and at the main entrance facing the Soviet Pavilion an elliptical pool with an Alexander Calder mobile and jets of water, surrounded by a paved area containing flowering apple trees. Two rows of flags honoring the thirteen original states dominated the lower apex of the site, just in front of the pool, and the flags of the other states were arranged at intervals around the building itself. The design team would make continuous alterations, but this would remain the basic layout of the American Pavilion. In exterior appearance, it owed a debt to the Beaux-Arts tradition, with its classicizing white and gold colors; to modernism, in its simplicity and restrained geometry; and to the traditional European plaza with its paving stones, pool, and jets of water.[5]

The State Department was eager to have a pavilion that would act as a silent ambassador for democratic ideals.[6] Stone was already part of the growing cadre of architects cultivated by the State Department's Office of Foreign Buildings Operations (OFB), which furthered diplomacy through person-to-person contacts and the adaptation of regional styles of architecture in the building of foreign embassies. These cooperative ventures helped to "demonstrate American know-how."[7] The OFB program assumed that the American way of life was embodied within a unique method of organization and systematic production. Exporting these principles was a way of building unity across disparate cultural groups. The State Department's Office of Foreign Buildings was developed in tandem with other technical-assistance programs and had the added benefit of soaking up some of the excess local currency acquired by the United States through a credit system adopted in the financing of trade-and-aid schemes. The OFB program was very cheap, like the Fulbright scholarships that used the same foreign credits.[8]

The OFB stepped up its policy of using contemporary architecture in 1954 with the appointment of an advisory board made up exclusively of architects. Chairman John Walker summed up the spirit of the AIA board when he said, "I am against anonymity, uniformity, and all the things that go to make up modernism."[9] Walker considered himself to be not a reactionary but a humanist, following the lead of Frank Lloyd Wright and the architects and industrial designers influenced by the new Bauhaus, who sought a wider social role for architecture. Stone's restrained but ornamental style made him a natural candidate for this program. The AIA advisory board offered its services to the government free of charge, and the

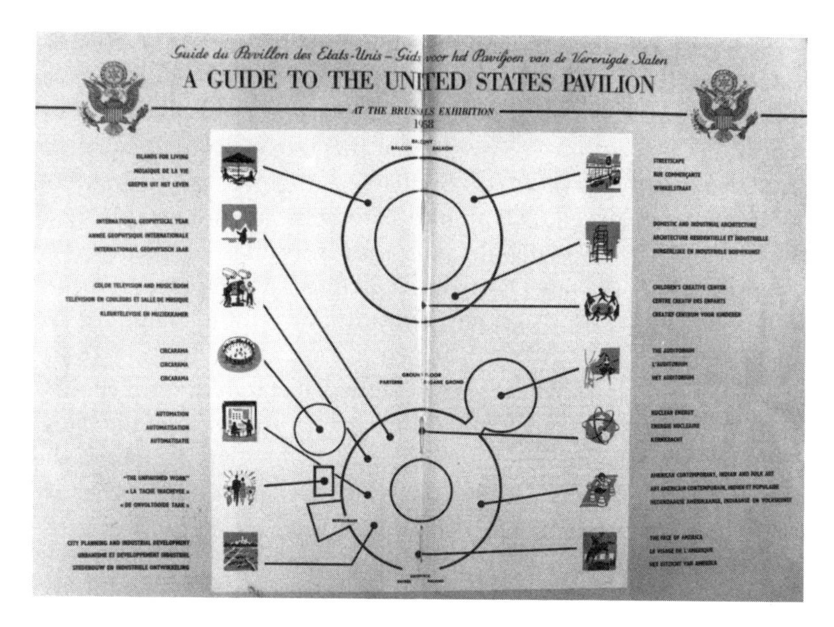

Guide to the U.S. pavilion at the Brussels World's Fair, 1958, that appeared in the official U.S. guide book. Collection of the University of Minnesota Libraries.

architectural press enthusiastically covered OFB commissions because they signaled the international acceptance of American architecture. By 1953 more than fifty embassies and other types of official residences were under construction through the OFB, with more to follow.[10]

The editors of *Architectural Forum* recommended that American architects working abroad use local contractors because it was difficult to get standardized parts outside the United States and locals were often able to rely upon a large reserve of craftsmanship to meet unexpected situations. Details from windows to radiators could be made to order at a low cost in most European cities, and slack building codes allowed for wide margins of error. Eventually, the State Department discovered that by using local resources, their foreign buildings fit into the regional culture, removing the sting of imperialism from the look of official buildings.[11]

By 1955 a clear set of objectives for OFB projects had been established. Two basic principles were adopted: to represent American architecture and to create buildings that "adapt themselves to local conditions and cultures so deftly that they are welcomed, not criticized, by their hosts."[12] Pietro Belluschi, a member of the first AIA advisory panel, urged OFB architects to make an in-depth study of climate and site in order to avoid any formulas or clichés. The "Americanness" of State Department architecture, in practice, meant simply absorbing local decorative traditions within a late-modern functionalism.[13]

The Brussels pavilion was designed in tandem with Stone's New Delhi project, and stylistically, it was the rectangular New Delhi Embassy made into a circle. But the cable-tension roof of the Brussels pavilion was a completely new departure and probably owed its inspiration to another OFB project, the Berlin Congress Hall, by Hugh Stubbins. Both the Berlin Congress Hall and the New Delhi Embassy provide insights into the dominant architectural trends within the OFB program during the late 1950s.

Seen from above, Stone's New Delhi Embassy could be described as a large rectangle with a hollow center. The inner light-well and central pool were decorated with overhanging tropical plants so that the work spaces surrounding them would have an airy atmosphere. A screen wall of perforated, ornamental terrazzo block wrapped around the exterior and gold pillars added a finishing touch. Stone hoped that the shape of the building would remind local residents of the nearby temples and that the white color, contrasted against the blue sky, would evoke the Taj Mahal.[14] At once a symbol of empire and the divine, the New Delhi Embassy was like a Roman palace. Stone liked adapting ancient (especially Roman) architecture for public and private use as his mature style developed—as if he were a modern Thomas Jefferson. But whereas Jefferson was drawn to the dignity and propriety of classical ruins, Stone, a romantic, had the courage to revive some of the raw sensuality and drama that those temples had when they were first erected.

Stone learned how to adapt regional styles and local traditions by working with industrial designers such as Russel Wright. In 1940 Stone was an adviser to Wright's "American Way" project, which sought to transform regional crafts in the United States into objects of mass appeal, mostly just through marketing techniques, but also by adapting crafts to mass production.[15] These were the skills that the State Department and other technical-assistance agencies needed overseas during the 1950s to help win the cold war. While Stone was hiring local craftsmen in New Delhi to help build a new kind of government structure, Russel Wright was in the Far East as an employee of the International Cooperation Administration, helping craft industries adapt to the Western market. Stone was part of a group of designers, architects, and—through his friend and fellow Arkansan Sen. William J. Fulbright—legislators who were personally committed to ending the cold war through person-to-person contacts, the exchange of ideas, and the creation of an international marketplace that would cement economic relationships between the United States and its allies.[16]

Stone commissioned local, New Delhi craftsmen to fabricate the mass-produced patterned terrazzo block used as a screen on the exterior of his embassy. The human touch combined with repetitive rhythm created a building that seemed smaller than its actual size and appeared less forbidding.[17] However, despite the regional character designed into the New Delhi Embassy, the architectural press was still quick to read into it all of the "American" characteristics that were becoming hot copy. National style had become a hobbyhorse of critics, who were suddenly convinced that the United States was not only unique but had an important leadership role to fulfill. This "uniqueness" was usually associated with technology and material progress. Stone, like many of his contemporaries, revealed that this technological excellence did not have to result in severe, strictly functional buildings. *Architectural Forum,* for example, described the New Delhi Embassy as the embodiment of "democratic vitality and romance, its pleasures as well as its power."[18] The editors of *Architectural Forum* were particularly impressed by the absence of the polished, the streamlined, and the mechanical aspects of typical government buildings.

The OFB helped create a legion of "silent ambassadors," ranging from sedate embassies to new dams and refineries. The patriotic *Architectural Forum* (published by Time Inc.) reported that the United

States was "building up the basic welfare of other nations, creating climates unfavorable to communism, readying countries for industrialization and democratic independence, making them prosperous enough to buy more of our products." As for the architects themselves, *Architectural Forum* found that the best of them had learned how to act as grass-roots ambassadors, showing that "America produces not only wealth, but technical and administrative abilities as well, and the willingness to share these assets with others."[19]

There were some forty housing specialists working through technical-cooperation programs sponsored by the OFB in 1955. In nine German cities, for example, these specialists introduced competitive bidding and FHA-type installment plans to produce and market more than 5,000 row houses in the strategically crucial Ruhr Valley. Germany was, of course, a special case, a cold war theater where the kind of East-versus-West confrontation so dramatically and obsessively hyped by the 1958 Brussels World's Fair had become a daily event.[20] Every OFB structure in Berlin, especially, took on the ideological responsibility of representing the United States, but none so much as Hugh Stubbins's Congress Hall in Berlin, designed to be a permanent symbol of democratic freedoms. The Congress Hall was the quintessential symbolic building, gaining much of its ideological vitality from a daring, prestressed concrete structure that was intended to complement the Western-style "freedom of expression" demonstrated within its conference rooms.[21]

The 1956 Berlin International Building Exhibition, for which the Congress Hall would be a crown jewel, celebrated "a complete redevelopment of a bombed-out area north of the Tiergarten with 8,000 permanent dwelling units shown in various stages of construction, architectural exhibits, festive pavilions, and cafés in a landscaped park."[22] At the center of the complex the Congress Hall, resembling a gargantuan bird lifting its wings to fly, dominated the Berlin skyline. Creating a symbol of freedom in postwar Germany was an iconological challenge for Stubbins. Many of the classical forms that Jefferson and other U.S. architects had found so amenable to the ideals of democracy during the revolutionary days of the late eighteenth century had been co-opted by fascism. Any building looking remotely like a Greek or Roman temple had to be ruled out. Stubbins decided to use prestressed concrete and suspension engineering in order to give his symbol of freedom a technological, or rational, emphasis.[23]

In 1955 *Architectural Forum* arranged a conference in which Hugh Stubbins; his structural engineer, Fred Severud; and Frei Otto, a German engineer and architect unrelated to the project, could debate the Congress Hall's design. The dynamic of modern buildings, Otto argued, was primarily a result of structural engineering. Modernism required new solutions and daring experimentation! In his opinion, the best of the new architecture used shells, light frameworks, and suspended roofs to keep the weight of a building to a minimum. This saved money, energy, and increased interior space. The American Pavilion at Brussels would have just the kind of soaring appeal, flexibility, and implied symbolic content that Otto praised in Stubbins's Congress Hall.[24]

In his autobiography, Stone recounted some of the choices that influenced his design strategy at Brussels. He considered the site to be "extremely fortunate" and described the eventual design as if it were the natural (rational) outcome of the challenges presented: the triangular dimensions, the trees, the relationship to the Soviet and Vatican pavilions.[25] A vast, translucent, circular building open in the center to allow light and air inside for the trees, did indeed satisfy the physical requirements and allowed for the virtuosity expected of a world's fair pavilion. Actually, the trees contributed to the outdoor-indoor effects he had already been experimenting with in New Delhi, and in private dwellings such as the Graf House in Dallas (1958), where the dining-room table floated on a circular island within a pool. But the American Pavilion would have the lushest interior of any previous Stone building, its plants and pool suggesting a tropical oasis or pleasure garden. Stone used new engineering technology, as had Hugh Stubbins, to symbolize freedom from tradition, but he combined this new technology with ancient motifs, rooting his symbolic statement within the familiar classical past in order to reassure his audience.

The *Architectural Forum* critic Peter Blake described the mid-1950s as a time of rapid transformation. "Whole groups" of modern architects, he wrote, no longer swore by function but embarked on one of the many directions made possible by the new materials, technologies, and challenging commissions presented by industrial expansion. "Modernism," according to Blake, changed and adapted to the "continuing revolution" of national life. Blake argued that "we are a nation with more space, more resources, and more left undone than any country in Western Europe. Why not invent a new architecture to meet our national aspirations?"[26] Modern, in this sense, was closely identified with the commercial spirit, with the changing forms of shopping malls, suburbs, international diplomacy.

Peter Blake tried to reconcile modernism with humanism (a term that the Brussels World's Fair would publicize as the central cultural issue of the decade) in a series of articles for *Architectural Forum* in which he associated *humanistic* with the indigenous and the vernacular: the Cape Cod saltbox and the Pennsylvania Dutch barn. Stone incorporated Persian motifs in the same experimental, ahistorical manner as did architects experimenting with the American vernacular, such as Alvar Aalto, whose dormitories for the Massachusetts Institute of Technology (MIT) used natural materials and irregular fenestration to lend a touch of the regional. Stone's modernism was part of the new globalism; his humanism was a revamped, pared-down version of the eclectic, imperial Gilded Age.[27]

During the 1950s Frank Lloyd Wright led the charge against the international style and the rectangle. Wright believed that his circular Guggenheim Museum of those years pointed the way to unity and the way out of "box-frame architecture" with "glassified poster-facades." In place of the rectangular box the Guggenheim offered "an atmosphere of the unbroken wave."[28] Unfortunately, it was also the architecture of a megalomaniac. The unbroken wave of the Guggenheim was such a powerful statement in itself that any competing work of art placed within paled by comparison. Stone's pavilion would be criticized for having a similar inflexibility by the U.S. deputy commissioner general, James Plaut, whose task it was to rein in the architect and prevent him from dominating the entire project.[29]

The notorious Guggenheim had been on the drawing board since the early 1940s, and while it was under development Stone cultivated the friendship of Wright, drawing inspiration from the older man's experience. During the 1950s Wright used the circular form for his Christian Science Church in Bolinas, California (1957), and his Greek Orthodox Church in Milwaukee (1956). Along with the Guggenheim, these two churches suggest that Wright thought of the circle as a way of encouraging fellowship and a sense of heightened emotion, which is how Stone would use it in Brussels. Eero Saarinen used the circle in a similar way in his domed auditorium and cylindrical chapel for MIT (1952).

Architectural Forum acknowledged that building in a circle was itself a challenge to rectilinear modernism. The Saarinen chapel, for example, was strange and haunting in a distinctly premodern fashion. Its emotional appeal resonated with "religion as far back as the temples of Vesta and beyond."[30] The circle seemed humanistic because of its association with ancient public auditoriums and domed gathering places but remained a pure geometric form in keeping with the stripped-down modern aesthetic. It appealed to architects searching for a way to subvert the rectangles of international modernism and was especially appropriate for a school that was pioneering the study of new materials and scientific processes essential for the growing international economy. Indeed, both the Stone office and the commissioner general's office would call on experts at MIT to lend their expertise to the planning of exhibits and the construction of the American Pavilion in Brussels.

In the spring of 1958 the editors of *Architectural Forum* endorsed the decorative impulse as if it were solely responsible for the revival of modernism, reversing a trend begun at the turn of the century when the Austrian architect Adolf Loos wrote that "the progress of modern man is measured by his removal of ornament from useful objects."[31] Loos was trumpeting the death of the Beaux-Arts ideal and the ascension of a style more suited to industry and technology, but his oft-quoted remark is perhaps best-loved because of its moralistic tone. The modern program promised an end to the trappings of wealth and class associated with the neoclassicism of the Ecole des Beaux Arts in Paris and took root in the United States during the Great Depression, when ostentation was inappropriate. The International Style, however, was too often pretentious, dull, and never as functional as the architects had promised. Writing in *Harper's*, Henry

Hope Reed Jr. complained in 1957 that "we no longer live in a world of scarce materials and financial distress but a world of expanding plenty, and there is need for an architecture which offers more than the functional."[32] Architects would never go back to the "White City" of Chicago's 1893 Columbian Exposition, but a new interpretation of the modern style was needed. Stone, whose Museum of Modern Art had long been an icon of international modernism, set out to reform the monster he had helped to create.

Architectural Forum distinguished the decorative elements in Stone's vocabulary: the pools, potted plants, and screen walls of patterned terrazzo blocks. The blocks were heralded as a brilliant adaptation of modern theory. They were not "applied decoration" but "patterned structure." They were decorative, but their application as a shading device and as a way of ensuring privacy justified their use.[33] Most important, they evoked the Near East: they were exotic; quite different from the acanthus leaves and columns associated with the Greeks, the Romans, American Republicanism, or fascism. To use these exotic elements in architecture was literally to put the "international" into "international modernism."

The American Pavilion was a symbol of imperial power: a gigantic, protective translucent circle, far more than just a shell. Stone designed a complete experience, establishing the way visitors to the pavilion would move within it, overwhelming them with subtle lighting effects and a vast, unnatural volume of space. Only minor details were to be left up to the exhibit designers. However, Stone did not anticipate the complications of a world's fair commission. So many individuals, government agencies, and private companies wanted to be involved that the project threatened to collapse under conflicts of interest. James Plaut represented the most serious threat to Stone's design because he believed that exhibits were as important—if not more so—than the building and hired the Peter G. Harnden design firm to redesign the interior. Harnden had already created many trade fair exhibitions for the Commerce Department and was familiar with the general problems of representing the United States overseas. But those exhibits had been within prefabricated buildings that were little more than enclosures. A difference of opinion between Stone and Harnden was destined to arise.

Stone's pavilion was constructed of new materials, engineered in novel ways, and adorned with eye-catching color. Tall, finned, gold columns were anchored into a circular foundation and supported a heavy, reinforced concrete ring about sixty-five feet off the ground. Descending from the heavy concrete "compression ring" was a metal high-tension trellis framework, holding in place a transparent acrylic wall and tying together the upper ring with the lower foundation slab.

The roof had an open, unprotected oculus in its center, created by a gigantic hollow steel cylinder. Cables were strung between the top and bottom of the huge cylinder and the encircling concrete rim. As the slack in the cables was taken up, the cylinder or "tension ring," was lifted off the floor and held suspended in the air. The vast size of the roof and the obvious weight of the cylinder astounded fairgoers (the ceiling looked like a giant bicycle wheel resting on top of the outer walls). The structure was a marvel of engineering; not as coherent as the geodesic domes, which were a runaway hit on the trade fair circuit, but with a similar gee-whiz appeal.

The surrounding circular wall was made from sets of metal strips laid diagonally across each other in a Beaux-Arts-inspired diamond-shaped pattern. Later, a third vertical metal strip was fastened to this shaky trellis, bisecting every other diamond. Transparent acrylic panels were sandwiched between an inner and outer metal trellis and cinched together by bolts along the vertical strips. The resulting wall equalized the tension of the roof with the compression of the outer concrete rim, the second-floor balcony, and the foundation slab. Recessed reflector lamps illuminated the trellis pattern from above, and because most of the bulk of the building was in the roof, at night the structure appear to hover.

To cover the roof, steel purlins (similar to lightweight I beams) were set onto the top set of ceiling cables in progressively larger circles radiating outward from the open central ring. Translucent fiberglass panels about four inches thick, hollow except for interior baffles, were fastened onto the purlins. This prefabricated roof required a rigid frame, but because the cables were always slightly in flux the seals leaked, and during the spring rains it was not unusual to see buckets set out to catch water.

Stone demanded spectacular effects but had little understanding of the difficulties of tension construction. The associates he sent over to Belgium to work with the engineering contractor had to improvise as the weight of the tension ring and the tensile strength of the cables were determined. The ring had to be light enough to stay aloft yet strong enough to resist the pull of the cables. Similarly, the cables had to be cinched tight enough to resist uneven wind loads but not to the point of warping, or even toppling inward, the outer walls. It proved a devilish structure to build and may have remained incomprehensible to Stone, who promoted the building but avoided the building site.[34] Stone evaded particulars and waxed poetic when asked to explain the virtuosity of the structure, crediting the inspiration for the design to the ancient Romans, whose Coliseum, he said, was probably roofed in just such a manner—only with rope and canvas rather than cables and plastic. He did not want to admit the extent to which he was indebted to the engineers on the project. Nor did he realize he was inviting negative criticism by evoking the Roman Coliseum—for Christian America a symbol of pagan decadence.

The American Pavilion was an experimental building: The tensile structure and the plastic and fiberglass components of the pavilion were not yet completely understood by architects (the Berlin Congress Hall, constructed with similarly experimental techniques, collapsed in 1980, injuring several people). A panel arranged by *Architectural Design* in 1957 to study the new synthetics announced that "the designer must forget all about known building materials and go back to fundamental needs."[35] Plastics were still expensive but they had the potential for liberating the architectural imagination, of allowing buildings to assume virtually any shape. The Monsanto "House of the Future," erected in June 1957 at Disneyland, California, demonstrated how dramatically different these new shapes could be. This futuristic model home looked like a giant mushroom on a squat stem with four pie-shaped slices removed to expose the interior. The circularity of the overall form and its plastic carapace were the last word in organic styling. It was a perfect expression of the nuclear family: the four wings of the home connected in the central kitchen, where Mom held sway at a command post. Monsanto, a chemical conglomerate, envisioned a future in which the miracle products of chemical engineering would be combined with inventive, novel applications to make Mom's tasks fun and easy. A scale model of the House of the Future was displayed in the American Pavilion's architecture exhibit.

The House of the Future had been developed at MIT under Monsanto sponsorship, but its eventual construction at Disneyland involved the cooperation of design teams from "a cross section of housing industry suppliers"—Chemstrand, Sylvania, Herman Miller Furniture, and other companies that were not afraid to cast "a frank eye on new markets for chemicals and plastics."[36] Since these were many of the same companies that contributed time, money, and materials to the American Pavilion—after Congress refused adequate funds—the pavilion was indeed a kind of big brother to the Disneyland house. Both buildings were jammed with push-button blenders, color TV sets, and futuristic gadgets. In the American Pavilion, even the clothes were apt to be made from the new synthetics. Chemstrand had donated the uniforms for the guides, transforming them into junior ambassadors of wrinkle-free Acrilan and nylon. Both the plastic "home" at Disneyland and the American Pavilion in Brussels were crammed with materials recently liberated from the laboratory.

The leading role played by science in the new humanism was the key theme of the 1958 fair, as dramatized by the "Atomium," the theme centerpiece of the 1958 Brussels World's Fair. The Atomium was a gigantic atomic sculpture-restaurant-panoramic tower that symbolized the colossal stature of chemistry and molecular physics in modern life. Scientists at Monsanto and other companies were learning how to deconstruct the molecular building blocks represented by this colossus and to refashion the universe into a more congenial, middle-class place. To stare up at the Atomium, especially at night, when reflections careened off its surface and tiny lights blinked in sequence around its orbs, was to exult in the potential of science: a realm of exciting new frontiers.

Stone and his associates were deeply concerned with the total effect of their pavilion: a symbol of the scientific and aesthetic marriage that constituted the new humanism. A rendering of the finished interior by Kenneth Frizzel, one of the assistants Stone had sent to Brussels, was published by *Architectural Forum*, revealing the comprehensive design the Stone office hoped to achieve.[37] Before Harnden became involved, the interior was spacious and uncluttered. The exhibits were integrated into the overall atmosphere established by the space, light, trees, and central pool. A mesh ceiling curtain of gold-colored aluminum discs suspended in luxurious billows from the lower cables helped to create a diffuse, dappled light.

The oculus—an allusion to the eye of God, taken from the Roman Pantheon—was a spectacular curiosity, and the architects, believing that the world's fair demanded glamour, fought with James Plaut to protect its embellishments. Silver lighting fixtures were placed against the gold-colored inner surface of the cylinder, creating a Las Vegas–style appeal. At night, powerful downlighting into the pool provided a column of light, dramatic in itself but especially so when it was raining and the shafts of illumination played across the precipitation falling through the open top. Plaut wanted a more conservative look, but Stone's associates stood firm and Plaut eventually had to yield to their designs.

Stone and his associates were overruled, however, regarding the design of the interior floor space. Preliminary drawings indicate that Stone wanted a large modernistic sculpture in the central pool, made from wiggly wire bars surrounded by jets of water—the creation of sculptor Richard Lippold. The prospect of his having the central commission of the sculptural program was destroyed, however, when James Plaut and Peter Harnden scuttled Stone's designs. As a last resort, Lippold wrote an open letter to President Eisenhower, *Life*, the commissioner general's office, and several popular tastemakers, praising Stone's intentions:

> It made me very happy to have Mr. Stone call upon me to collaborate with him on the development of a sculptural concept for the very center of this building, where all of its visual and structural forces concentrate on a great void, awaiting a core, or heart, to give it life. Our mutual agreement . . . resulted in . . . a gigantic golden form, resting on the brilliantly illuminated center of the great pool, opening up its component parts to the daylight-lit vast opening in the roof. This image is expressive of the unfolding, golden flowering of American culture. It concentrates the sources

> of its energies at human eye-level, lifts its forces toward the ceiling, which, capturing them, draws them back down the glistening walls to the pool again, thus enveloping the spectator in the total experience provided by the inseparable unity of form of the sculpture and architecture.[38]

Even long after the interior had been taken over by Harnden, Stone kept pleading with Plaut to let him have just one fountain, in order to provide a strong vertical element at the heart of his circular composition and provide an element of gaiety, beauty, and continuity with the jets of water outside.[39] By March 1958 Plaut was tired of arguing with the architect and decreed that there would be no fountains anywhere within the building.[40]

The disagreement over the design of the central pool, which Harnden filled with props of his own liking, aggravated Stone, but Stone was shocked when Plaut informed him that a concrete runway for fashion models was going to descend from the balcony level onto a slab positioned halfway across the pool like a dock on a pond. The ramp horrified Stone's associates, who dubbed it the "sheep dip" and the "cattle chute."[41] They complained that the ramp was too narrow, too steep, too "brutally detailed." Even the exhibits team had to concede that they were disappointed with the final results.[42] But Plaut had the concrete ramp painted white and the pool area redesigned to accommodate the fashion models. Decorative partitions were extended across the pool, transforming its circularity into a series of fragmented rectangles.

Plaut sent a letter to Stone, asking the architect to forgive the meddling with his blueprints. But Plaut was too embarrassed to tell Stone the truth: that the launch of *Sputnik* had thrown the commissioner general's office into total confusion, forcing the exhibits team to place a greater emphasis upon American popular culture. The fact that the Soviets had beaten the Americans into outer space disturbed the U.S. public enormously. The United States was still the world's undisputed leader in the production of peaceful consumer products, however—the victor of the nylon war if a loser in the space race—and so a daily fashion show was made to be the single most important event inside the pavilion. It was a risky ploy, because critics would be looking for the U.S. answer to *Sputnik* in the pavilion's displays. But the United States, whose military power was as frightening as it was formidable, had everything to gain from concentrating on "the good life" in its displays and pretending that *Sputnik* was of little consequence. Stone and his associates, however, were not pleased that their work was going to be upstaged by glamorous girls in slinky costumes.[43]

Although Peter Harnden's exhibits transformed the interior, the exterior of the pavilion stayed the way that Stone had designed it. The paved area at the front of the pavilion's triangular site created a spacious setting and isolated the building from other pavilions, which Stone felt were too crowded. And the apple orchard planted around the edges, coaxed into bloom during opening week, provided a tasteful but informal atmosphere. Evergreen shrubs, yews, and flowers were used as details. The landscape contractor Charles Middeleer was able to get an American company to donate more than 750 native roses for the fourteen beds at the main entrances.

Stone retained a degree of influence over sculpture commissioned for the pavilion, although he had to work closely with the commissioner general's office. Alexander Calder, at Stone's behest, created two mobiles: a large, solid black sculpture for the outside pool and a smaller one to hang in the theater foyer (which visitors entered from an exit in the main pavilion). The mobile in the outside pool was placed on the center line of the pool, among jets of water, where it was visible from the two primary approaches.

In Calder's sculpture the cynicism of dada and the irony of surrealism had been replaced with a confident formalism relying on the innate fascination of movement, color, and shape. And in the pool, revolving among the jets of water, his mobile shared in the dispensation of bliss generated by the water jets as their cooling mist settled over an international hot spot—the crossroads between the American, the Vatican, and the Soviet pavilions. If the rest of the art and artifacts inside the American Pavilion had accomplished as much in the way of good public relations, the commissioner general's office would have been saved a great deal of embarrassing controversy.

Stone, with help from the commissioner general's staff, obtained murals by Saul Steinberg and Al Hirschfeld for the inside of the pavilion that served much the same function as the Calder mobile outside: They were not supposed to make earth-shattering claims for American art but merely to contribute to the over-all atmosphere of insouciance and innovative modernism. The decorative Hirschfeld mural—really just a collection of previously published drawings enlarged and pastiched together into crowded groupings of theatrical celebrities—was inconspicuously placed on the wall behind the bar in the theater lobby. By contrast, Steinberg's mural was the most prominent artistic statement by any single person inside the pavilion. His European background (he was born in Romania and trained as an architect in Italy) enabled him to explain American foibles in an endearing manner. The commissioner general's staff had decided that Europeans were only too well aware of America's industrial might, military power, and wealth, but too little exposed to American popular culture. Steinberg was enlisted to portray Americans as easygoing kinds of people who did not take themselves too seriously, who were aware of their shortcomings but making progress in spite of them.

Steinberg's mural was placed on the pavilion's main floor near the pool. As people walked by the mural (divided and staggered so the viewer was virtually inside the mural sections), they were confronted with whimsical scenes drawn from the U.S. landscape. Called *The Americans,* the mural consisted of eight panels with separate themes and titles. The panels were ten feet high and from twenty to seventy-two feet long. They were constructed out of photographic blowups of drawings (some already published in Steinberg's books *The Labyrinth* and *The Passport*) mounted on plywood and then variously altered with heavy brown paper and applied newspaper comics. The final touches were drawn in by hand, and then everything was coated with clear plastic. Odd shapes emphasized flat pattern and the dramatic play of graphic possibilities. Steinberg evoked baton-twirling majorettes, the bizarre landscape of Las Vegas, and dour, pseudo–Grant Wood farmers in bib overalls. He poked fun at Main Street, U.S.A.; at Shriners, trailer parks, and traffic jams; at all those things touted by the other pavilion displays. With just a touch of irony or satire these would have been cutting-edge heralds of the Pop Art movement. But Steinberg's sensibility

19 THE SOVIET UNION'S NATIONAL DAYS

SPUTNIK

3. SOVIET ART AND CULTURE

WRITERS - at the Round Table !

SAMSON BREAKING HIS FETTERS

MONUMENT TO SPUTNIK

IN THIS LIES OUR HAPPINESS!

LANGUAGE OF ART IS INTERNATIONAL

WE GIVE WHOLEHEARTED SUPPORT TO MIKHAIL SHOLOKHOV

The first page of Sputnik, *August 11–13, 1958, the Soviet newspaper at the Brussels World's Fair. Edward J. Orth Collection, National Museum of American History, Smithsonian Institution.*

was essentially romantic, and he was too respectable to create the blasé imagery soon to be made famous by Andy Warhol's generation. Like those artists of the 1930s who searched for Americana on Coney Island or on Manhattan's skid row, Steinberg still viewed the United States as a sort of noble freak show.

As the pavilion was being constructed, the Belgian office of the USIS kept a wary eye on the USSR program. A daily Soviet newspaper, *Sputnik,* promised to be an ideological headache, as did the concert halls and theaters that local promoters said the Soviets were renting. Panic set in for the understaffed USIS officers, who realized that Washington would never provide them with the money and resources available to their Soviet counterparts (reportedly some $60 million), unless the prestige of the United States was severely threatened. American journalists were alerted that a scandal was brewing and began cleaning their typewriters. The USIS probably encour-

Interior of the American Pavilion at the Brussels World's Fair, 1958, showing crafts in foreground with view of Steinberg mural in background. National Archives.

aged the press to inflate the importance of Soviet displays in order to force the hand of congressional appropriation committees.[44]

One of the first in-depth press reports on the American Pavilion revealed how the State Department had sat on the project for nearly two years before appointing Cullman, and how Congress had been withholding funds. The *Saturday Evening Post* reporter Ernest O. Hauser uncovered the discord between the architects and the exhibit designers. Hauser explained that "our design team was hired when it was too late to change the structure, and, being stubborn individualists, they went ahead and squared the circle, constructing a rectangular world within the drum, and leaving foreign visitors with an impressive insight into our wonderfully democratic way of doing things."[45]

If Stone had been allowed to design exhibits, the interior would have remained open and sophisticated, expressing through light and spatial effects those mystic vibrations that only architecture can ever hope to conjure. Still, Peter Harnden and his associates were not solely responsible for the controversial interior. Harnden's exhibit designs would affect the public reception of displays, of course; but the content of those displays had been decided by the commissioner general's staff and the USIA at theme-planning sessions at the Massachusetts Institute of Technology in the spring of 1957. The American Pavilion and its exhibits had to accommodate the ideological themes devised by the USIA and the Advertising Council over the previous few years. Despite all the compromises that Edward Durell Stone was forced to make, however, the American Pavilion became a popular hit. Many U.S. tourists would condemn Harnden's interior, but few criticized the amazing pavilion itself, which was presented to Belgium after the 1958 World's Fair ended and, although considerably altered, has remained in continuous use as a warehouse and television studio.

4 Exhibit Planning

The American Pavilion at the 1958 Brussels World's Fair

In order to ensure a high-class cultural program—in contrast to the Commerce Department and USIA exhibits featuring productivity themes, ideal families, and model homes—the State Department asked Howard Cullman to be the commissioner general of the 1958 Brussels World's Fair. Cullman, a prominent New Yorker, had been the honorary chairman of New York's Port Authority, but he was best known as a Broadway producer and as a director of the Metropolitan Opera.[1] His involvement with show business began with the renovation of New York's Roxy Theater during the Great Depression, and it was while he was arranging productions for the Roxy that he met his wife, Peggy, who had been Bonwit Teller's publicity director and the associate editor of *Stage* magazine. Shortly after their marriage they combined forces and began producing plays. Their first big success was *Life with Father,* and by 1957 Cullman could boast to a reporter that theatrical productions had earned the couple more than a million dollars.[2] The Cullmans certainly had enough contacts in show business and retailing to orchestrate a major production for the State Department; they were lacking only in political experience and the knowledge of how to project a positive national image.

Before Cullman was hired to supervise the U.S. exhibition the most important decision had already been made by Edward Durell Stone: the design of the U.S. Pavilion. In addition, the State Department and the USIA had for some years been developing a national image of the United States tailored especially for Europeans, and Cullman's ideas would not be allowed to compromise that scenario.

To complicate matters further, whenever he accepted the help of an outside group Cullman risked embroiling his office in unexpected debates. The fine-art displays, for example, required guidance from several of the most prestigious museum directors in the United States and cooperation from artists, galleries, and critics. Although he had professional assistance from his deputy commissioner, James Plaut, the former director of the Institute of Contemporary Art in Boston, Cullman had little hope of remaining in control when so many egos, so many commercial and ideological agendas, came into conflict. Many of the exhibits were influenced by matters completely unrelated to the world's fair. It was Cullman's task to smooth over differences, repackage shopworn exhibit ideas and tiresome and trite slogans like "Atoms for Peace" and make everything seem either brand new, or time-honored, hallowed Americana.

The State Department and the USIA assisted Cullman by arranging a series of interviews with prominent Americans, such as Nelson A. Rockefeller, during January 1957 and then by organizing a round-table discussion at the Massachusetts Institute of Technology, where the exhibit themes were finally established. The group that met there over the weekend of April 27–28, 1957, was called the Cambridge Study Group, and the essential purpose of the brainstorming session was to update the image of the United States especially for the Brussels World's Fair.

The Cambridge Study Group was composed of Cullman, Plaut, Harnden, and other members of the commissioner general's staff, who were teamed with experts from the MIT faculty, including Dean John E. Burchard, School of Humanities; the historian Elting E. Morison; the physicist Victor Weisskopf; and, most important, the economist Walt Whitman Rostow, Ithiel de Sola Pool, and Max F. Millikan from the MIT Center for International Studies (CENIS). The Cambridge Study Group broke into teams on the first day, to focus on themes such as culture, science, and technology. On the last day, they met as a group to combine their findings and reach a consensus regarding the overall message of the exhibition.

The theme of the Brussels World's Fair was "A World View—A New Humanism." In a more specific directive sent to U.S. planners from the Belgian Information Service, the hosts indicated their desire to create a "crossroads of the nations," a place where the "duty of co-operation" between all nations would be given a new meaning. According to the Belgian commissioner general, mankind needed to be reminded of the population explosion, the deeply disturbing structure of "economic and social relations," as well as the bright promise of atomic energy, information science, and the electronic media. The material progress of mankind, the Belgians believed, had been achieved before spiritual maturity. In order to help redress the contradictions of the modern world, the Belgians asked the United States to send exhibits emphasizing international cooperation and a renewed humanism.[3]

The Belgians wanted to present their nation as the temporary "world capital" and promised to welcome those organizations dedicated to international cooperation. Their exhibition would become a "universal museum," they hoped, a place where individuals from around the globe could discover what they had in common with others. This was to be, as much as any historical world's fair, a celebration of "one-world" sentimentality, only with an emphasis placed squarely on Western Europe as the new center of world civilization. By 1958 jet travel had indeed made the globe accessible for many middle-class people who believed that they could have an effect on world peace by building international friendships and business contacts. This was naive, in many ways, but trade fairs, jet travel, "people to people" programs, and the establishment of the United Nations did revive the ideal of global unity that had been dashed by the failure of the League of Nations during the 1930s. The ideal of a unified planet was as good a reason as any to host a world's fair.

Small nations like Belgium, wedged between the superpowers, had little to gain from the cold war. Seeking to position itself as the bureaucratic center of a unified Western Europe, Brussels, at least, had much to gain from a world characterized by peaceful negotiations. Placing the American and Soviet pavilions across from one another at the fair was therefore a deeply symbolic act, forcing a temporary thaw in the frigid realm of international relations. This arrangement also simplified the political landscape of that era, removing the buffer zones between the two superpowers and encouraging the staff and visitors from the United States and the USSR to discover what they had in common. The idealistic promotion of international understanding is what made the fair a popular attraction.

Records of the staff discussions in Cullman's office from early November 1956 indicate that he had already received some counseling from the USIA on how U.S. culture should be presented. The ideal exhibits suggested to Cullman focused on respect for the individual, the contributions of immigrants, religious diversity, the family unit, and medical and educational advances. From the beginning, Cullman was encouraged to think in terms of a unified overall design, both physically and psychologically, to look for exhibits that would carry forward the unity expressed in the architecture.[4] "Life, liberty, and the pursuit of happiness" was one of the themes that Cullman and his USIA advisers hoped could weave exhibits into a single powerful statement. But the concept was far too vague to be of much use. "Youth" was a promising alternative motif because it suggested that Americans were focused on the future, and, thanks to Elvis Presley and James Dean, a youth theme built upon perceptions many Europeans already had of Americans. A youthful theme could argue that although Americans were naive they were receptive to change and that although American society was full of social inequities, these were the natural concomitants of social mobility, of progress.

The USIA advised Cullman to devise animated, rather than static exhibits, to use live actors or interactive participation. Eventually, youthfulness was expressed in the American Pavilion by a children's art room, an exhibit for American artists under forty, and the mural by Saul Steinberg, which poked fun at American foibles instead of exalting American virtues. Most important, the theme of youth would encourage exhibit design that emphasized contemporary fashion trends. Generally speaking, Cullman was guided to plan exhibits using what advertising executives called the "soft sell," a marketing strategy that relied on understated, even self-deprecating, images and alluring objects rather than slogans, labels, and reasonable arguments.[5]

When Nelson Rockefeller was interviewed in January 1957 by the USIA and Cullman's staff, he encouraged planners to recognize American cultural achievements such as radio, TV, and Elvis Presley, as well as the new upscale social programs of the Museum of Modern Art. And he hoped Cullman would show how the modern movement had found its clearest expression in the new corporate architecture sponsored by companies like Seagram. Rockefeller was a proponent of People's Capitalism ideals: He wanted exhibits to show how unions were developing "self-improvement workshops" and to tell the story of the whole do-it-yourself fad currently sweeping the country as ex-urbanites tried to personalize the often dull sameness of inexpensive suburban real estate. Rockefeller recognized a unique aspect of American culture in this self-improvement trend and wanted to portray popular culture as the real wealth of the nation, a wealth made possible by an increase of leisure time created by the capitalist economy.[6]

A more thorough consideration of how Europeans thought and felt about America was offered by Eugenie Anderson. As the former ambassador to Denmark, she had firsthand knowledge of how the United States was regarded by Europeans. In her opinion, most Europeans pictured America as it was before the New Deal and had little understanding of the progress that had been made since World War II. She therefore encouraged exhibits that emphasized a process of constant change and improvement, demonstrating that the United States was a dynamic society that rewarded hard work. The most tragic misconceptions about America she blamed on "cheap movies and an irresponsible press." The fair, she naively believed, was an opportunity for the government to state its case without the press interfering. Most important, she considered this an excellent chance to explain away racial disharmony. The most popular speeches she had given in Denmark were on the "Negro problem." Her experience taught her to confront the segregation issue head-on, and so she advised Cullman to give a short history lesson that emphasized the progress that had been made since the 1860s and that expressed the "deep feeling of moral obligation" that Americans harbored toward people of color. Progress, in other words, should be the keynote in any attempt to put a brave face on racism. Her advice would have a profound influence on the *Unfinished Work* exhibit and in the selection of an integrated staff.[7]

Anderson was one of the few people who recommended a focus

on domesticity. She hoped that Cullman could dispel the notion that American children were spoiled with some kind of an exhibit on child development, demonstrating that the freedom permitted children was an attempt to develop their individuality. Her advice aimed at dispelling criticism of the United States in very specific areas, especially home and family. The home, or the lack of an ideal home, turned out to be a major point of contention later when male exhibit designers, disillusioned with the ideal image of family life promoted by trade fairs and the People's Capitalism campaign, refused to use the type of prefabricated home that had proven so popular around the world. But the Children's Creative Center, which demonstrated progressive theories of child rearing, became one of the unequivocal successes of the pavilion.

Walt W. Rostow, who would also be a member of the Cambridge Study Group that April, suggested that the exhibits tackle the challenges of the immediate future: education, integration, and the reconstruction of urban centers. America the military power and America the wealthy should not go on display. Instead, Rostow wanted the United States of Carl Sandburg and Walt Whitman, a vivid, energetic nation of individuals; contemporary problems would then seem like a natural part of America's sprawl and energy. A good-neighbor image could be enhanced with quotes from speeches by Franklin D. Roosevelt, Truman, and Eisenhower, illustrating how the last three American presidents wanted a democratic way of life for the world at large. Rostow also wanted to debunk the notion that American culture was becoming standardized and monolithic with exhibits that demonstrated that individuality was enhanced by mass-media organs such as television, mass-produced periodicals, paperbacks, recordings, and the like.[8]

The labor leader Victor Reuther agreed with Anderson and Rostow that the presentation of American shortcomings, such as the history of race relations, would lend credibility to exhibits, so long as they were contained within a progressive narrative, ending with new technological trends such as automated factories. According to Reuther, automation was a force that would benefit the whole society "and not one economic group alone." He betrayed no anxiety regarding the replacement of labor by automation devices. Indeed, he was concerned that European workers might be critical of U.S. corporations and he wanted to find a way to alleviate any bad impression Europeans might have regarding Wall Street and other symbols of dehumanized capitalism. To humanize large capitalist institutions, he recommended exhibits featuring racially integrated factories, the benefits of community organizations, and the forty-hour work week, which he considered to be an important American innovation. He cautioned against medical exhibits because the rising cost of health care suggested that the average person would remain unprotected. Ironically, later on, when segregation displays inside the *Unfinished Work* exhibit became too controversial, they were replaced with public-health displays.[9]

Arthur Schlesinger Jr., a professor of American history at Harvard University, shared Eugenie Anderson's fear that Europeans still thought of the United States in terms set down by such left-leaning authors as Jack London, Upton Sinclair, Sinclair Lewis, John Dos Passos, and Erskine Caldwell, who were still popular in the Eastern bloc. In their works the United States was denigrated as a society of robber barons, petty businessmen, and crazed dirt farmers. He urged Cullman to find some way of refuting the idea that communism was the only humane way to apply the industrial revolution, recommending do-it-yourself exhibits and paperback exhibits of contemporary authors. Do-it-yourself exhibits would illustrate that technology was not just the property of wealthy capitalists; the paperbacks would exhibit new literary visions of post–World War II America.[10]

Lewis Galantiere, a publicist for Radio Free Europe and one of the advisers to those involved in the People's Capitalism campaign, recommended that the planners give the Europeans what they least expected: humanism, religion, values. He warned that Europeans were worried about the "spirit-killing effects of mass production." To allay these fears, Galantiere advised an emphasis on the new leisure activities, such as travel, Sunday painting, and amateur music, which strengthened individual happiness. Galantiere's exhibit ideas indicated the extent to which subtle, soft-sell techniques had begun to take precedence over rhetoric within the propaganda community. He even advised using an exhibit of American food. His personal recommendations included waffles, oyster stew, roast turkey, hash, pancakes, cheese, California wines, and a soda fountain that served sundaes and hot dogs. A glorified drugstore, gay, cheerful, and with service by Americans might be just the thing, he suggested. When the Brass Rail Restaurant was hired to run the pavilion's food concessions, Cullman, following Galantiere's advice, made sure they provided regional dishes. And a drugstore soda fountain serving soft drinks and ice cream was put in near the "Streetscape" section on the balcony level.[11]

There is a striking similarity in many of the preliminary interviews (of course the same questions were asked of each subject). C. D. Jackson, a vice president of Time Inc., recommended that exhibits show both how the individual has greater opportunity in the United States and how there are private areas of workers' lives that unions do not control. Like Rostow, Reuther, and Anderson, Jackson recommended that the overall theme of the exhibits should be "America's unfinished business," because this presented social shortcomings in progressive terms, as works in progress, instead of as final achievements. American society could be presented as an "unfinished revolution."[12]

While the commissioner general's office was interviewing prominent citizens, the USIA approached John Ely Burchard, the dean of humanities at MIT, and asked his advice on how to integrate science into the cultural program inside the American Pavilion.[13] Soon a USIA representative and the commissioner general's staff would make a special trip to Cambridge in order to discuss their ideas with a faculty group Burchard assembled at MIT.

The various planning groups convened at MIT for the first time in March 1957, but they did little more than introduce the problems. Burchard realized that a more lengthy session was needed and so asked John Slocum, the coordinator of public affairs in the commissioner general's office, to set aside an entire weekend during which the World's Fair Committee could meet with MIT faculty members, who would be asked to formulate some concrete ideas. Max F. Millikan, from the MIT Center for International Studies (CENIS), was asked to work out contractual details, and the historian Elting E. Morison was asked to act as chair for the group. The date for this weekend session was finally set for April 27–28, 1957.

When the USIA and the State Department decided to present their rather vague notions regarding the role of the United States in world culture to the faculty at MIT they were obviously searching for more substantial ideas than those proposed by the Advertising Council, whose People's Capitalism campaign had simply provided a new image for the status quo policies of the Eisenhower administration, encouraging complacency and compliance instead of substantive developmental aid for the Third World, for instance, and a more aggressive response to Soviet expansion. There was only one reason for the Brussels World's Fair Committee to go to MIT and that was to probe the minds of the scholars at CENIS.

The MIT Center for International Studies was seething with new proposals for U.S. government action. CENIS had been launched in 1952 with grants from the Ford and Rockefeller foundations for the express purpose of exploring the "economic, social, and political processes" of the developing countries and with the intention of having significant proposals regarding U.S. foreign policy ready by 1958–59. Millikan and Rostow's *A Proposal: Key to an Effective Foreign Policy* had in fact made the rounds in Washington, D.C., as early as 1956, when an important foreign-aid bill was before Congress. The influence of Millikan and Rostow's ideas, which would not really come into their own until the 1960s, were probably what brought the fair committee to their door.[14]

Millikan and Rostow's book was prepared at the request of C. D. Jackson, who approached CENIS shortly after resigning as special assistant to the president for international affairs (a position subsequently taken by Nelson Rockefeller) and returning to Time Inc. Jackson's goal was to find a way that "the U.S. might play a more positive role in the building of a stable world."[15] While the proposal was being written, Millikan and Rostow also worked with Jackson and Rockefeller on the Open Skies Proposal, which Eisenhower presented to the Soviets at the 1955 summit conference in Geneva. When the Soviets rejected Open Skies—which had proposed the mutual inspection of military installations by the United States and the USSR—Rockefeller concluded that the Soviets had no desire to pursue peace and that the United States had to prepare for confrontation. Rockefeller enlisted Millikan and Rostow to organize a symposium at which a new foreign policy could be outlined; the symposium convened at the Quantico Marine base in northern Virginia in September 1955.[16]

In his history of the events at Quantico, Rostow stated that the participants set forth four basic principles: that there should be: a "full disclosure of the dangers confronting the country . . . in order to rally the national will"; a dramatic increase in military spending; "economic aid to build up the free countries so they can eventually contribute to the defense effort around the world"; and constant pressure on the Communists, with an emphasis on counteracting their propaganda. But these expensive foreign-policy plans were opposed by George Humphrey (secretary of the treasury), Charles Wilson (secretary of defense), and Herbert Hoover Jr. (under secretary of state), who did not think that the nation could afford these new initiatives or that they were necessary. The *Sputnik* launch in late 1957 would swing public opinion into line with Rockefeller's proposals, but by that time he had left the Eisenhower administration and formed a new coalition centered on a "large-scale public version" of the Quantico report, subsidized by the Rockefeller Brothers Fund.[17]

Rostow called the group of influential business and labor leaders, foundation officials, academics, scientists, retired military men, and lawyers (from both political parties) that Rockefeller brought together to formulate his 1956–57 "panel reports," "a kind of shadow cabinet in opposition," backing an "alternative program against the president."[18] Once it became apparent that Rockefeller himself was not going to run for president in 1960, both John F. Kennedy and Richard M. Nixon would try to harness the energy of this new coalition. Nixon would have a tough time convincing moderate Republicans that he was willing to steer the nation in a new direction. Kennedy, with considerable help from Rostow and other intellectuals, gathered the activist coalition together under the slogan "Let's get this country moving again."[19]

In the late 1950s Rostow became an adviser to Senator Kennedy and eventually entered the White House as assistant to the national security adviser, a position that enabled him to put into practice some of the ideas adumbrated at CENIS, which he then published in 1960 as *The Stages of Economic Growth: A Non-Communist Manifesto.*

Rostow's designs for U.S. intervention abroad sprang from the theory that all healthy societies grew in stages, culminating in the stage of mass consumption. He contrasted these (capitalist) stages with Marx's: feudalism, bourgeois capitalism, socialism, and communism. In effect, *The Stages of Economic Growth* was the ideological handbook that Theodore Repplier and the Advertising Council had been searching for during the development of the People's Capitalism campaign. Repplier would have been pleased with the importance that Rostow attributed to the mass-consumption society. Activist and conservative groups may have differed in their strategies, but they all wanted the same eventual outcome of world prosperity and international capitalism.[20]

In the spring of 1957 the CENIS staff, especially Millikan and Rostow, were deeply involved in the "schizophrenic" public policy debates over foreign aid.[21] Rostow's and Millikan's notions regarding the stages of economic growth indicate that military and diplomatic pacts were hardly as important to them as was coaxing other countries into the mass-production stage of economic maturity. Economic interdependence was the best way to ensure international security and the only way (other than direct confrontation) of thwarting Soviet expansion. Insofar as CENIS was concerned, the United States had to support economic development with all due haste. This was not only a matter of national security, but a spiritual, moral mission that could be denied only at the risk of "spiritual decline." Millikan and Rostow concluded their *Proposal: Key to an Effective Foreign Policy* with the warning that if the United States turned its back on the developing countries it risked losing "some of those basic spiritual qualities which have been historically linked to the nation's sense of world mission . . . its distinction, its transcendent quality." A sense of imminent crisis and transformation filled the thoughts of Millikan and Rostow when they met with the rest of the Cambridge Study Group in April 1957.[22]

At the MIT meeting five teams were formed to tackle exhibit concepts and find ways of representing them in a three-dimensional manner. The commissioner general had decided that exhibits could be divided into five categories: the land and the people, life and work, American idealism in action, science and technology, and culture. At least one person from the commissioner general's staff sat on each subcommittee. Robert Warner, from the exhibits program, was on the Land and the People subcommittee; Peter Harnden, the exhibit designer, attended the Life and Work session; John Slocum, from public affairs, was part of the Idealism in Action group; James Plaut was on the Science and Technology subcommittee; and Bernard Rudofsky, Harnden's chief associate, was on the Culture subcommittee. The five groups prepared reports on the themes, and later these were condensed and forwarded to the commissioner general's office.

The Life and Work subcommittee worried that anything portraying working women, even women in volunteer club activities, might reinforce stereotypes of the masculine American woman. Women, they suggested, should only be shown fulfilling traditional roles as wives and mothers. Some of this could be accomplished with displays in shop windows and model homes. The fashion show, which would eventually become the most talked-about exhibit at Brussels, satisfied some of these requirements by exhibiting "feminine" women (the models were actually Europeans) in association with domestic appliances, which the models sauntered through on their way to the display ramp. But the actual women's program in the American Pavilion would not be as restrictive as these advisers wished. That program, separated from all the other exhibits, would not take shape until Katherine Howard was appointed as the second deputy commissioner, long after the MIT sessions were over. Her guidance turned the women's program into a showcase for working women.[23]

The Idealism in Action subcommittee members developed the *Unfinished Work* exhibit. They wanted it to be of the highest quality, but not necessarily very large, and "soundproofed, and as solemn as a religious shrine."[24] Inside this shrine they wanted to place displays explaining the segregation problem and urban blight. Racial woes, for example, were to be cushioned by exhibits demonstrating the progress of African Americans since the Civil War. And American slums were to be presented in conjunction with information touting the foreign-aid programs aimed at Third World nations. Troubled American communities were to be linked with problems throughout the developing world, demonstrating that Americans were trying to raise the living standards of all underprivileged people, not just those living in the United States, by slowly broadening middle-class ideals. Rostow suggested that the exhibit could actually be created out of *Life* magazine photographs and quotes from politicians and famous authors.

Time Inc. provided the design and funding for the *Unfinished Work* exhibit resulting from this planning session. Leo Lionni, the art director at *Fortune,* designed the exhibit, retaining the substance of the ideas outlined by Rostow and the Idealism in Action subcommittee—basically the same ideas that *Fortune* and other Luce publications had long promoted. Racial equality, urban renewal, modern agriculture, and a burgeoning middle class were exhibited as the fruits of American foreign and domestic policy.

The Science and Technology subcommittee chose as its unifying theme "man exploring the universe." The group's first consideration was to show that, although science had always been an important part of the American tradition, many of the current scientists in America were actually immigrants. A focus on immigrants would win friends for the American scientific community abroad and garner sympathy for U.S. objectives, such as the peaceful application of nuclear power. But the members did not want science to appear as if it were an elitist pursuit. They urged Cullman to create an amateur astronomy exhibit, something that would interest armchair scientists and backyard tinkerers. Similarly, they suggested an exhibit on genetics and antibiotics that demonstrated that the United States was a nation deeply committed to the welfare of the world.[25]

A nuclear reactor exhibit would become the key element in the American presentation of benevolent technological progress, revealing how abundant, inexpensive energy would fuel the life of a small town. In an understated fashion, science was the cornerstone of many of the exhibits in the American Pavilion, from the plastic chairs on the terrace to the Acrilan uniforms worn by the guides. Science and technology were, indeed, the foundations of the international capitalist democracy promoted by the American Pavilion. Americans had been the undisputed world leaders in science and technology, especially in regard to the mass production of the consumer products that gave People's Capitalism a ring of truth. But this leadership would be shattered by the Soviet launch of the space satellite *Sputnik 1* on October 4, 1957, an event that shocked the American public and threw Cullman's exhibit designers into temporary chaos. There was no way to match this Soviet scientific achievement. At the last minute the American program was weighted even heavier in the direction of "peaceful" cultural displays and alluring consumer goods. Cullman even promised President Eisenhower that he could create the cultural equivalent of *Sputnik,* if the president could get him the requisite funds.[26]

The Culture subcommittee, oddly enough, wanted to exclude the fine arts so that culture would be seen as part of everyday life, as a core component in all the exhibits. It wanted to show how things in America were intimately connected with mass-distribution outlets. Paperbacks, for example, simultaneously demonstrated the medium of mass production and American literature. And the Culture subcommittee hoped an accent would be placed on significant new forms: jazz, news photography, industrial design, interpretive dance, and architecture—even toys, beach paraphernalia, camping equipment, lawn and garden artifacts. Using these guidelines, James Plaut enlisted the help of colleagues at the Boston Institute of Contemporary Art to assemble a spectacular array of novel items that gave the material culture exhibits in the pavilion a casual, fun-filled appearance. The fine arts were inevitably included, but ironically, their inclusion brought accusations of elitism down on the head of Howard Cullman, proving that the Culture subcommittee members had actually been wise in their desire to exclude the type of esoteric objects normally only seen in museums.[27]

After the MIT convention, the commissioner general's office had plenty of concepts to sort through: the USIA reports, the advice from leaders in the business and publishing world, and finally, the recommendations of the Cambridge Study Group. The commissioner general's office and the Peter G. Harnden design firm had to synthesize these imaginative suggestions and determine which proposals could actually be constructed, given the shape of Stone's pavilion, the lack of time, and the financial restrictions.

Despite everything, the pavilion opened on time. Those who began their tour of the pavilion at the main entrance found touchstones of American culture—tumbleweeds, a Model-T Ford, a gold nugget, cowboy boots, and an Idaho potato—arranged beneath a 100-foot-wide wire map suspended from the ceiling. Exiting this introductory exhibit, and following a path that circled the central pool, visitors next encountered a 480-page edition of the Sunday *New York Times* displayed on panels. This pre-Christmas issue (November 24, 1957) illustrated the role of the free press and provided dramatic evidence of the culture of material abundance. Arranged so that it could be taken in at a glance, the visitor had no sooner gulped down this black-and-white whorl of fashion and consumer culture than he or she was confronted by the American art exhibition. The art exhibition was divided into four sections: folk art, Native American art, contemporary painting, and sculpture. In the Native American section the curators took pains to stress regional and tribal variations in order to dispel the myth of the Indian as a creature exclusively of the Plains—as little more than a savage foe of white settlers. Likewise, the forty-three contemporary paintings and twenty-six modern sculptures demonstrated how people in the various regions of the United States had met the challenge of modernism in unique ways. The paintings occupied a special exhibit area built out from the curving wall, but the sculpture extended across the floor and into the central pool itself. Nearby was Saul Steinberg's large mural in several freestanding sections.[28]

Continuing along a circular path, visitors encountered the nuclear energy exhibits inspired by the Atoms for Peace programs that had been touring Europe for the last few years. These included irradiated food, a hospital's "cobalt-60" radiation unit, and the popular "electromechanical hands" used to manipulate radioactive material. The robotic hands allowed visitors to translate the motion of their own fingers to the steel hands behind a protective shield. By playing with radioactive substances, visitors, it was hoped, developed confidence in American scientists and learned that radioactivity could be contained and manipulated. Atoms for Peace exhibits during the 1950s were designed to show that atomic energy had many peaceful benefits. Placing the International Geophysical Year exhibit next to the nuclear section extended this peaceful analogy to space research. In a dim, air-conditioned room, black lights helped to simulate a polar environment in the portrayal of the exploration of the South Pole region for an exhibit titled *Nations Working Together.*[29]

Several display areas on the ground floor translated science into layman's terms by showing how new technologies were fueling a "continuing industrial revolution" in the United States. The automation display, for example, used a group of integrated computers, control mechanisms, and testing devices to demonstrate how far automatic technology had progressed beyond the old assembly line. One card-playing computer beat all challengers at bridge. The IBM Ramac computer acted the role of idiot savant by typing out, in ten languages, the most important historic occurrence of any year between 4 B.C. and 1958. A small, animated display of the New York Stock Exchange revealed how automatic tabulating devices had become the heartbeat of the democratic marketplace.[30]

Behind a glass partition, RCA recreated a closed-circuit television studio that broadcast interviews, science demonstrations, and documentary films. Visitors could see color television, often for the first time, and catch a glimpse of the fascinating, behind-the-scenes activities of a broadcasting studio. Next door, a soundproof room furnished with ultramodern Harry Bertoia wing chairs (provided by Knoll International) invited the visitor to relax and experience the wonder of hi-fi music—another product that RCA was introducing into the European market.

Finally, the ground floor featured two urban planning exhibits. There was a 300-square foot model of the city of Philadelphia with an automatically operated "flip-over" feature that replaced a blighted ghetto with a planned, modernized city center. Dioramas, maps, and panel displays outlined the history and development of the city. In an adjoining section, a complementary exhibit on new industrial parks revealed how grouping factories outside of town in modern suburban facilities near transportation arteries improved both civic and commercial life.[31]

Before leaving the ground floor, the visitor could enter the attached theater through the foyer that displayed the hanging Calder mobile. The film version of *South Pacific,* which appropriately dramatized the romance between a Frenchman and an American woman, opened there on May 1, 1958. Performances by artists such as Benny Goodman and Harry Belafonte offered popular versions of jazz and calypso music. Live performances attracting a large number of people garnered excellent coverage in the press and were sometimes taped for television broadcast. The theater was the best-equipped facility of its kind at the fair, so good that the Belgians kept it standing after 1958 and eventually transformed it into a television studio. It was also the perfect setting for special events and addresses by important persons. The Women's Program used it for presentations by prominent American women in order to show the scope of their contributions to the nation's life.[32]

Three stairways on the first level led up through ample circular openings to the second floor. Here more than 1,000 objects of daily life—home and office furniture, kitchen equipment, household appliances, sporting goods, toys, outdoor appliances, craft products—revealed the delights of consumer culture and the talents of craftsmen and industrial designers. These items were arranged in groups, or "islands," as they were called, each with a distinctive theme. The fashion runway, descending down to the pool from the second-level displays, integrated the fashion show with the appliances and appurtenances of the housewife. The fashion models actually had a dressing room among the "islands," so when they emerged wearing new costumes they paraded through the appliances before descending to the pool. The fashion show ran on and off for most of the day, every day, and became a wildly popular event, jamming the pavilion with spectators. It was a great competitor to the Soviet Pavilion's science displays but nevertheless enraged many U.S. tourists who felt that some kind of military hardware, instead of mink coats and American ready-to-wear fashions, should have occupied the focal center.

"Streetscape," the mock-up of a main street, was located on the balcony level across the open circle from the "islands." This "street," paved with asphalt, had directional signs, mail boxes, manhole covers, and twelve store windows, featuring a variety of American products. Two shops in this area sold books and magazines, and a drugstore soda fountain served ice cream, Coke, and Pepsi. Huge photomurals of city scenes mounted in curving, panoramic displays, helped convey the look of American urban life. Nearby, architectural exhibits, including scale models of homes, skyscrapers, churches, schools, and shopping centers, gave visitors a peek at both the utilitarian and experimental architecture of the United States. The last big exhibit on the second level was the Children's Creative Center, where parents could leave their children with specially trained art teachers.

Also on the second level was the Brass Rail Restaurant. Visitors could exit or enter on this level at the back of the building. The pavilion had been built into the rising slope of the hill behind it, so above and below it was flush with pedestrian walkways, where some forty entrances and exits provided for unstructured circulation and minimized any sense of entrapment—one of the methods devised by the architect to express symbolically the freedom of American life.

Those who left the building on the second level came out near the freestanding *Unfinished Work* exhibit and the round Circarama theater featuring the 360-degree Disney film, *America the Beautiful.* The *Unfinished Work* exhibit conveyed the idea that the spirit of the American Revolution was still alive, inspiring miracles in scientific agriculture and the prevention of natural disasters. The exhibit also promised visitors that although many individuals in the United States, especially southern blacks, were not able to share in the wealth and civil liberties for which the Revolution had been fought, the basic principles of government guaranteed that someday there would indeed be equal opportunity for all Americans. The exhibit demonstrated how Americans were working to bring basic amenities such as food and housing to the underprivileged and how a constantly expanding number of blacks were being brought into the middle class.

Complementing this dose of cold war rhetoric, the nearby Circarama theater provided novel entertainment for some 1,800,000 visitors. Inside the building, visitors were treated to a transcontinental tour of the United States as thirteen synchronized projectors created a totally circular film environment. This cinematic update of the painted panoramas familiar to the nineteenth century was the most popular of the U.S. exhibits. The standing audience was swept over New York harbor, the Grand Canyon, and the Golden Gate Bridge as if on a magic-carpet ride. Children cried and parents gasped as a row of grain threshers advanced toward them in the prairie sequence. Circarama was so popular that while waiting in the hot sun for a chance to get in, people actually fainted rather than give up their place in line.[33]

Films were an important method of conveying information and were used in several ways. Both documentary and entertainment films played in the pavilion theater. The "Cavalcade of American Films" program, for example, began with the most primitive early films and ended with the latest Cinemascope marvels. And scattered throughout the pavilion were "loop films," or short films on selected American topics that played over and over all day.

Ostensibly, the pavilion provided an objective, detached portrayal of the United States, but many exhibit materials were provided by companies that wanted some sort of recognition for their efforts. Although the American Pavilion had nothing like the typical layout of merchandise and corporate logos seen at trade fairs, it was still a display of commercial culture, illustrating the behavior of people to whom buying and selling, getting and spending, were central concerns. Taking a cue from the commercial environment in the nation itself, the American Pavilion combined entertainment, glamour, even relaxation and a sense of ease to sell its primary product: the American way of life. It was an apt symbol for its day, mirroring a domestic environment in which it was becoming more and more difficult to distinguish between commerce and culture. But it also shared attributes with American propaganda exhibits, presenting a society in which the divisions of history, class, race, and gender were being overcome by technology, upward mobility, creativity, and equal opportunity.

5 Victor D'Amico's Creative Center

Kindergartens staffed by the wives of U.S. military personnel were popular features of the trade fair program, beginning with the fair held in Paris in 1955. The kindergartens advertised progressive toys and demonstrated in a lively, interactive manner the care lavished upon U.S. children by their mothers (whose free time was ensured by the abundant society). No ordinary kindergarten would be good enough for the American Pavilion in Brussels, however; at the Brussels World's Fair, U.S. methods of child rearing and education itself would be on trial. The American Pavilion featured the Children's Creative Center, sponsored by the Museum of Modern Art (MOMA) and staffed with specially trained attendants.

Adults were not allowed into the Creative Center except for a few teachers, the press, and VIPs. At the door to the exhibit children passed through the "enchanted gate": a white metal rod shaped like a contour drawing of a four-year-old and a twelve-year-old walking side by side. Unless a child could fit through the gate without crouching, he or she was not admitted.[1] The gate was a convenient method of separating children from their parents, but it also symbolized the entrance into the world of childhood—a world that most people were psychologically incapable of reentering after puberty. The Creative Center was designed for those children who had not yet traded in their imaginations for conformity.

The center accommodated up to twenty children, who often had to reserve places ahead of time with guides posted at the door, for sessions lasting one hour and fifteen minutes. Inside, children were introduced to unique educational toys and encouraged to create mobiles and modern paintings much like the ones on display in the U.S. art exhibition. Informally organized school groups passed through the center all day, seven days a week. The staff took fifteen-minute breaks in between classes to clean and replenish art supplies.

Victor D'Amico, director of the Museum of Modern Art's Department of Education, designed and installed the Children's Creative Center and then returned to New York, leaving his handpicked staff in charge. In substance, this exhibit was another version of the Children's Holiday Carnival, an annual event at MOMA during the 1950s and itself an outgrowth of programs D'Amico was continually refining through the museum's Department of Education. The Children's Creative Center, in a modified version, had already been tested abroad at trade fairs in Milan and Barcelona, where it had scored a public relations coup for the U.S. Department of Commerce.[2] At trade fairs, the Children's Creative Center was intended to demonstrate progressive education methods, but it also taught important lessons about the American way of life.

At the 1957 trade fairs in Barcelona and Milan, one wall of the exhibit was made of glass to provide an unrestricted view of children from all races and classes eagerly learning how to paint and sculpt. A pamphlet called *Our Children and Productivity* explained to parents the parallels between an abundant economic system and healthy, happy children. The pamphlet also encouraged ideas long promoted by the Marshall Plan and the various Mutual Security Agency organizations that were designed to enhance European economic and military strength through mass production. Promoting capitalism and the American way of life abroad often provoked Communist or nationalist reactionaries. D'Amico's progressive education exhibit was a subtle way of convincing Communist-leaning Italians and Spaniards that the bounty of democracy enhanced the life of the lower classes. Most important, the Children's Holiday Carnival—in its various manifestations—demonstrated that democratic freedoms had a personal dimension. Finally, the unrestricted laughter of children rising up out of the Holiday Carnival, like the aromatic steam from a pot of soup, made the hard-sell claims of other American exhibits easier to swallow.[3]

Trade fairs exhibited the benefits of mass production: model homes, ready-made clothing, beautifully designed products. But no exhibit had the dramatic impact of the Holiday Carnival, which demonstrated how a new generation of American children was growing up with the artistic and cultural opportunities formerly reserved for the upper classes. Italian or Spanish children playing behind a glass partition dramatized the benefits ahead for the people of Europe once they emerged from the post–World War II rebuilding phase and entered into the leisure culture of abundance and consumption enjoyed by Americans.

The Children's Holiday Carnival of Milan and Barcelona was redesigned for the Brussels World's Fair and renamed the Children's Creative Center. Like other trade fair exhibits, it was revamped to fit in with the new strategy at Brussels. By 1958, the Soviets were claiming that they could produce almost as much as the Americans. So the American planners focused their exhibits less on productivity and more on the ways in which productivity benefited the average person. Thus D'Amico was allowed to emphasize the advanced teaching methods he used at the elite Museum of Modern Art.

The glass wall of the Holiday Carnival was replaced with a wall pierced by little portholes, which gave the children more privacy and added an aura of mystery. The parents, peering through the portholes into the enchanted realm, observed a classroom in which the normal rules did not apply. In the Creative Center, children stood before an array of strange devices manipulating colors and shapes. Or they sat at tables discussing their paintings with teachers, exploring the relative merits of collage, or the singular importance of an event that may have occurred on their way to the fair that morning. The Creative Center was not just a place where art objects were made. It taught children that their lives were unique, that their decisions and choices mattered, and that daily events could be important experiences.

The Creative Center consisted of two rooms painted in primary colors, each wall a different shade. First, the children entered a semidarkened room painted in deep blues and greens, filled with toys either bathed in pools of light or illuminated from within. Musical recordings enhanced the mood in an atmosphere of "magic and fantasy," reminiscent of a "friendly forest, cool and quiet," full of delightful surprises. In this "inspiration room," the child was encouraged to experiment with specially designed toys that taught aesthetic fundamentals without "words or dogma of any kind."[4]

The toys in the inspiration room were of three basic types: one group emphasized the sense of touch; another, color composition; and a third, spatial relationships. A "fantasy zoo," designed by Ruth Vollmer, introduced several kinds of tactile experiences through a toy cat, rooster, and caterpillar. The cat was made from rabbit fur stretched over a wire base. When stroked, the cat responded by arching its back, thereby stimulating the tactile sense. The rooster was made from wire spirals and danced when a lever was jiggled. And "Chenille," sixty-eight inches long and three inches in diameter, was a caterpillar made from horsehair and feathers, with two bone balls for eyes and seven sets of wooden balls for feet. When a knob was pushed, Chenille wiggled, thereby demonstrating a form of automation and a sort of tactility different from the soft, responsive cat or the manually operated wire rooster.[5]

The Design Color Window consisted of variously shaped pieces of colored Plexiglas on an illuminated, translucent Plexiglas table top. Children rearranged the colors in experimental designs and color compositions. A similar device, the Color Player, was constructed like a piano with keys and pedals. Abstract shapes reminiscent of bird and animal forms were hung by the child on two treelike structures in a large upright box, and then a window was lowered over the front. By playing different keys, the child could then manipulate cool-colored lights on one side of the frame and warm on the other. Pedals like those on a piano allowed the child to set the trees in motion. Color, shape, and movement interacted inside the Color Player.

The Space Ship Design Projector was the largest mechanism in the gallery of toys and had room for two children to sit inside its "cockpit." Three projectors behind the cockpit passed light through

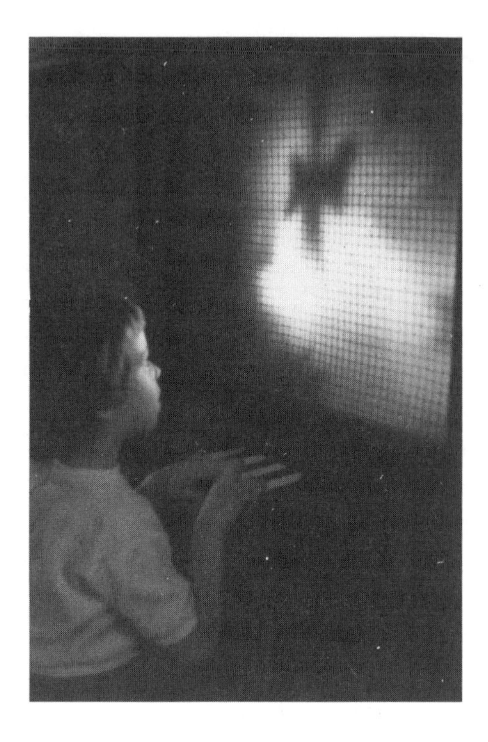

Child using the Color Player in the Creative Center, Brussels World's Fair, 1958. Photograph by Lois Lord.

colored cellophane, sandwiched between plastic discs, onto suspended forms suggesting planets in front of the children, creating the sensation that the operators were flying through space. The "pilots" controlled the changing colors and moving patterns by turning the steering wheel or working the pedals and panel switches.[6]

Composition lessons were taught with a large shadow box that had elastic strings emerging from a hole in the center of its base. The strings could be stretched up to several hooks on the ceiling or the sides of the box to form three-dimensional compositions. Little foam balls on the strings helped give the box an "atomic" look and added visual interest to this strictly black-and-white space. An even simpler compositional device used elastic bands stretched over a Peg-Board. The elastic strings could be pulled into angular shapes by wrapping them around golf tees set into the Peg-Board. The last

Child with the cat in the Creative Center, Brussels World's Fair, 1958. Photograph by Lois Lord.

compositional toy was the Giant Builder: a set of wafer-thin wood squares with slots cut into them that could be pieced together to build little structures or abstract figures.

These creative toys were designed to appeal to different facets of the imagination and the senses. They were simple to manipulate and encouraged children to begin thinking abstractly about color, shape, texture, and design and contributed to their ability to work without adult guidance. Once sufficiently primed, the children were led into the Construction Room, where they painted at easels or gathered around tables and made mobiles. They created tiny animals—entire zoos—out of straws, string, felt, fine mesh, cellophane, feathers, paper, pipe cleaners, and glue. Whatever they made was packaged up by the attendants and sent home with them as a souvenir.

The Construction Room was brightly colored in red, yellow, and

Child painting in the Creative Center, Brussels World's Fair, 1958. Photograph by Lois Lord.

gray-blue. There was no ceiling on the room and so it was flooded with natural light and the sounds of the fair. Easels in contrasting colors (yellow easels were placed against red walls and blue easels against yellow) and adjustable heights invited children to paint. And in the center of the room, two circular tables with pie-shaped lazy Susans in the middle provided materials for three-dimensional masks, mobiles, and collage. Above each table was a suspended hoop for hanging the mobiles the children made, adding a festive touch to the atmosphere.

As in the first room, the staff (composed of equal numbers of professional artists and art teachers) encouraged the children to keep working without worrying about results. And there was plenty for them to work with: poster paint, cartons of drawing paper, pipe cleaners, colored tissue, corrugated paper, gold paper, straws, burlap, and yarn. Children were given assistance when they did not know how to operate a toy, how to start a collage or construction, or did not seem happy. To coax children into working with paint or collage the teachers asked open-ended questions: "Have you seen anything interesting today?"[7] The intention was to lead children toward unique subject matter and topics they would not normally associate with art.

Eugene Grigsby, an African American staff member, observed a great initial rigidity in the children from local schools. "All the girls," he said, "drew houses at first."[8] And European boys were even more determined to draw boats than were their American counterparts to draw cars and airplanes. This subject matter had been encouraged by strict teachers. Indeed, some of the teachers who were invited into the Creative Center with their classes would begin telling children what to do, even holding the brushes and guiding the hands of children as they painted. European teachers had to be forced to stop controlling their students and pay attention to the unobtrusive American methods, which suppressed traditional discipline in the hope of teaching social skills, individuality, and creativity.

Encouraged to paint things fresh in their memories, or things that seemed especially interesting to them, the students explored the meaning of their own lives while they learned about the visual arts. But if a child could not get beyond the stereotypical boat, he or she was asked, "Where do you most often see boats?" Every effort was made to help children see beyond the clichéd subjects that they had been taught to associate with art. Thus a child who insisted on painting a boat would be encouraged at least to create an authentic local setting to moor it in.[9]

Children who came to the center learned to hone their perceptions, to paint things unique to their own experience, and to become "individuals" in the American sense of the term. Some children turned into violent abstractionists. Others, coaxed along in their private visions, put together representational scenes. Many children drew pictures of the Atomium, the bizarre building in the form of an iron molecule that towered over all the other structures at the fair. The teachers in the Creative Center studied these paintings in order to learn about cognitive development. One of the staff members, Lois Lord, photographed some of the paintings and arranged them in sequences for her own study and for the benefit of other teachers. For the staff of the Creative Center, artwork was like a window that enabled a trained instructor to peer into the psyche of children.

Lois Lord measured progress in terms of expressive power. Children were not taught to use perspective or color theory unless they needed a little technical assistance in order to become more articulate. However, because they were not judged according to their grasp of traditional techniques, or their mastery over technical skills, students often developed expressive methods that were just as good as perspective, or better, and that were more in keeping with their personal idiosyncrasies (such as a penchant for design). So although some paintings looked bizarre they were judged successful when they showed evidence of a personal sense of style.

Jane Cooper Bland, another teacher in the Creative Center, had published a book on the developmental stages that the Creative Center teachers expected to nurture. Bland's *Art of the Young Child: 3 to 5 Years,* which was sold through the souvenir store in the American Pavilion, taught parents and teachers how to recognize and accept varying degrees of ability according to age or development; how to encourage their students and present new challenges; how to help the child weigh choices—"to discriminate, to both use and understand the things that make up his or her everyday world."[10] Bland wrote that even scribbles were extremely important because of the meaning they had for the child. Those private meanings were respected because progress manifested itself in numerous ways: some social, some psychological, some technical. Bland cautioned instructors to think of growth in the long term and not to worry about sudden digressions into sloppiness or scribbling because the youngster might be in the process of working out a new idea.

Some basic developmental stages were taken for granted. Very young children, for example, cannot concentrate for long and were not allowed into the Creative Center. Four-year-olds were about the youngest children admitted. They were expected to be able to manipulate materials and have the power to transform ideas as they worked. Poster paint was used to help them change their concepts: it was opaque so new colors could be painted directly over old ones. Bland believed that the first major step for children was the making of definite forms, such as circles, and the placing of colors in relation to one another. At four, most children had also learned to use the entire sheet of paper and to start with a specific idea or be able to elaborate one as they worked.

At five, children were expected to be able to concentrate for almost an hour, to make positive shapes (even designs), mix colors, choose and cut collage material, notice how materials affected one another, and realize how their imagination could transform raw materials into something of their own making. Bland urged parents and teachers not to worry about paintings as if they were IQ tests but to strive to understand what the child was saying. The main thing was not to tell the child what to do. "Creativeness is hindered or even destroyed by indoctrination." The child would grow in a natural manner unless the parent somehow gummed up the works.[11]

Despite the lack of emphasis on "art," children in the Creative Center were indeed learning how to create in the modern tradition. Their work was not very different, for example, from that of the American artists Saul Steinberg and Alexander Calder. Calder and Steinberg, whose art was on display just outside the Creative Center, were themselves often photographed in ways that made them appear to be childlike. They had become celebrated examples of the notion that the creative potential of childhood needed to be cultivated throughout one's entire life. Indeed, photographs in *Life*, showing Steinberg at work on his comic collage mural for the pavilion, make him appear nearly indistinguishable from the images of children making constructions in the Creative Center.[12] Steinberg and Calder represented an ideal type of artist: They were innovative but not pretentious, satirical at times but never offensive. Most important, they were vital members of society. Steinberg's cartoons appeared daily in international journals, and Calder's sculptures were often created specifically for corporate lobbies. Steinberg and Calder were the paragons toward which the teachers in the Creative Center directed their efforts.

Adults perplexed by Steinberg's strange murals or Calder's whimsical mobiles may have actually looked into the portholes of the Children's Creative Center for clues to deciphering modern art forms. George Staempfli, in charge of the fine-arts exhibits inside the

The Americans, *by Saul Steinberg (1958). Detail of a mural in sections for the interior of the American Pavilion at the Brussels World's Fair, 1958. © IRPA-KIK-Brussels.*

American pavilion, should have probably recommended sessions at the Creative Center to the members of Congress and tourists who demanded that a more realistic form of American art be displayed in the pavilion's exhibition spaces. Bowing to pressure from these critics, Staempfli eventually hung a few "realistic" paintings around the pavilion. One day, the staff of the Creative Center arrived to find a Norman Rockwell painting, *Mrs. Effie McGuire Reading to Her Pupils at Oak Mountain School,* hanging over the appointment desk outside the enchanted gate. Lord was angry enough to badger Staempfli daily to have it removed. Not only was this depiction of an old-fashioned one-room school house the most tired sort of composition, but its sentimental depiction of pioneer children huddled around a wood stove, taking dictation from a central authority figure, was exactly the type of education the Creative Center hoped to replace. Particularly upsetting to Lord were the tiny, cliché-ridden children's paintings that Rockwell had painted onto the walls in his mythical schoolroom.[13]

The Rockwell painting was indeed out of place. After all, the purpose of the American Pavilion was to help prepare the European population for the automated, push-button world ahead. In keeping with the American attempt to teach Europeans about the managerial, scientific, and information age toward which the hoped-for post–cold war world was heading, the exhibits in the pavilion argued for an economy of leisure, planned obsolescence, and abundance on the American model. And all this was accomplished with a sense of naturalness. It was not an accident, for instance, that the reporter Hughes Vehenne, writing for the French-language newspaper *Le Soir,* found that everything presented itself to him with "an easy-going-style." Or that he felt compelled to "relax" in one of the hundreds of cozy armchairs instead of rushing about to see new products.[14]

As Vehenne slipped off his shoes and settled into one of the hundreds of mass-produced fiberglass Eames chairs, he was experiencing the new American way of life. The easy-to-maintain colorful chairs were a practical application of the new creative principles demonstrated beyond the enchanted gate. These nearly indestructible versions of the middle-class throne demonstrated to tired feet the rewards of rethinking all types of design and material culture—not just painting or sculpture. The American way aimed at refashioning cultural standards for the atomic age, using new materials, making things that had never seemed possible before. The Children's Creative Center explained how the things on exhibit were produced; it was the ideological map that laid out the method at work in the new things displayed, even in the building itself. Abundance provided leisure; leisure nourished creativity; creativity allowed people to fulfill themselves, to discover the meaning of their lived experiences.

But the middle-class American utopia displayed at Brussels was

A guide explains the operation of a nuclear reactor to visitors in the U.S. Pavilion at the 1958 Brussels World's Fair. National Archives.

not an accomplished fact. Critics noted that, to the extent that it actually did exist, the ideal American way of life was threatened from both without and within: Externally, the Soviet Union was becoming increasingly powerful, while internally, the growing conformity of business culture was creating dissent among minorities and the younger generation. At least one prominent American, Sloan Wilson, the author of *The Man in the Gray Flannel Suit* (1955), blamed the nation's problems on the educational system.[15] The American government was eager to show off the impressive education strategies implemented by D'Amico in order to demonstrate that Americans had begun to address the problems that accompanied affluence.

Complaints about life in America centered upon the new managerial class, composed of the men and women who had survived World War II and returned to upward mobility, the suburbs, and television—only to find themselves mired in conformity. William H. Whyte Jr., assistant managing editor of *Fortune,* fingered conformity as the enemy of the age in his book *Is Anybody Listening?* (1952). The leaders of the new democratic utopia, Whyte feared, were suffocating in the faceless corporations that characterized the consumer society. Managers were in danger of losing their dynamic initiative. "A new respect for individuality must be kindled," said Whyte. "A revival of the humanities perhaps or a conscious effort to accommodate dissent" was needed to revive the everyday life of Western democracy.[16]

Conformity and anticonformity became key issues of the decade. While Gregory Peck in *The Man in the Gray Flannel Suit* (1956) and James Dean in *Rebel without a Cause* (1955) dramatized the psychological trauma of both new and old generations trying to fit in without totally losing a sense of personal identity, Whyte counseled the business community and its legions of gray-suited managers that a circular form of organization had to replace the hierarchical, pyramidal structure characterizing old forms of capitalist enterprises. As applied to the corporate structure, Whyte's circular, or "flat," organization used more executives and placed fewer people beneath each manager, avoiding the lopsided power structure of man-at-the-top organizations and allowing for the creative participation of a larger number of people.[17]

The American Pavilion was itself a large, symbolic representation of the utopian, circular power structure Whyte described. So were the tiny round tables in the Children's Creative Center, where children of many nations played together. The children made funny hats; they exhibited brotherly love; they acted out a one-world drama, becoming ambassadors of the new global democracy that many people hoped might soon become reality. Any evidence of a hierarchical structure inside the American Pavilion—although one certainly existed—was hidden from view.

Soviet imagery at the Brussels World's Fair, by contrast, suggested that Soviet society was as pyramidal as any old-fashioned capitalist organization. Typical of Soviet imagery was the huge statue of an earnest Lenin in an overcoat, looming over the crowds at the USSR Pavilion. The windswept, gargantuan portrait of the mythical Soviet pioneer was appropriate in that collection of heroic achievements—*Sputnik* among them. By contrast, the abstract art and the fashion models who occupied center stage in the American Pavilion seemed to advertise the wildest extremes of liberty. As a purely symbolic statement of communism—an ideal society striving for equal opportunity—the Soviet Pavilion sent conflicting signals. The rectangular structure with its idealized leader towering above displays of industrial production looked like something out of a Victorian exhibition dominated by local robber barons.

The American (and Soviet) obsession with production had inevitably led to boredom and dissatisfaction, to "work and its discontents," in the words of Daniel Bell. Bell attacked the "cult of efficiency" that the cold war encouraged and remarked that although mass production gave Americans appliances and gadgets, the factory jobs that produced these things provided none of the innate satisfactions once associated with craft.[18] Bell's criticisms were aimed at the People's Capitalism slogans, which promised that higher wages, better working conditions, and the increase of leisure time provided by automation would alleviate the problems accompanying factories. Similarly, John Kenneth Galbraith's influential *The Affluent Society* (1958) pointed out that the "conventional wisdom believes in material progress but it would seem that real progress is actually taking place in the values of people who want more productive lives in terms of fun and interesting work not just dollars."[19]

Critics of the abundant society rarely speculated on the environmental or political consequences of mass production and global distribution. Whyte, Galbraith, and Bell, for example, were primarily concerned with how abundance and affluence affected character. The educational reforms on display in the Creative Center addressed the criticisms set forth by these disgruntled social observers by showing that children could learn to work cooperatively without totally losing their sense of individuality; that Americans could live in an environment packed with material enticements without becoming overwhelmed; that the younger generation could be taught to develop a sense of individuality from the choices they were offered—instead of falling prey to alienation.

In trying to formulate a prescription for the new individuality, Daniel Bell relied on the ideas of David Riesman and his model of inner-directed/other-directed behavior. At issue in Riesman's *The Lonely Crowd* were the psychological and sociological effects of the new society of abundance, in which the baby boomers were being incubated.[20] In contrast to the society of scarcity in which their parents had been raised, and which encouraged discipline and careful personal choices, the boomers were being raised in a more permissive manner that encouraged the insatiable need for approval.[21] For these "other-directed" children, fashion was replacing the morals and customs of their ancestors. Behavioral cues were being absorbed from their peers, from ads, new products, and institutions. They were, in short, being raised to become consumers of the first water. What kind of society would they create? That was the question on everybody's mind.

Frederick Pohl and C. M. Kornbluth's science-fiction novel *The Space Merchants* (1952) envisioned the other-directed generation ultimately falling prey to Big Brother corporations led by admen. In the authors' futuristic world of determined behavior, advertisers had become will-zapping villains, and the masses enslaved consumers who had fallen prey to various forms of subliminal control. Later in the decade, Vance Packard's *The Hidden Persuaders* (1957) warned that Pohl and Kornbluth's fantastic vision was closer to reality than anyone could have predicted.[22]

Appropriately called "the soft sell," the new advertising was characterized by the principle of friendly persuasion. The circular American Pavilion itself, with its promises of abundance, was a type of subliminal advertisement for consensus capitalism and the American way of life. Whereas a visitor to the rectilinear Soviet Pavilion was able to form a clear idea of what communism offered—of what the USSR had accomplished and in what direction it was headed—a visitor to the American Pavilion often left with no such experience, no sense of having handled, confronted, or understood the product of "Americanism." The soft-sell atmosphere in the American Pavilion invited visitors to relax and enjoy themselves, thus subliminally conveying to them that life in the United States was so technologically advanced that it was almost effortless.[23]

Some educators in the United States viewed the tactics of advertisers and manufacturers with alarm. D'Amico responded to the aggressive tactics of merchants, and the need for new social skills, with a variety of techniques that were grouped under the rubric of *progressive education,* a term derived from a distinctly American reform movement initiated by John Dewey, who has been called the "most influential American philosopher of the twentieth century."[24]

A central tenet of Dewey's belief was that ideas should be tested by practice. He created the Laboratory School, part of the Departments of Psychology and Pedagogy at the University of Chicago from 1894 to 1904, to apply his ideas regarding education. The most influential methods developed in the Laboratory School derived from the commitment to "occupations" rather than "studies."[25] Students at the Laboratory School were treated as growing, changing individuals within a specific nexus of social forces. During art classes, for example, teachers sought the "child's own motivations as a point of departure."[26] The progressive-education movement that grew from Dewey's pragmatic methods was always controversial, but by the end of the 1930s Dewey's influence prevailed in many public and private schools.[27]

After World War II, progressive education came under attack. Dewey had taught educators to respect children as individuals, to explore the ways in which children absorbed and manipulated knowledge instead of placing undue emphasis on how much they mastered of a traditional curriculum. But despite Dewey's emphasis on fostering democratic behavior in his students (or possibly because of it), when rebellious teenagers appeared in unprecedented numbers during the 1950s, progressive education was blamed for the breakdown in social order. It was easy for critics to draw parallels between the lack of authoritarian discipline in the schools and the lack of respect youth were showing toward the status quo.

Dewey's great crime, in the eyes of his detractors, was to have encouraged teachers to replace traditional values with a progressive relativism. The progressive style of education trained students to discriminate among relative values in the hope that they would learn to think independently and become truly democratic citizens. Dewey replaced indoctrination with pragmatic inquiry. He encouraged teachers to stop posing as authority figures and to act as "interpreters or guides." Such ideas were bound to offend conservatives, to whom matters of tradition, theology, patriotism, and scientific progress were best pursued through discipline, faith, and obedience. In 1959 President Eisenhower himself warned the American people "to abandon the educational path that, rather blindly, they have been following as a result of John Dewey's teachings."[28]

D'Amico's methods clearly derived from the pragmatist notion of "learning by doing" that had become the basic characteristic of progressive education. But D'Amico found the methods of most progressive educators too lax, and so his art classes became a mix of experimentation and discipline. Teachers in the Creative Center were amateur psychologists. They had to know the proper moment to intervene, to teach techniques only when they were needed.[29]

D'Amico developed the exercises in the Children's Creative Center over a number of years in programs at the Museum of Modern Art, such as the People's Art Center (for all ages) and the annual Children's Holiday Carnival. The art classes he organized at MOMA began as ways to subvert traditional stumbling blocks in the education process. The trick was to open some avenue of creative endeavor in each student. Those who liked the feel of materials were introduced to clay, for example, or collage, and they were encouraged to make "feeling and seeing pictures."[30] If a student found this difficult to grasp, D'Amico drew parallels between the way one selected materials for an art object and the way in which one selected clothing to wear or the things that made up the unconsciously created environment at home. The only crime was copying the work of another artist, no matter how celebrated.

In a comparative review in *House Beautiful* of the methods used by D'Amico and other children's educators, Joseph Barry wondered how different the depression-era generation might have been had they played with color and texture, forms and shapes. "We might have reached a state of culture never before seen in history, a culture achieved by individuals over a whole nation rather than by an elite of wealth or pedigree."[31] Barry had been especially impressed with a sign he read on the wall during the 1955 spring exhibition of children's art at MOMA: "Copying destroys self confidence, builds false skills, hinders initiative, atrophies the imagination." Barry's comments reveal the extent to which the Creative Center participated in the utopian dreams that sustained modernism in all its manifestations. And Barry was exactly the type of critic whom D'Amico hoped to attract. After just a glimpse of a few paintings by D'Amico's students at MOMA, Barry walked away a convert, his head full of populist ideals.

The modern environment tripled the threat of conformity through television, motion pictures, radio, and comic books. To compete with the media environment, D'Amico felt that educators needed to aim their lessons—as marketers did—directly at the target audience and their interests, in this case children. His goal was to set up sequences of challenging situations that enabled children to recognize their unique talents and to use them to overcome the clichés pressed upon them by an information-intensive society. The teacher's job at the Creative Center was to urge the child toward a deeper synthesis of inner abilities and the outer environment. The Children's Creative Center was ostensibly an art school, but it was also a training ground for the modern, democratic citizen.[32]

By conceiving of the Creative Center as a land apart, as an enchanted place, a world into which adults could only hope to peer (through portholes), D'Amico was expressing certain cultural preconceptions regarding childhood. The anthropologist Helen B. Schwartzman writes, "Every culture develops its own view of children's nature, and with it a related set of beliefs about how best to 'culture' their 'nature.'"[33] Like many Americans, D'Amico's faith in "natural" child development predisposed him to think that children everywhere lived in a natural utopia. Hence his desire to protect them from adults—the vehicles of culture (and therefore of divisiveness).

Faith in the natural goodness of children had become a popular middle-class notion in the United States after the publication of *The Common Sense Book of Baby and Child Care* (1946), by Benjamin Spock,

M.D. Spock's permissive ideas and his faith in the innate wisdom of mothers regarding most problems (and in experts for the rest) came after many years of contradictory advice to parents from the psychological profession. Spock's handbook was the best-selling how-to book for parents ever published. Spock, like D'Amico, urged parents not to worry about theories they did not comprehend but to have patience with toddlers, lest they induce some "complex" through nagging and discipline. Spock urged parents to break with longstanding traditions of child rearing. Instead of training children to guard against inner, corrupt desires, parents were urged to preserve and protect them from corrupting influences outside of themselves. The child was "by disposition friendly and reasonable" and naturally disposed to becoming a "free, warm, life-loving person." This model of child rearing struck another blow to the old model of vigilant attention and discipline that had already been severely eroded by the Dewey Laboratory School and its successors.[34]

Why were parents eager to adopt the new techniques of education and child rearing that D'Amico and Spock popularized? Probably because both "experts" promised to help children become better citizens. D'Amico urged adults, even grandparents, to join their children in making art, and Spock placed social skills above everything, even academic skills. "The main lesson in school," Spock wrote, "is how to get along in the world." A good school "wants to teach democracy . . . as a way of living and getting things done." Both D'Amico and Spock emphasized methods by which the child could become a respected member of the group.[35]

Spock provided a handbook for parents who wanted their children to become white-collar members of the middle class, a group for whom organizational and social skills were more important than skilled labor.[36] D'Amico was less influential than Spock, but he sought to encourage the same social trends. His art classes gave lessons on developing new sensual equipment for enjoying the abundant society. D'Amico's textbook, *Art for the Family* (1954), for example, urged those of all ages to modernize themselves by indulging their eyes, ears, fingers, and noses. For D'Amico, art training was boot camp for the good life. Becoming an artist in the old sense of the term—a practitioner of a craft, or servant of the muses—

hardly mattered. Spock and D'Amico modified Dewey's radical prescriptions for training democratic citizens and so helped to bring progressive education into the age of consensus capitalism.

European teachers were eager to adopt the methods they learned at the Creative Center and begged the staff for any leftover supplies that they could use in their own classes. D'Amico and the Creative Center staff worked hard to sell themselves to Europe through a small but high-quality media campaign. From the outset European teachers were encouraged to come and meet the staff at the center. Letters were sent out to about one hundred schools in the area explaining the nature of the enterprise, and a preview for the press was held with representatives from both the French and Flemish media in attendance. The U.S. commissioner general even paid the entrance fees into the fair for the first school groups of French and Flemish children that came to the Creative Center.

The press liked the Creative Center. Television and radio reports aired on both local and foreign stations, helping to drive up attendance. By July the center was full all day long. On August 22, the arrival of the ten-thousandth child was celebrated, and soon afterward the Belgian minister of public education sent letters to schools all over his country imploring children to attend a session. In the last weeks of the fair, four to five school groups a day were arriving, and many had to be turned away. The tremendous interest brought school inspectors and teachers for special sessions. Some teachers returned with different groups and were themselves keen students of the Creative Center.[37]

The appearance of the Children's Creative Center in published articles was important to D'Amico. He borrowed Lois Lord's photographic slides to illustrate his teaching methods, and her pictures eventually formed a record of the center that was used in promotional efforts. At first, Lord just tried to capture children as they worked, avoiding their tendency to pose, but candidness was not as interesting to D'Amico as were the group shots that documented cooperative activity; shots of the toys—most of which D'Amico had invented and that distinguished the center from traditional classrooms; and especially shots of "types" of children—different nationalities and races working together.[38]

As his photography instructions to Lois Lord reveal, D'Amico tried appealing to the one-world sentiment fashionable in the liberal community. In a progress report submitted to MOMA, he wrote, "regardless of nationality, children immediately comprehended the meaning of the Children's Creative Center and participated freely." Children, he said, "can be taught creativity regardless of their previous background. Creative children are the result of an education that develops creativeness: uncreative children are the victims of indoctrination. It is that simple."[39] These statements were undoubtedly relished by Edward Steichen and the staff members of the museum who had worked on the *Family of Man* exhibition; they probably earned a nod from Nelson Rockefeller (the president of the board of trustees), too.

D'Amico was trying to build the Department of Education at MOMA into a local and even national resource. By 1958, as the chairman of the Council of the National Committee on Art Education—an organization of leading art directors, supervisors, artists, and teachers—D'Amico had, in fact, become an influential figure. This organization tried to spearhead educational reform and credited itself with being the "first to expose the danger of contests, copy books, and the paint-by-number kits," while pioneering "better television, art programs, and improved education for the classroom teacher."[40]

The Children's Creative Center was a popular hit at Brussels. Few critics attacked it. Visiting parents liked watching their children have fun, and the children were enthralled by the strange toys and lavish attention. It might have been more popular in the United States, too, had not *Sputnik* sent a wave of panic through the American educational community. The Creative Center was not immune to the attacks aimed at progressive education even though it celebrated the arts, an area in which Americans had only recently achieved international recognition.

D'Amico and his followers believed that the authoritarian model of education was obsolete, but they were in the minority. D'Amico's career would fade into obscurity. However, the Creative Center was perfect at a place where—just a stone's throw away—the Soviets were dangling *Sputnik* with its air of martial rectitude before the eyes of anxious Europeans. The international, interracial groups of children playing together inside the Children's Creative Center provided a spectacle of hope for those who believed that international peace would be fostered by people-to-people programs rather than missiles guaranteeing mutually assured destruction.

6 Men's Gadgets, Women's Fashions, and the American Way of Life

On June 26, 1957, the State Department's deputy chief of protocol swore in Mrs. Katherine Graham Howard as Howard Cullman's second U.S. deputy commissioner general. Howard was a talented fund-raiser and she provided some token representation for women; but her character profile and her professional accomplishments hint that the most important reason she was brought on board was to restrain James Plaut (the other deputy commissioner) and the exhibit designers, Peter Harnden and Bernard Rudofsky, whose interpretation of U.S. culture had become too radical. This was not a pleasant assignment and required a certain type of person, but the photograph of Howard that appeared that day in the *Washington Post and Times Herald* suggested that she would probably be equal to the task. Her square-jawed determination, her forthright character, and her Republican virtue were captured perfectly by the photographer, Jim McNamara.[1] She was wearing a softly rounded pillbox hat with a black bow that nestled primly on her unruly dark curls. The shawl collar on her fitted dress and the double-strand pearl choker around her throat gave her the perky but conservative look popularized by Mamie Eisenhower and Pat Nixon. Even the silver-dollar-sized polka dots on her dress and the charm bracelet on her wrist could not soften the moral rectitude of her demeanor, or the aggressive confidence that had made her one of the nation's leading Republican women. Howard was the ideal person to uphold the conservative views of the Eisenhower administration.

Katherine Howard had been the secretary of the 1952 Republican Convention and the only woman on Dwight D. Eisenhower's policy and strategy committee. But although she had held many powerful positions they nearly always involved women's groups, women voters, women's needs—ancillary to male interests. Her job on the Republican National Committee, for instance, was to "coordinate campaign activities among women's groups." After Eisenhower's election she was rewarded with the position of deputy federal civil-defense administrator, a job she defined as "a crusade against fear of the atomic bomb, which is something we can live with, and recover from." In order to stave off the psychological and social disintegration caused by the threat of nuclear attack, she adopted "home-by-home civil defense protection" and called on women's clubs and parent-teacher organizations for cooperation. As a woman in the Republican administration, her task was to bring government policy into the homes of the United States and infuse daily activities with a respect for government policies. She did this through her network of women's clubs and by the authority she wielded as a role model.[2]

With Katherine Howard's leadership more than half the contributors to the Republican party in Massachusetts, in 1950, were women. In 1951, because of her efforts, the first three women in history were appointed to the Republican National Finance Committee. In their book *Ladies of Courage,* Eleanor Roosevelt and Lorena A. Hickok sketched a profile of Howard in order to show that "masculine hostility" need not hold women back. They described how Katherine Howard first gained national attention during the televised 1952 convention when the camera caught her going about her duties without wearing shoes. As the secretary of the Republican National Committee, she often found herself in the spotlight with Joseph W. Martin Jr., chairman of the convention and Speaker of the House of Representatives. In heels, Howard towered above Martin. Shrewdly aware of how this might appear on television, she kicked off her shoes and went about in stocking feet. Her autobiography would be titled *With My Shoes Off,* appropriately summing up her life as a dutiful Republican lady.[3]

Katherine Howard had been married since 1921; she was fifty-nine years old and the mother of two children at the time of her swearing-in. Her husband was the Massachusetts banking commissioner, and her brother would soon become the atomic energy commissioner. Her swearing-in was witnessed by Under Secretary of State Christian A. Herter, who had been co-chairman of the Eisenhower-for-President Committee at the time that Howard was working on the Eisenhower campaign. The *Washington Post and Times Herald* described the two as "long-time acquaintances," but they were also long-time allies, both intimately involved in the political apparatus of Massachusetts and the Republican party. After the 1952 election, Herter became the Republican candidate for governor of Massachusetts and in November 1952 defeated the Democratic incumbent, Paul A. Dever.[4]

Herter became the under secretary of state on February 21, 1957, just as the planning sessions regarding the American Pavilion were getting under way. Herter had been born in Paris and began his education there. He had worked in Europe for the State Department as long ago as 1917, helping to negotiate a prisoner-of-war agreement with Germany. In 1919 he assisted Herbert Hoover as executive secretary of the European Relief Council. When Hoover became secretary of commerce in 1922, Herter became his assistant. After World War II, Herter became a key player in setting up the Marshall Plan.[5]

An internationalist who believed that technical assistance programs and foreign aid were essential weapons of the cold war, Herter was an avid supporter of economic and cultural ties between nations.[6] On July 4, 1958, he brought Herbert Hoover to Brussels to give an American Independence Day address emphasizing international cooperation. Hoover was so well thought of in Belgium that the government declared a "Hoover Day" in his honor. While Hoover delivered his address on international understanding, Herter was busy behind the scenes twisting the arm of Howard Cullman until he closed down the *Unfinished Work* exhibit. The State Department wanted the American Pavilion to promote goodwill between the United States and Belgium, not to advertise the deeds of segregationists and lynch mobs. But Herter did not have time to stay in Brussels and watch over the American Pavilion. Katherine Howard did this for him. She argued with Cullman, Plaut, and the exhibit designers and tried to ensure that the American Pavilion did not deviate too much from State Department policy goals.

About the same time that Howard was taking her oath of office, *Vogue* asked the willowy socialite Lee Canfield to be their representative at the fashion show in the American Pavilion, which *Vogue* had been asked to organize and oversee. Canfield was something of a jet-setter, long before the term became common currency. While Howard wore her clothes like a uniform, Canfield expressed her creativity, wealth, and taste by flaunting her knowledge of style; one was individualistic and adventurous while the other was predictable, reliable, a team player. As a representative of the United States, Howard demonstrated the ability of women to wield power outside the home while simultaneously protecting family values. Canfield, by contrast, lived in England, was on the verge of a divorce, childless, and radiated the kind of lithe international stylishness Audrey Hepburn had come to symbolize in films like *Funny Face.* The two women had little in common. With such contrasting personalities directing the presentation of consumer products designed for female consumption, it is no wonder the American Pavilion sometimes resembled a battleground.[7]

In the commissioner general's office Howard spent most of her efforts fund-raising but found time for the creation of an American Women's Program—a special tribute to working women that included a fashion show at which diplomatic employees and the commissioner general's female staff modeled their own working attire. Katherine Howard's fashion show was dramatically different from *Vogue*'s. Its intent was to show how fashionable attire helped women gain control over their social roles, as did normal fashion shows, but Howard championed the working woman and so made sure that the women who modeled the clothes were the most important feature of the program. In the *Vogue* show, the models were just animated clotheshorses. But in Howard's fashion show the models stepped up to a podium and discussed career goals.

Katherine Howard was pestered with questions about women's exhibits soon after being appointed. At first she was perturbed by the constant assertion that women needed special treatment. To her way of thinking, women were "interested in all the exhibits" not just in things that would be particularly related to their sex. The idea of gender-specific exhibits seemed demeaning, maybe because she assumed they would preclude leadership roles. "Nowadays," she said, "women's interests incorporate everything from kitchens to atoms for peace." Howard changed her point of view after meeting Betty Barzin, a Belgian radio commentator and director of women's activities for the Belgian-American Association. The Soviets had asked Barzin to help organize an exhibit on Soviet women, but she had refused and then encouraged Howard to organize a competing show. Barzin eventually worked closely with Howard, urging European women to attend the American women's events, using her connections in the local media for publicity. With Barzin's assistance, Howard had an opportunity to embarrass the Soviets. After years of civil-defense work, this was the kind of battle Howard could understand. It was not a question of fighting for equal rights for women, which was a contentious, divisive issue. This was a matter both of defending the United States from Soviet propaganda and of asserting the professional accomplishments of American women.[8]

By March 21, 1958, Howard had formulated a plan that was inexpensive and simple to implement. She envisioned a conference program featuring outstanding American women leaders who would be invited to come at their own expense, maybe during a vacation or business trip they had already planned. It would create an opportunity for international networking, and since it would cost very little there would be no ill-feelings created between herself and her male co-workers—who had allocated no money in the budget for women's activities.

In her proposal to the commissioner general, she drew up lists of potential participants such as Clare Boothe Luce, former ambassador to Italy, and Eugenie Moore Anderson, former ambassador to Denmark (who had been consulted by the planning committee). Women in government, publishing, community service, science, education, medicine, business, and the arts were all included. She promised the commissioner general that the candidates would be "not only capable . . . but excellent representatives of 'America, the

Land and the People.' What they are will speak even more plainly than what they say." Her goal was to reserve the American Theater for August 12–13 and hold an international women's conference. Women who could not make it at that time but who could come earlier were to be filmed in the pavilion's television studio and then presented at the conference on TV screens. When her initial presentation received a green light, she was left with a tremendous amount of work to do and very little time. She immediately wrote to Alice K. Leopold, a friend back in the United States, asking for help.[9]

Leopold and Howard had both worked their way up through local politics and the 1952 presidential election. In 1952 Leopold became a policymaker in Eisenhower's campaign. After the election, she was appointed director of the Women's Bureau of the Department of Labor. Leopold could be blunt when arguing for the dignity of women. She told the American Society of Women Accountants, in April 1954, "When we have more women taking an active part in politics, we'll have better people running for office." She could be persuasive but less caustic when addressing a more conservative crowd. Speaking before the District of Columbia League of Republican Women in February of 1954, she said, "I don't happen to be one of those who believe women want equality. Equity seems to me, as a worker for legislation which protects and frees women, a much more important point of view."[10]

Leopold's published addresses and opinions revealed that Republican women like herself and Howard had achieved their positions only after tremendous sacrifices. In an article for *National Parent-Teacher* magazine, Leopold explained her recipe for success. Young women should prepare for a life lived in three stages: they should train to be professionals, then give up their professions to become housewives, mothers, and community volunteers, and finally return to the work force once their children were grown. She had confidence in the growth of the American economy and its ability to sustain women in all these phases.[11] "Womanpower" was what she called the theme of her 1958 campaign.[12] It was a slogan she used without any of the irony women later implied by the term *superwoman,* but it amounted to the same thing. It was a vision for women that allowed for few mistakes and presumed not only that all women wanted the same things but that they all had the same opportunities. It a was pro-family stance and totally excluded the option of birth control or independence from men. As a Republican woman, Leopold urged others to make their families the basic social unit, the control center of American society from which all good deeds sprang and by which the ultimate worth of legislation could be measured. She had done this herself—but it was a tough act to follow.

Leopold believed that the burgeoning power of the United States gave women unprecedented opportunities to affect global politics. Applying the logic of her internationally minded colleagues in the Eisenhower administration to her own concerns, she attempted to shape an international women's movement. She visited Europe in 1954 under the auspices of the Foreign Operations Administration to study "women's economic problems and their effects on family life."[13] In 1954, 1956, and 1957, she served as adviser to the United States delegation at the annual meetings of the International Labor Organization, held in Geneva, Switzerland. Back home she urged young women to think internationally. A speech delivered at Douglas College, Rutgers University, on April 17, 1958 (opening day of the Brussels World's Fair), reveals that she believed traditional domestic roles could be given a wider application. She asked an audience of college women to

> strive unceasingly to help achieve understanding and cooperation among peoples the world over. . . . As the heart of the home, women are responsive to human needs and changing conditions. They have developed within the course of their everyday tasks a leadership that is outstanding. This leadership, if transferred to broader realms of activity can be an immeasurable aid to women in other lands, particularly to those who live in countries which just now are emerging as free nations.[14]

Leopold wanted more representation for women in U.S. programs abroad and so encouraged the USIA to integrate women in equal numbers with men, at foreign posts. In the fall of 1957 she helped get Virginia Geiger appointed as the USIA's first women's affairs adviser. Leopold was convinced the USIA would discover that women were powerful molders of public opinion, despite their often inferior status.[15] Soon the USIA was proclaiming ladies' days in places like Trivandrum, India, where women came in groups to see the *Family of Man* photography exhibition at the USIA library. At other posts, women's magazines were imported from the United States and cooking classes were held featuring American cuisine. "When the women of Jakarta start worrying about calories and diets—then we'll know they've gone completely American," said a USIA official in the fall of 1958.[16]

Katherine Howard's appeal for assistance came at a time when Leopold was eager to move into the international sphere more aggressively. "What we do here" [at Brussels], she wrote back to Howard, "may well set a pattern for regional conferences in other sections of the world."[17] But if Leopold hoped that Katherine Howard had provided a way for her to circumvent the usual bureaucratic apparatus, she was wrong. The USIA and the American Embassy in Brussels had already persuaded Howard to drop her idea of a ground-breaking two-day conference and replace it with a series of low-key talks spread out over the life of the fair. The government officials she consulted were panicky. An international women's conference was just too radical an idea.

Howard gratefully accepted her advisers recommendations and passed them on to Leopold.

> [L]et the program grow naturally . . . In this way the program might become an 'in' event—not something to accept or reject, or judge. . . . The atmosphere in Europe is very different from the United States. The women here are not conditioned to conferences of this kind, and the men have a built-in resistance. . . . [L]et the word get out and feature each particular woman as she comes[18]

If the word got around, Howard believed that prominent American women would begin writing to her with their itineraries, and she hoped that a few key speakers, like Leopold, would attract others. When women did write, she made it appear that she was doing everything in her power to help potential participants find a place in the spotlight at this international event. This enabled her to retain veto power, but those who were rejected were not able to take it personally.[19]

Alice Leopold asked Virginia Geiger to compile a list of American women headed to Europe that summer. She also called George Meany's office to see if she could persuade the AFL-CIO to finance a few women labor representatives who might be willing to participate in a fashion show. Meany's assistant, George Brown, liked the idea and thought it might be a way of enlisting the interest of the International Ladies' Garment Workers' Union.[20] Brown agreed that a fashion show of working women would diffuse some of the press criticism directed at the *Vogue* fashion show, which many Americans believed to be too frivolous and generally ill-advised, given the perilous nature of the cold war. Then Leopold took the initiative and tried to drum up active support for a special women's exhibit inside the pavilion, aside from the program Howard was organizing for the theater. But she met with killing bureaucratic indifference. "The USIA, the State Department, and the Labor Department," she complained to Howard, "are equally guilty of complete failure to provide anything which has the dignity and newness to be suitable."[21]

When all was said and done, August 12, 1958—the date Howard had originally hoped to inaugurate an international woman's conference—did indeed become the highlight of the Women's Program. Alice K. Leopold came to Brussels and stayed at the Time Inc. apartment. She gave her address, "The Mutual Goals of Women," in French to an audience that included many leading Belgian female politicians. Afterward, twelve American women plucked from various jobs around Brussels modeled clothes "from their own wardrobes, made in America." After a stroll across the stage, each model spoke briefly to the audience about her work and private goals.[22] And despite the State Department's fear of the press, Betsy Talbot Blackwell, editor-in-chief of *Mademoiselle,* one of *Vogue*'s chief competitors, was invited to close out the American portion of the program with a talk "on the scope of her magazine, and the work, interests and outlook of young American women." Finally two Belgian women, both national senators, were allowed to respond with European views in a program entitled "Women Who Work."[23]

Betty Barzin ensured excellent media coverage, as did the

American Public Affairs Office, enabling Howard to steal a considerable amount of fire for the United States on one of the Soviet Union's national days, when all eyes would have normally been focused on the special events in the Soviet Pavilion. For Katherine Howard, this accomplishment, at least, made the Women's Program worthwhile.

Once the Women's Program had been transformed into a series of talks, participants treated it like any other event of the social season. Betsy Talbot Blackwell explained to the readers of *Mademoiselle* that she had been going to Paris anyway, to see the new fashion collections. From Paris she was whisked by helicopter to the fairgrounds, where she was met by a guide and taken directly to the American Theater. There she was presented to "the representatives of 42 nations" along with other "outstanding American women." Afterward, she was interviewed on television with the Soviet official Klimenti E. Voroshilov while reporters "flocked around her." Ordinary souls asked for autographs; an artist from the *London Times* sketched her portrait. Later she was feted along with Howard and Leopold at the Cullmans' residence before taking a whirlwind tour of the town. The next day she caught the first plane to London.[24]

Under Howard's stewardship, "The Continuing Women's Program," as it came to be called, stretched from May to October. On May 16 the program kicked off with May Roper Coker from Hartsville, South Carolina, receiving the 1958 American Mother of the Year Award, which was dispensed annually by the American Mothers Committee, a Republican-oriented organization of which Mamie Eisenhower was the honorary president. On September 4, the Honorable Edith Green, a Democratic member of the U.S. House of Representatives from Oregon, invited the Belgians to participate in the 1959 Oregon International Trade Fair, and Eleanor Roosevelt spoke on international cooperation.[25] These sedate affairs, attended by visiting dignitaries from other pavilions, were preceded by the playing of the respective national anthems and ended with coffee in the Commissioner's Lounge. They were photo opportunities aimed at the media and so-called opinion molders from other countries. To some extent they were the kind of networking opportunities that Leopold, especially, had hoped to create, but the program remained conservative and focused on honoring the achievements of women more than it argued for any basic changes in gender relations. For the hard-working, politically minded Republicans in charge of the Women's Program, women were limited only by their own energy and resourcefulness. The program featured ideal mothers, doctors, lawyers, publishers, and politicians, who demonstrated that women could be successful without being radical, that the basic model of the American system was worth emulating.

Vogue's fashion show drew much more attention because it was aimed at the typical visitor and it took place everyday. And the models, like Lee Canfield, excited envy and admiration. Canfield, née Lee Bouvier, was the 1950 Debutante of the Year. In 1953 she married Michael Temple Canfield, who became the private secretary to Winthrop Aldrich, the United States ambassador to the Court of St. James, in London. American women could keep abreast of her adventures in the gossip columns and through articles in magazines such as *Ladies' Home Journal,* which ran an article in December 1957 on her new English wardrobe, comparing it to that of her sister, Jacqueline Kennedy, in Washington, D.C.[26] In 1958 Lee Canfield was a fashionable woman in search of a glamorous career. Her *Vogue* portrait shows a waifish, impeccably dressed and coiffured upper-class pixie standing behind a row of trunks over which she has tossed her coat. In her gloved right hand she clutches a tiny purse to her chest and looks skyward as if to say "free at last!" She was young and liberal, as different from Katherine G. Howard and Alice K. Leopold as John F. Kennedy would be from Richard M. Nixon in the next presidential election.[27]

The outfits in the *Vogue* collection emphasized social roles. The goal was to provide a range of outfits for female "types" the reader was expected to emulate.

> There's the super-wife dress, for instance, that might walk the children to school or cruise the local A&P or Grand Union supermarket. There are dresses for parties, blue jeans for the country, a dress for golf, suits for swimming, pants for being at home, and the famous American split-personality dresses—they go on from where you are to where you're going: Red Cross meeting to lun-

> cheon, P.T.A. to dinner, office to cocktail party to theater. They're the American look.[28]

Instead of emphasizing career goals, *Vogue* encouraged women to express their modernity by being girlish, or a little silly—and above all, consumers. The important thing for *Vogue* was not "woman-power," but "the American look" (which could be purchased). The fashion industry depended more on selling clothing—on appearances, that is—than on the personal achievements of its customers. The outfits in the pages of *Vogue* were like the magical caps in fairy tales, promising to transform women into successful "American" women—the most powerful and privileged women in the world. But to achieve that success, the women needed certain physical attributes and a considerable amount of spending money.

Vogue never pretended to be the Sears, Roebuck catalog. Its clothes were for the woman whose role as wife, sexy consort, or social organization volunteer was predicated on free time, a healthy income, and lots of energy. In deference to the populist atmosphere of the fair, *Vogue* announced that the "most American look on two legs" was indeed within everybody's price range: a pair of turned-up jeans and a plaid Western-style shirt. In the pages of *Vogue,* however, as on the runway, the jeans were worn by models as thin and good looking as Lee Canfield, with short hair and no hat—hardly everyday attire for women of the 1950s.[29] *Vogue* promoted jeans probably because they had been directed to by the exhibit designers. Blue jeans had an inexplicable way of winning friends for the United States. Blue jeans and plaid shirts, icons of rock-and-roll and the Western tradition, were sewn up on the spot at trade fairs from Poznań to Bangkok on Singer sewing machines and given away as souvenirs of Americana. In fact, this was *Vogue*'s fourth international show for the U.S. government (some 270,000 Berliners saw *Vogue* fashions at the German Industries Fair in 1955).[30]

Reporting on the jeans appearing at the Poznań Fair, held in June 1958, the *New York Times* noted that "ordinary Poles, we may assume, wondered what the blue jeans cost to produce and what they cost when bought at stores. And perhaps some of them—emulating Walter Mitty—had fantasies of themselves bedecked in blue jeans

A designer label for American blue jeans displayed at the 1958 Poznań International Trade Fair. Collection of Charles H. Clarke.

and on a horse herding cattle to market. . . . Perhaps even the Russians realize that what people are most interested in are things they can use and enjoy."[31] Encouraging fantasies was exactly what the USIA and the U.S. Department of Commerce intended to accomplish under the pretense of dispensing information and selling products. Blue jeans became one of the most potent conveyors of the American mythos because they enabled foreign teens to dress up like the heroes they saw in magazines and movies. The handmade jeans given away at the 1958 Poznań Fair even had special designer labels that made the fantasy complete.

Vogue organized their outfits at the fair into collections that were later made available to more than 175 shops across the United States. The "Young American Look," for example, featured jumper dresses, cone-shaped coats, and moderately priced sweater-dresses, day woolens, and skirts. Another collection featured a line of inexpensive ready-to-wear clothes in the $4-$25 range, which included sportswear that the models exhibited with tennis rackets and golf club props. As they descended the runway to the center of the pool, an attendant held up the price of the ensemble on a large white card affixed to a pole. The *Vogue* models lounged around on the balcony level in the home-furnishings area, relaxing and chatting with visitors until it was time to work the runway. Here the public and the press could get a close-up view of the fabrics and ask the European models for their personal opinions. Coaches helped the models say all the right things, especially to the press: "Just wearing these clothes makes me more anxious than ever to visit America," remarked the Parisian model Denise Girard. Press releases noted that she liked the "relaxing and refreshing change of pace offered by American sportswear."[32]

The chemise dress, in its many variations, was the most predominant style in the *Vogue* wardrobes at the American Pavilion. Across the street, the Soviets advertised chemises, too, although their sales pitch was rather crude. One of their brochures boasted, "Girls will be girls! In all countries and all latitudes they attach just the same importance to the way they dress." Through text and illustrations, this pamphlet explained how the modern Soviet woman could now "argue which style of dress is the best . . . give preference to one over another." Illustrations showed a woman trying on a close-fitting sheath while an attendant helped her choose the right size. But although the Soviets wanted to compete with the West, they were ambivalent about the social ramifications of consumerism. The text pointed out that all this freedom of choice created "a dilemma as to which dress to choose; others have the same problem about furnishing their new flat."[33] The Soviet exhibits had variety, but the emphasis was on availability and their many ethnic styles. This ethnic variety was quite different from the opulent excess and planned obsolescence of the U.S. market. The ethnic styles emphasized a respect for the many cultures in the USSR (not Paris or New York). In their pavilion, up-to-date sheaths were displayed next to more traditional or folk outfits such as a white silk dress-suit trimmed with traditional Ukrainian embroidery.[34]

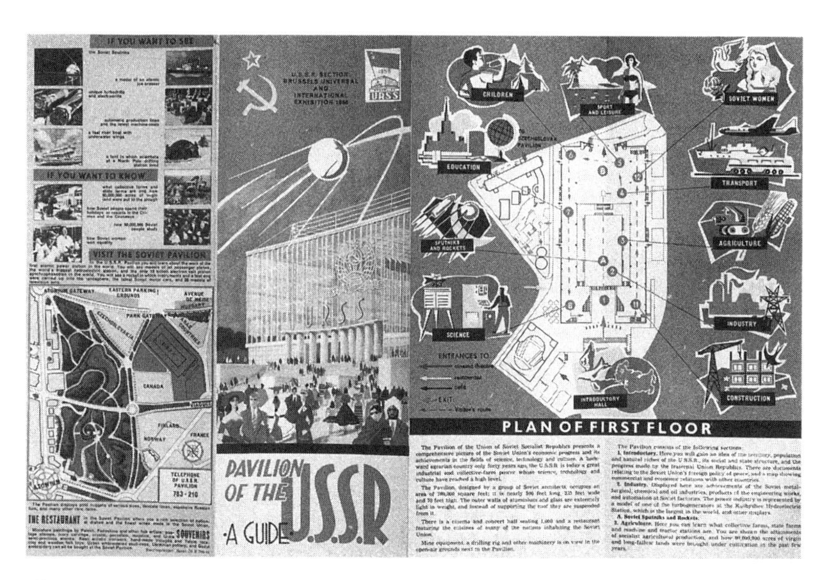

Illustrated map of the USSR Pavilion, featuring an exhibit on Soviet Women (top right). Edward J. Orth Collection, National Museum of American History, Smithsonian Institution.

The U.S. planners hoped that their daily fashion show, with the occasional splashy mink coat or ball gown, would act like a magnet to the passing crowds. *Industrial Design* reported that "a cautious canvass of non-Americans revealed that in most countries fashion shows are open only to wealthy clients of exclusive designers."[35] By contrast, here was a chance for ordinary people to participate in an elite experience. The *New York Times* reported that the new collections attracted "spellbound audiences" standing three and four deep in a ring around the pool . . . watching selected European models "slither up and down" the runway in outfits valued from $15 to $7,500.[36] Although an attempt was made to show how the American ready-to-wear industry had democratized fashion by making a wide variety of clothing easy to obtain, the fashion show also gave the lower classes a glimpse of Shangri-La with its furs and evening gowns. *Vogue* revealed how the United States brought wealth and happiness to those who worked for the American way of life.

Ironically the ball-gown fantasies on the runway had been brought to life with the help of Peter Harden's designer Bernard Rudofsky, an admirer of the fashion designers Elizabeth Hawes and Claire McCardell. The catalog for his 1947 exhibition at the Museum of Modern Art, *Are Clothes Modern?* makes it clear that Rudofsky was an enemy of the obfuscation caused by the admixture of fashion and nationalism. Rudofsky was a modernist. He believed that the problems of dress should be studied from a functional viewpoint, and he advocated a return to fundamentals, reserving his highest praise for radical designers who were willing to tackle basic problems such as the relation between dress and movement. For Rudofsky, style was either an attribute of function or an expression of good craftsmanship.

Rudofsky hated the fashion industry's use of mass production for maximum profit and the demise of hand tailoring. He despised the "baby talk of the fashion editor and fashion advertiser."[37] It seems incredible that he could have helped create what may well have been the longest-running American fashion show of the 1950s! Like a nightmare come to life, the American Pavilion embodied exactly what his *Are Clothes Modern?* exhibition had condemned. "Fashion," he wrote in his book *Are Clothes Modern?* "is based on envy and the urge of imitating the envied. It presupposes the existence of an aristocratic minority—aristocratic in the sartorial sense—that sets the style and the pace of style rotation. Newspapers keep the reader informed of the momentary wardrobe of such pacemakers."[38] Rudofsky mocked the so-called Americanness of clothes and the claims of the fashion press: "Fashion is democratic, sounds the contumacious repetition in the fashion writer's infantile or anile report. Fashion is democratic, echoes the dress-industrialist. Dresses-for-every-purse, the stock phrase of the trade, is taken as incontestable proof for the democratic nature of domestic apparel."[39] Rudofsky assumed that people believed this nationalistic cant only because they were envious of the Lee Canfields of the world; that *Vogue* was taking advantage of a snobbery that reached unprecedented heights in a society with no rigid class system. Ironically, his critique, despite its bitterness, would have been a great handbook for State Department officials and USIA exhibit designers—had they cared to read it—because it explained, even as it condemned, the interrelatedness of ideology, economic forces, and style. The fact that he was allowed to work on the U.S. Pavilion reveals a great deal about the way the State Department screened employees: Subversive types were valuable so long as their work could be controlled.

Richard B. McCornack, a historian at Dartmouth College and a former member of the State Department's Office of Intelligence Research, writing for the *Foreign Service Journal* in the spring of 1958, tried to put the role of fashion in diplomacy into historical perspective. He explained how dress had long been a potent symbol of America in the European courts, stemming from an 1853 order to American diplomats from President Franklin Pierce, who encouraged foreign ambassadors to "appear at court in the simple dress of an American citizen." This meant abandoning cocked hats and knee breeches for ordinary hats and "the very proletarian long pants." According to McCornack, this had resulted in the Swedish king's refusal to admit American diplomats to the court (the king called the new dress code "Republican propaganda"). The future president James Buchanan countered such remarks with the assertion that "it was altogether improper for a representative of a republic to ape the fashions of royal courts."[40]

In another attempt to explain the political ramifications of fashion, during the summer of 1958, *Life* noted that by promoting the evolution of the sack dress into the high-waisted Empire revival, Parisian fashion leaders had found a way of asserting French authority among the anti-French people of Cairo and Beirut. In this tongue-in-cheek article, *Life* editors noted that the French "dictatorship" of fashion was actually far more effective than any of their attempts at military conquest.[41] But while the Empire revival had odious associations with imperialism, some American designers were learning to absorb and incorporate the traditions of dominated countries. The U.S. designer Tina Leser, for example, was represented in the *Vogue* fashion show by a housedress of yellow linen with pink silk lining, based on the Japanese kimono, and in the *Face of America* exhibit by a pair of Bermuda shorts. Tina Leser's borrowing from international sources was not much different from Edward Durell Stone's ransacking of history and the Far East to fuel his romantic reworking of modern architecture. Along with many other architects, designers, musicians, and artists, Tina Leser and Edward Durell Stone were remaking the United States into an exotic, polyglot culture—an odd reflection of the far-flung ambitions of the Eisenhower administration. The original meaning of the foreign styles was radically altered through transposition because authenticity was not an issue. Foreign cultures were made into harmless, stylish commodities by the artists who borrowed motifs from around the world.

The spring Sears, Roebuck catalog, which was also on display in the American Pavilion, introduced the chemise as the splash of the season. But while *Vogue* promoted the sophistication of the chemise, Sears exploited associations with Parisian couture. "The chemise look bears the Paris stamp. Completely new from every angle . . . subtly fitted in front, loose in back, shorter . . . the chemise dress is young, easy, becoming . . . inspired by Paris, made for Sears in the USA."[42] For the Sears customer, clothes had to be inexpensive, easy to maintain, and stylish. Sears, Roebuck was proud of its ability to take an elite European style and transform it into a mass-produced, mail-order, easy-to-care-for "American" dress of the people. If a *Vogue* chemise was made out of silk or cotton, a Sears "American" knock-off would typically be 75 percent Dacron or Acrilan. The catalog made a great display because it showed exactly how modern technology served the masses. *Vogue* expressed Americanness through comfort, wealth, youth, and taste, whereas Sears, Roebuck emphasized the proper application of science and technology in the service of the masses.[43]

Life reported that the chemise accounted for 80 percent of all moderately priced 1958 spring dress sales in the United States (this estimate included variations, such as the sack dress). But a backlash had already begun. Protesters in Birmingham, Alabama, burned sack dresses and demanded a return to curves.[44] These sack saboteurs did not like the self-confident sophistication of the chemise, which appealed to society women and college girls and looked so different from the bombshell fashions made popular by Jane Russell,

Marilyn Monroe, and Jayne Mansfield. The chemise played fast and loose with gender stereotypes. Men generally hated all permutations of the chemise craze. One reporter complained that a women in a chemise "has no waistline, no bosom and no hips. Let us hope that she is a nice gal inwardly because outwardly she looks a little bit monsterish."[45] Joseph West was quoted by *Consumer Reports* as saying, "It used to be that when a pretty gal waltzed by, you could take a look and say to yourself 'There goes a lot of woman.' Now, you don't know; it's kind of like looking at a tent."[46] And James Roosevelt, a member of the House of Representatives from California, had a friend's letter inserted into the *Congressional Record* that stated, "We have an excellent thing in having 200 cheerful, dedicated college girls on duty [in the American Pavilion]. But why dress them in the worst looking sack dress uniforms possible?"[47]

Exhibit designers knew that animated shows had eye-catching appeal. The fashion show was used to get people inside the pavilion, where they could be introduced to the Atoms for Peace exhibits and more serious things. Glamorous models in fashionable clothes were often used, back in the United States, as advertising props in the attempt to sell products like cars and boats.[48] The strategy here was much the same. When models were not parading up and down the runway, they lounged in an informal recreation-room section of the home-furnishings exhibit. Called an "island for living," this exhibit was arrayed on three levels inside a structure that looked something like a contemporary split-level home. This was just one of the material-culture exhibits scattered around the pavilion, all of which were nicknamed *islands*. Plaut, Harnden, and a specially appointed design committee decided that the toasters, cameras, dishwashers, and lawn mowers would be grouped on these islands so as to express mobility, portability, flexibility, and the other qualities that the planning sessions had determined to be characteristically American. By having the fashion models interact with the furniture and appliances on the islands, they hoped to extend the excitement of the fashion show and generate an even more powerful sense of how the dynamic free-market economy was propelled by dreams, dissatisfaction, novelty, and invention.[49]

For Katherine Howard, domestic appliances and home furnishings were crucial elements of a conservative domesticity. But the exhibits team directed by Harnden and Rudofsky wanted to emphasize themes and aesthetics. And there was no model home in the exhibits, as Howard wanted, because the exhibit designers wished to avoid an ideal image of the United States in order to point out instead some of the "many local and regional characteristics which stem from our differences and perhaps even act as links to our European forebears."[50] There was no model kitchen because the current trend among designers and manufacturers was toward the open-plan domestic environment, in which the boundaries of the kitchen dissolved into the living room and even the backyard. The new appliances, in theory anyway, no longer required a woman's specialized knowledge. Before Howard arrived on the scene, the men in charge of the American Pavilion had already reduced the role of women in the domestic environment to glamorous accessories (fashion models), and put the emphasis instead on design, technology, and gadgets.

The commercial products were removed from the women's sphere of influence—the traditional domestic environment. But this was no "best products" show. For every Eames chair there was a humble-looking vernacular product, such as the Coleman kerosene lantern or a rural mailbox. The idea was to express the variety of products on the market in the United States and not just the aesthetic perfection of a few masterpieces. The chief vernacular exhibit was called a "Streetscape" and featured street signs, store windows full of merchandise, and even parking meters. Americans hardly gave these things a moment's notice, but they were unique to Europeans. Just as the art exhibits were divided between the latest abstract styles and Saul Steinberg's wacky mural, so too the material-culture sections contained the latest in Westinghouse mixers side by side with educational toys and novelty items like the pogo stick.

The islands contrasted the forms, functions, and aesthetic values of objects in relation to one another, resulting in displays that must have often seemed perplexing. Durable goods were set next to disposable goods; the hand made was contrasted with the machine made. Mailboxes, outboard motors, and portable barbecues were allowed to stand as emblems of the culture that produced them without overly determined justifications or explanations.

The poolside island, which had a surreal beach theme, featured a stiff-jointed female mannequin reclining in a hammock, wearing a black mask as if she were at a masquerade ball. But for the most part, the islands were designed to express consumer values. One island consisted of three lawn mowers set on a bed of gravel next to plastic Tupperware containers, a six-pack of Coke, a "Delighter Deluxe" aluminum deck chair, and a General Electric portable television. Because the objects seemed unrelated, their design values jumped out and their incongruity created a dynamic study in contrasts. But they also revealed the effect of marketing ideas or cultural trends (mobility, flexibility, portability) on material culture.

The three mowers, for example, each had unique features and illuminated the choices available to U.S. consumers. Two of them were sit-down mowers, which manufacturers back in the United States were calling "power-units," or "packages of power."[51] The central power unit was really just a portable engine that took several attachments, like the old Electrolux vacuum cleaners, which seemed to mutate into whatever cleaning appliance happened to be needed. These quick-change yard units were important symbols of suburbia. They became mowers, then snow throwers, lawn aerators, edge-trimmers, tillers, and sprayers. Their technological sophistication reflected the enthusiasm lavished on suburban yards.

These lawn mowers were part of a manufacturing trend that was trebling the number of appliances on the market. Variations of this idea included the stationary kitchen power units built by NuTone. These allowed blenders, mixers, knife sharpeners, and other accessories to be plugged into a countertop motor, enabling consumers to purchase highly specialized attachments for precise tasks. Products on the islands revealed how manufacturers aimed at every segment of the market and how consumers enhanced their sense of individuality through technology. With these machines, consumers could become even more mobile, productive, and efficient.

Throughout the 1950s members of the industrial design profession had been agitating for greater recognition of their accomplishments. Theodore S. Jones, the director of design at the Boston Institute of Contemporary Art, wrote to the American Pavilion selection committee to express his conviction that it was time to give appliance designers full recognition "just as the names of architects, craftsmen, artists, and other designers are usually identified with their works or models of their works."[52] This was a reasonable request, but it may have prompted Harnden and Rudofsky to feature the aesthetic values of industrially designed objects a little too much, thereby alienating some of their audience.

Katherine Howard believed the home, and specifically the kitchen, to be the foundation of American society. The emphasis on designer fashions and styles infuriated her. To her way of thinking, what counted was efficiency and affordability. But James Plaut would not listen to her entreaties, and Peter Harnden probably considered her a nuisance. There is a tone of exasperation in her pleas to Howard Cullman on this point. She warned Cullman that she did "not want to be held responsible by an irate press, Congress, and the White House for an avant-garde treatment of how America lives."[53] Her instincts were sound. Bernard Rudofsky estranged people by creating a bathroom of the future, featuring a throne-like tub lined with a foam-rubber lounge mat, which one reporter described as "a porcelain casket." The tub had a high-winged back at one end to cradle the head and rested on the floor without benefit of legs. Worst of all it made no provision for plumbing.[54] In his eagerness to recreate a stylish Roman bath, Rudofsky only made himself into a laughingstock. The home furnishings area where the tub appeared was shut down a week after opening day because, according to Marjorie Harlepp of the *New York Times,* American tourists were complaining they had never seen such a thing. Plaut denied hearing any criticism and stubbornly insisted that "a delay in receiving building materials and display items" had prevented the completion of the exhibit. Nevertheless, the tub was gone when the exhibit reopened.[55]

Rudofsky's sensibilities ran counter to those of mainstream America. Undoubtedly his goal was to influence the development of taste and not to document the popular culture of the United States (which he reviled). The bathroom of the average American house was so little to his liking that he devoted a chapter to its reform in his book, *Behind the Picture Window.* Americans did not derive any pleasure out of bathing, he argued. "We wash" and abhor sensuality. "The motions we call bathing are mere ablutions, which, formerly, *preceded* the bath." He was a sybarite at a time when hedonism was shunned.[56]

When the home-furnishings area reopened, it remained essentially an abstract version of a split-level suburban environment with three levels of toys, modern furniture, and an occasional antique. The antiques provided a historical dimension and lent their aura of warmth to the gleaming modern objects. A Shaker tilting chair, for example, had specially constructed back legs inset with wooden balls, which allowed a person to tilt backward (hence the name). It was a precursor of the modern furniture on display in the sense that Shaker craftsmen had developed their design in conjunction with a functional requirement.

By avoiding a model home and creating a skeletal split-level, Harnden and Rudofsky were able to display many more objects, of a wider variety and utility, than the trade fair model homes with their family-oriented exhibits. Those exhibits tried to show that everyone in the United States could achieve a certain level of comfort. This exhibit tried to show the amazing variety of comfort levels that were within the modern consumer's reach. The freedom to choose, or construct, an individualistic environment from consumer products was perhaps the most important of the "American" values the islands tried to express in material terms.

The selection of modern furniture featured a Charles Eames easy chair veneered in walnut, with tufted leather upholstery and a polished aluminum swivel base. It imparted a sense of "dynamic repose," which suggested that leisure could be a positive, creative activity. There was also Eero Saarinen's pedestal chair, one of the classic expressions of the "organic" style, rising up from the floor in a sweep of proportional balance. Accompanying it was a pedestal marble-top table, also by Saarinen, which looked a little like the initial stage of an atomic blast. Both table and chair were poised in dynamic balance on a single supporting stem, which left plenty of leg room.[57] Saarinen's tables and chairs, a George Nelson desk, and a Harry Bertoia wing chair shared with the overall architectural statement a gravity-defying buoyancy that Sigfried Giedion claimed was as innate to the modern period "as the buttress to the Gothic and undulating wall to the Baroque." Certainly the pavilion itself exhibited this combination of strength and ethereal beauty.[58]

These high-style items were grouped on the upper two levels of the split-level "island for living," which included a squarish, carpeted lounge area where the models could rest. On the bottom level, toys like the Ideal Toy Corporation's "Robert the Talking Robot" were featured along with a "Junior Playdome" by Geometrics, Inc.: a skeletal dome made out of metal rods that could be climbed on or turned into a little ultra-modern playhouse. These educational toys made rudimentary science, geometry, engineering, and architecture into fun and games.

Katherine Howard begged Cullman to add a model-home-type kitchen to these avant-garde exhibits. "The modern American kitchen," she said, "has profound sociological and psychological implications. It is one of the wonders of the modern world. It has been the focal point of interest in other international affairs." This last statement was buttressed by Robert Warner of the USIA's exhibits program division, who had advised Howard that not long ago, when he was leading Nikita Khrushchev and Nikolai Bulganin through an American pavilion at a trade fair, Khrushchev had refused to leave the kitchen until he had made a thorough study of it. He had spent more time in the American kitchen than at any other exhibit.[59] Knowing that ordinary Soviet visitors would probably be as impressed as Khrushchev had been by practical, attractive amenities, Katherine Howard wanted to make a simple but potent statement: that social justice was meaningless without an equality of goods and services. Howard argued that this was the greatest propaganda statement they could hope to make.

But the exhibits team did not care about propaganda. Their displays featured the imaginative aspects of American design, which they believed were more alluring, more telling, than ordinary kitchens. The final displays revealed that the United States was full of delightful things that were beautiful to look at and a wonder to behold. The United States was not just a nation that loved labor-saving devices! Harnden and Rudofsky's displays were intended to astonish and amaze people, especially those Soviet visitors who were normally not exposed to products like geodesic playdomes and Saarinen furniture.

Katherine Howard was never won over by the point of view held by the designers:

> To my mind, as a woman and as an average citizen, this is the one part of the exhibition that must have reality. . . . [W]e must not lose sight of the fact . . . that first and foremost we are engaged in a psychological battle to win the uncommitted nations to the free way of life. This is the main reason Congress brought us into being, and why the United States is participating in this exhibition. . . . It is one of the wonders of the world that Americans in every economic strata have kitchens with labor-saving devices which free the American woman from drudgery, which make the kitchen the heart of the home.[60]

In the final design of the kitchen area the consumer products embodied the commercial character of America and the variety of materials available to manufacturers. Innovative design was demonstrated by novel products and through the contrast of old and new. The setup revealed how quickly American inventors, designers, and manufacturers improved and transformed their products. Sleek, chrome-plated, portable appliances dissolved the kitchen by transporting cooking to the rest of the house. These new devices promised to make even gourmet cooking idiot-proof. The product displays in the American Pavilion mirrored the drive by manufacturers and women's magazines to make the art of cooking into the same sort of technological fantasy experience that General Motors had made out of driving.

The Harnden and Rudofsky exhibits team, with the administrative support of James Plaut, portrayed the kitchen as a place where technology reigned—not skilled housewives. Their appliances suggested that the symbolic importance of the kitchen was all but obsolete. Anyone could cook efficiently with new gadgets: the clubwoman, career lady, the male bachelor. Saul Steinberg depicted one of these newly independent men in his illustrations for a 1954 article on appliances called "Is the Kitchen Disintegrating?" Steinberg's bachelor sits at a table with the evening paper drinking coffee, virtually surrounded by appliances, which are perched on footstools and plugged into an overhead ceiling lamp. The self-satisfied bachelor with his harem of automatic devices crooks the baby finger of his cup hand to indicate his mastery of the domestic sphere.[61]

The modern-minded Alice B. Toklas, a resident of France for forty-five years, was quick to see the revolutionary potential of the new electrical appliances. After American friends sent her an electric blender she wrote that it had dramatically improved her daily life and "liberated" her from "the struggle of finding time to do what must be done." She wondered if her friends realized what a transformation in her life they had wrought. "For them the blender is a reality; for me it is a miracle. . . . [I]t is possible to prepare with it most of the great French dishes in no more time than it does the simplest of food without it and . . . it permits one to cook, to serve and to be free to remain at table with one's guests."[62] Alice B. Toklas probably liked to spend the occasional day cooking, but her desire "to do what must be done" indicates that she shared with many modern women a desire to use cooking shortcuts so that she could pursue other interests, like writing magazine articles. Manufacturers and advertisers promoted this freedom from domesticity, even while conservative matrons like Katherine Howard (who probably kept a maid) tried to protect traditional, labor-intensive lifestyles.

At trade fairs, simple blender demonstrations brought the miracle of cooking with appliances to admiring crowds who had little appreciation for industrial design. But if it was a weakness in the design strategy at Brussels not to have hands-on, animated appliance shows, the Brass Rail Restaurant more than made up for it. The Brass Rail ran its restaurant as if it were a material culture exhibit. It even rivaled trade fair supermarkets as a demonstration of how technology and mass-production techniques in the United States had revolutionary cultural implications. Plaut and his supporters could point to the Brass Rail and say that if anyone wanted food demonstrations, they could find them there. Of course, the restaurant was a full-blown commercial food factory, not a cozy little kitchen. Like the new fast-food chain restaurants back in the United States, the Brass Rail was trying to show that home cooking was obsolete. Why not eat out every day of the week when it was cheap, fun, and there was nothing to clean up afterward? In the end, the only kitchen in the American Pavilion was the one in the Brass Rail, which served up fancy alcoholic drinks, and frozen, prepackaged fast food.

The Brass Rail was a food company that operated many institutional concessions, restaurants, and coffee shops in and around New York City and had had five restaurants at the 1939–40 New York World's Fair. Inside the American Pavilion, it operated a soda fountain in the Streetscape area, a bar in the theater lobby, and a large coffee shop on the second floor, which included a cocktail lounge and another bar adjoining the terrace.[63] The company brought in its own design team—Eszter Haraszty, a Hungarian-born color stylist, interior decorator, and clothes designer, and her associate, the muralist Al Herbert—who worked in conjunction with the Brass Rail's Department of Planning and Edward Durell Stone to create a deluxe dining area that presented an edible, drinkable, feast of Americana.

Working closely with Stone, the Brass Rail drew up some thirty sets of plans before settling on the idea of a central coffee shop with a cocktail lounge and an outdoor terrace, each allowing for maximum seating and the fastest turnover. The cocktail lounge featured exotic beaded glass curtains, stained glass panels, dramatic red carpets, and a fabulous black bar that had a glass top with red underlighting set in a torchy background of magenta, orange, and black appointments. The rug was shot through with alternating metallic orange and pink fibers like the new Lurex designer fashions.[64]

In the cocktail lounge, the sparkling hues, colors, fabrics, and beads symbolized fun and illicit pleasure. The lounge overwhelmed the visitor with emotions of grandeur, in a way consistent with the feeling of opulence generated by the superabundance of space inside the pavilion's central court. The bar on the terrace was tame in comparison, with its yellow-and-white-striped awnings shading sunny Eames fiberglass chairs. Haraszty was a believer in mood colors. Each area—cocktail lounge, coffee shop, terrace—had its own color-coded emotional tenor.

In the central coffee shop, luscious colors were reflected in luminous Formica countertops supported only by corner posts, providing for a maximum amount of leg room and imparting a sense of openness. Diners could watch the chefs preparing food in the mirrors suspended over the work stations. As was true of the original McDonald's back in California, mass-production methods became a display of considerable interest. The mirrors afforded a view of the latest in electronic cooking: king-sized barbecues, rotisseries that cooked glazed chickens, ventilating systems, and dishwashing machines. Like the agricultural equipment sold off after a trade fair, the world's fair provided American manufacturers a way of introducing their products into the European market. The vice president of the Brass Rail, David J. Berge, boasted in a trade journal that "the equipment which has proved to be such a star attraction for visitors to the American Pavilion, has also been seen and appreciated by European restaurateurs. In fact, enough equipment has been sold so that we suspect we may have changed the eating habits of the world."[65]

Fast food was the most contested, worried-over aspect of the Brass Rail operation. Test shipments of victuals from New York determined that food demands in Brussels would have to be anticipated by four weeks: Few quick adjustments would be possible. Eli Elbert, general manager of the restaurant, conducted local surveys in Brussels to determine the availability of suitable supplies. He decided that American beef would have to be frozen and shipped over because the local meat did not have the high fat content and "marbleized grain that produces a more succulent beef" associated with the American table. European sausages, encased in gut skins and shorter than the American hot dog, were completely unacceptable. Prepared foods, such as syrups, shortenings, beverages, baked beans, cranberry sauce, catsup, chili sauce, relish, and mustard were also imported from the United States, and the Brass Rail manufactured its own ice cream—up to 300 gallons a day—mostly for the snack-bar concession. The European staff was given a fifty-five-page manual with minute instructions on the handling, preparation, and presentation of the food. Intensive training gave them precise directions on the size of each dish, the way to carve meats, safety and cleanliness requirements, rates of pay, and hours of work. Nothing was left to the imagination. The Brass Rail was a fully mechanized restaurant with an American veneer that turned modern food processing and traditional recipes into a Disneyland-style experience of usable history, painless fun, and maximum profit.[66]

The menu featured American hamburger and hot-dog buns (soft and fluffy compared with the local breads). Freezing and shipping quadrupled costs, but local bakers could not produce the white bread that was an essential component of fast food. When it came to the systematic production of food, every element had to be predictable and everything had to be adaptable to the assembly line.[67]

The greatest Brass Rail controversy was caused by the hot dogs, or "H-dogs," which *Reader's Digest* called "America's Super Weapon." In a breathless account, the reporter Leslie Lieber recounted the "inside story" of hot-dog diplomacy: At the first meeting with Brass Rail officials in November 1957, someone from the State Department asked that the hot dog be made a prominent menu item. Edward Levine, the president of the Brass Rail, was apparently horrified because hot dogs did not travel well "without losing taste and texture."[68] He may also have been worried about the same inconveniences that had persuaded the McDonald brothers to avoid hot dogs. Since hot dogs were a kind of open-faced sandwich, they begged to be customized. People inevitably fiddled with their hot dogs, and this resulted in messy, unsanitary countertops. Hamburgers were far more amenable to the mass-production process.

In order to make hot dogs into seductive agents of Americanism, the patriotic president and vice president of Brass Rail made a personal trip to Brussels in search of a first-class local supplier. They were frustrated to learn that not only were the best sausages too thick and short for American rolls—they were encased in Russian sheep-gut! Working against a short deadline, they had the restaurant manager, Eli Elbert, attempt to teach a Belgian sausage maker the secrets of hot-dog making. Meanwhile, the executives contacted Catherine Personius, head of the Department of Food and Nutrition at Cornell University, to find a foolproof recipe "for all-beef frankfurters with garlic." Despite everything, the first batches of red hots made by four different European sausage makers all failed. They were "soggy, off-color, oversized, and under-spiced." In desperation, the Brass Rail decided to fly fresh, raw hot dogs to Brussels from the

United States, daily if necessary. Apparently it was not the distance that affected the dogs, only the freezing.[69]

The final product, developed especially to "yelp freedom's message overseas" and be "grilled into juicy testimonials to the American way of life," was made by the New York manufacturer, Trunz, Inc. It was a skinless, all-beef hot dog and, according to rigorous tests by *Consumer Reports,* superior to any on the American market. This frankfurter, for foreign consumption only, had a relatively high water content (61 percent), the highest protein content of all hot dogs tested, and a relatively low fat content (19.8 percent). It scored tops in flavor, texture, appearance, and absence of defects in a field of some twenty-eight other brands (but it still did not outsell the hamburger at Brussels).[70]

The Belgians were very strict about letting foreign food into their country. Until they could determine exactly what the U.S. hamburger meat was made from, it was impounded in Antwerp, thirty miles away from the fairgrounds. The U.S. Embassy wrangled with the Belgian authorities until the meat was released, and it arrived just twenty minutes before opening ceremonies. The British "banger" was less fortunate. This traditional pub sausage was denied entry into the fairgrounds after the fair was under way, thus causing a public embarrassment. Belgians insisted that imported sausages consist of at least 90 percent meat. The banger, a mysterious combination of pulverized bone, cartilage, offal, and on average only 50 percent veal or pork, fell woefully short of this standard. British butchers had to develop a special sausage under the expectant eyes of their countrymen. Their new sausage, also for export only, was dubbed "the British Banger Mark II."[71]

The menu given away by the Brass Rail as a souvenir explained some of the finer points of American food ways to visiting tourists. Aside from its normal purpose of listing the daily dishes, the menu tried to brush in the details in the overall picture of American cuisine. It pulled details together into one unambiguous statement and defended aspects of the restaurant that seemed vulnerable to criticism. The emphasis on quickness, time-saving devices, and efficiency presented something of a problem to the restaurant, for example, because Europeans were notorious for their love of long meals. In self-defense, the Brass Rail explained in its menu that Americans did not just "gulp down food" but could eat at their leisure—the fast-food concept only applied to preparation. "America relaxes—and eats!" The menu explained how the coffee shop, or snack bar, was a fixture of the American landscape, providing quick and easy snacks at the beach, ball games, along highways, and at shopping malls. "Although the picnic is still a time-honored institution in the U.S. the homespun hamper full of laboriously prepared food and drink has been supplanted . . . by this convenient, efficient oasis." People did not need to cook any more, according to the Brass Rail: Snack bars throughout the land provided instant nourishment.[72]

The Brass Rail coffee-shop menu presented the U.S. corner restaurant as the metaphorical "melting pot," where all types of people, all classes, old families and new immigrants, businessmen and bohemians alike could find something to suit themselves. The Brass Rail wanted people to believe that neighborhood coffee shops and drugstore soda fountains prevented the polyglot culture of the United States from flying apart, that the cooks in such places were like neighborhood social workers who tossed ethnic and regional tensions into the same pot, simmered them awhile, and served up peaceful "American" cuisine. And more: The soda-fountain stools often "became upholstered clouds" upon which boys and girls could perch and dream away their adolescence over cool ice cream sodas or banana splits. Accompanying the menu notes were cartoon-style drawings by Henry Boltinoff depicting a Cupid-lipped teen-age girl enthralled by her crew-cut date, a carhop waitress in a short skirt approaching a diner in a car, and similarly innocuous views. In reality, the whole idea of fast-food dining was an attempt to replace waitresses with self-service, and lingering teenagers with high-turnover, high-volume sales.[73]

Part of the strategy used to make fast food comprehensible to Europeans involved explaining the European origins of the hot dog and hamburger so as to make the Brass Rail versions of these foods seem like regional variations of local dishes. There was also a brief explanation on how agricultural science, animal husbandry, and the meat-packing industry were combined in America to produce similar foods on a nationwide scale. The Brass Rail celebrated the food-processing industry and its most up-to-date technologies, hinting that this was the wave of the future. Many of the biggest names in the industry, including Coca-Cola, Nestlé, and Pillsbury, were contributing sponsors.

Belgians were so curious about this mass-produced American cuisine and the so-called American way of life that a local paper, *Le Peuple,* sent a reporter, Maurice Haurez, on a journey across the United States in the summer of 1958 to see if the displays inside the American Pavilion had any veracity. One of the articles he sent back detailed a few days of feasting with the Goodwyns, a typical American middle-class family (Mr. Goodwyn sold electric appliances, Mrs. Goodwyn was a housewife, and they had two children in school). The article was accompanied by two photographs that told most of the story. One photograph showed Mr. and Mrs. Goodwyn standing before a table piled high with groceries. Everything was in an industrial-designed package. Haurez assumed that this packaging was part of a pervasive fear of germs, a fear of "earthiness." Generally speaking, however, Haurez admitted to enjoying the American love of novelty. His second photograph shows Mrs. Goodwyn with an Elsie the Cow mask over her head playing cards at a weekend costume party.[74]

Belgian food ways were indeed different from those demonstrated by the Brass Rail. The commissioner general's wife, Marge Cullman, reported that her maid, for example, considered it a disgrace not to buy fresh household food everyday. In order to save time Cullman attempted to introduce her maid to convenient frozen foods. She bought a new refrigerator with a big modern freezer, installed it in their home, and ordered a large quantity of beef and lamb. But when it came time to show the woman how to thaw and prepare frozen foods, Cullman discovered that all the meat was missing from the freezer. The Belgian maid, having not been informed of Cullman's intentions, had come across the meat in its rock-solid condition, decided that something was wrong with it, and tossed it all in the garbage.[75]

Despite her love of modern conveniences, Marge Cullman detested the Brass Rail. At a specially prepared meal one afternoon in the commissioner general's quarters, the Brass Rail chefs had somehow earned her eternal scorn. "To cap it all," wrote Cullman, "in a country where the merest scrap of bread is fresh, crusty, and appetizing they had imported, at great pains, quantities of pale, limp hamburger buns." Cullman says little more on this subject, reserving her description of food for the fabulous wines and gourmet dishes the Belgians served her at dinner parties. She was a food snob. But it is hard to criticize her preference for artichokes in mousseline sauce over cheeseburgers. She was the polar opposite of those who enjoyed basking in the glow of Americana; who flirted with mysterious strangers in the Brass Rail cocktail lounge, or sipped Shaeffer World's Fair Special Edition Beer on the terrace in the sun. The Brass Rail was not for the gourmet. But it did not pretend to serve aristocratic cuisine to 20,000 people a day, either. The Brass Rail promised food for the masses. Gourmet stuff could be had in town.[76]

The material culture exhibits worked with each other to illustrate the ideals of mobility, portability, flexibility, and the other so-called consumer values deemed uniquely American by the exhibit planners. Commercial products demonstrated how American mass-production, distribution, and marketing techniques would have revolutionary consequences for any nation that cared to adopt them. Unlike a trade fair, however, mercantile values were masked by the razzle-dazzle of culture (there were no Chamber of Commerce booths set up to take buy and sell orders). This made some business-minded American visitors impatient. Robert Letwin, editor of *Sales Management*, for example, thought that the American Pavilion suffered from the lack of a succinct message. He liked the IBM computer, the mechanical hands that enabled visitors to handle isotopes, and Circarama, but he found them little more than entertaining. Letwin claimed to be unaffected by soft-sell techniques. He admired the Soviet Pavilion, wherein every display made a matter-of-fact statement regarding the excellence of national goals and commercial products.[77]

Robert Letwin found the American Pavilion a waste of time because it did not feature specific products that retailers could order. Indeed, the American designers had constructed their displays to provoke curiosity and encourage Europeans (who might have been suspicious of American motives) to relax and enjoy an ideal "democratic" atmosphere. Individuals like Letwin did not understand that the internationalism promoted by the U.S. Pavilion did not depend on selling specific American products so much as on selling ideals and promoting consumerism. Critics of the U.S. Pavilion wanted to protect nostalgic American virtues; the planners of the U.S. displays, by contrast, wanted to sell liberal capitalism.

7 The *Unfinished Work* Exhibit

Walt Whitman Rostow, Leo Lionni, and the New Liberal Consensus

The New York Stock Exchange exhibit in the American Pavilion (part of the "automation" section on the first floor) was not much different in spirit from what had been developed for the visitors' center in the New York Stock Exchange itself. The New York exhibit, designed to show the role of investors "as share owners in the future," was opened in March 1957 in a new million-dollar gallery that included a glimpse of the trading floor. Eight female guides conducted tours through the exhibits and into the new theater that featured films on stock buying. The stock exchange invited corporations to set up displays in their new gallery, which demonstrated the relation between investment capital and consumer products. American Telephone and Telegraph, General Motors, and Standard Oil contributed fanciful displays built around the People's Capitalism ideal. Consolidated Edison sponsored an animated atomic power plant; U.S. Steel emphasized the important role that small investors played in research and development.[1]

A monthly publication, *The Exchange,* compared the stock-exchange displays inside the U.S. Pavilion at the Brussels World's Fair with the nearby voting-machine exhibits that demonstrated how elections were held in the United States. Together, these two exhibits explained the interrelation of commerce and government and demonstrated how the choices of free citizens determined their own fate in a capitalist democracy. The theme of the stock-exchange exhibit was "America's Business Is Everybody's Business," dramatized by the film *Your Share in Tomorrow,* which was projected on a two-by-three-foot screen and explained how buy and sell orders reached the

Visitors in the American Pavilion at the 1958 Brussels World's Fair examine the exhibit of the New York Stock Exchange, equipped with an operational stock ticker. National Archives.

Wall Street trading floor from 2,400 member offices around the United States. And just as the voting machines mixed their educational intent with entertainment (visitors "voted" for their favorite actresses, musicians, and statesmen in private booths that were just like the booths used in real elections), the stock-exchange exhibit personalized cut-throat capitalism by entering visitors' names onto the flow of ticker tape and then projecting the names on the "trans-lux" screen—the first "big board ticker ever to operate in Europe." Afterward, copies of the ticker tapes were given to visitors as souvenirs so that they would remember how they had become, symbolically, participants in the flow of capital.[2]

A crowd of visitors at the six voting machines in the American Pavilion at the 1958 Brussels World's Fair. National Archives.

The stock-exchange exhibit invited Europeans to join Americans in a prosperous democracy, thereby extending an image of corporate culture that was already very much a part of corporate public relations in the United States, where General Electric, for example, urged its blue-collar employees (especially women) to use stocks to put themselves on an equal footing with management. Articles in the *General Electric Review* featured testimonials by employees who had found that a new sense of responsibility came with stock ownership.[3]

Into the late 1950s the ideology generated by the People's Capitalism campaign continued to be an important public relations tool for corporations, both domestically and internationally. The basic message of the campaign was that the United States was controlled from the bottom up by worker-capitalists instead of from the top down by some type of central committee, as in the Soviet Union. The constant theme in People's Capitalism rhetoric was that social or economic problems were never structural, only superficial. At trade fairs, in domestic advertisements, and in the statements of pet journalists and intellectuals, workers were urged to participate in stock buying and in family-oriented pursuits, which strengthened the American way of life. The greatest threat to this ideology was not the willful resistance of Communists, however, but the fact that millions of Americans (especially racial minorities) were unable to participate—as capitalists—in the burgeoning Western economy.

At Brussels the influence of the People's Capitalism campaign would not have extended much beyond the stock-exchange exhibit except that the Soviets had panicked the Americans with their weekly newspaper, *Sputnik*. The Cullman administration reacted by producing an official guidebook (it went on sale about June 1, 1958), subsidized by Chemstrand, Singer Sewing Machine, and IBM. The souvenir guidebook was mostly an explanation of exhibits and a guided tour through the pavilion, but it also slanted the meaning of exhibits toward People's Capitalism themes—especially in the supplemental section entitled "The Land and the People," which featured photographs of a Levittown-style model home, workers leaving a factory, a labor-management negotiation session, and an oil refinery. The guidebook described Henry Ford as an example of the Horatio Alger myth, a person who was able to use the "unparalleled" opportunities in America to fashion his car company. Other aspects of the United States, such as the system of government, free public education, religion, and recreation were given brief descriptions.[4]

The ideal image of the United States presented by the guidebook went beyond the normal emphasis on abundance and profit sharing. Folded into the guidebook was a map of the United States entitled "The Land and the People," which presented the country as an ideal society of racial and ethnic harmony—not a melting pot but a place where people from Afghanistan to Albania, Yemen to Yugoslavia, shared folkways and enjoyed the natural resources of the land. Across the top of the map, with hands joined from sea to sea, were drawings of foreign people in ethnic dress. These fanciful illustrations brought the country to life: Off the coast of Florida, Greek sea divers hunted for sponges; in New York City (emblazoned with the crest of the United Nations) the map revealed Belgian, German, Irish, Syrian, even Russian, communities living side by side. The map could be dismissed as simple-minded propaganda; but it was also a positive step toward revising the old melting-pot idea, asserting a heterogeneous United States instead of a single Anglo-Saxon culture that absorbed all immigrant groups. It was certainly an appealing image of the American way of life (especially to foreigners). The map argued that the United States had become the crossroads of the world, a place that drew its character from the unique talents of immigrant groups.

In an attempt to explain the philosophy of the Office of International Trade Fairs, Charles H. Clarke, an exhibit designer who had worked for both the Department of Commerce and the USIA, once said that "the American Tobacco Company never sold one Lucky Strike by advertising cancer."[5] Clarke was expressing the commonly held belief among government exhibit designers that negative displays were detrimental, even foolish. Few such exhibits, if any, ever showed up at trade fairs or propaganda exhibitions. However, world's fairs addressed such a large audience, and the racial tensions in the United States were becoming such a hotly debated issue abroad, that one exhibit in the American Pavilion was allowed to depart from the ideal image exemplified by the guidebook and reveal the "cancerous" aspects of the United States: the "unfinished work." The reverse side of the souvenir map explained that the title of the exhibit came from a passage in Abraham Lincoln's "Gettysburg Address": "It is for us the living to be dedicated to the unfinished work." Next to this brief statement was a drawing of a white middle-class couple, with children in tow, walking toward the rising sun, which surrounded the family with its circle of glory. "America," said the caption, is determined "to solve her problems."

The *Unfinished Work* exhibit was relatively gutsy, especially in its attempt to explain racist behavior; however, unlike other controversial exhibits, *Unfinished Work* finally had to be shut down. Segregation problems, exemplified by the crisis in Little Rock, Arkansas, where Gov. Orval Faubus had called out the National Guard to prevent black children from attending a whites-only school, were portrayed in this exhibit and it was not long before this drew criticism from powerful southern members of Congress. Worse, a photograph in the exhibit mocked the U.S. Congress: It showed black children playing in the slums of Washington, D.C., against a distant view of the Capitol dome, revealing shameful conditions in the nation's first city.

Planning for the *Unfinished Work* exhibit began with Walt Whitman Rostow and the Idealism in Action theme committee at MIT, where Rostow had tried to mold the exhibit into a showcase for the ideals of the Center for International Studies, especially regarding the role of the United States in developing nations. All the MIT sessions had been influenced by Gunnar Myrdal's *An American Dilemma: The Negro Problem and Modern Democracy* (1944)—but none more than the Idealism in Action subcommittee. Myrdal's book pointed out that the new climate of internationalism made it imperative that the United States demonstrate to the Third World that American blacks were achieving social and political equality. Myrdal predicted that race relations in the United States would soon come under a microscope, that any and all concessions to black civil rights in the next phase of history "will repay the nation many times."[6] By 1957, when preparations for this exhibit began, the situation had become inflamed by the new prosperity enjoyed by white society and the flagrant denial of black civil rights in Little Rock. *Fortune* sponsored the exhibit; its art director, Leo Lionni, who had helped Edward Steichen produce the mass-market book version of the *Family of Man* exhibition, became the designer.[7] Rostow, Lionni, and the supporting staff from Time Inc. probably viewed this exhibit as an opportunity to publicize the views of the liberal coalition forming around Nelson Rockefeller—the coalition Rostow would later call the "shadow cabinet in opposition to the President."[8]

The *Unfinished Work* exhibit had been designed as part of the displays inside the American Pavilion but eventually ended up outside, on the terrace next to the Circarama theater. It was divided into three adjoining sections—visitors entered a shadowy, black-and-white interior from the front and proceeded directly through the three rooms to the exit in back. In the first room, three major social problems were set forth: the difficulty of self-government, the dilemma of American blacks "who have yet to win all of the equal rights promised them by American democratic theory," and urban congestion. These national shortcomings were specified in an impressionistic collage that covered the angular, faceted walls with newspaper clippings, featuring headlines like "Fellow Governors Treat Faubus Like Flu Carrier" and "Dixie Governors Join in Opposing Troops." A few captions written by John Jessup, an editor for *Life*, clarified the intentions of the display.[9]

The second section was a simpler polyhedron shape with larger, fewer facets in brighter colors and with more lighting, explaining how Americans were confronting the social problems exposed by the free press. Its overall theme was "the people take action." Charts and photographs in this section explained "the public and private war on prejudice." Captions assured visitors that blacks were beginning to participate in the new prosperity and rather bluntly noted that "the doom of the American caste system is in sight." Portraits of President Eisenhower, Adlai Stevenson, Rev. Martin Luther King Jr., and Walter Reuther adorned the walls. The portrait of King was accompanied by his words: "This is not a war between the white and the black, but a conflict between justice and injustice. It is one of the greatest glories of America that we have the right of protest." Reuther's statement supported King's, and he promised that "The job of the AFL-CIO will not be finished until there is equal opportunity for one and all."[10]

It was also in the second section where the embarrassing photograph of Washington, D.C., appeared, along with another cluster of graphs, charts, and captions describing how privately owned model homes in the suburbs and new apartment complexes in the cities were replacing the filth of congested slums. "Home building soars in the U.S.," one caption proclaimed. Another boasted that "Six of every ten Americans own their homes." These displays were followed by panels and photographs on farming and the environment, detailing the American "alliance with nature."[11] Lionni and Jessup's claim that independent farmers, corporations, and the federal government had adopted a policy of conservation and cooperation for the general good was a little optimistic, even for a couple of Time

The Unfinished Work *exhibit at the 1958 Brussels World's Fair. National Archives.*

Inc. staffers, but the goal was to present a model for developing societies, not to probe the relative merits of progress. By exposing social ills in the United States they wanted to show that it too was a nation still developing—that the solutions found there could be applied elsewhere.

Section three, the last room, expressed the "hope for the future." Here there were no statistics, no graphs or charts—just large photomurals of the type that had proved so effective in the *Family of Man* exhibition, and a few captions illustrating the idyllic appearance of a modern society that had solved the problems introduced by the first two rooms. This room expressed the hope that "democracy's unfinished business, already partially mastered, will get done on a na-

Newspaper headlines express outrage over resistance to integrated schools in Little Rock, Arkansas, in the first section of the Unfinished Work *exhibit at the 1958 Brussels World's Fair. National Archives.*

tional scale." The room was painted in alternating tones of blue and white on the exterior, and inside, on matching blue walls, were hung three large photographic blowups. The first photo showed farms that used conservation techniques; the second mural displayed a modern apartment building; and the third depicted a racially diverse group of children dancing in a meadow holding hands. In sum, section one revealed, literally, the bad news Americans had been forced to confront in recent years. Section two revealed the reaction to those problems. The concluding section envisioned a modern utopia as the outcome of current reforms.[12]

Photomural of children of different races dancing a ring-around-a-rosy in the third section of the Unfinished Work *exhibit at the 1958 Brussels World's Fair. National Archives.*

Rostow's ideals and Lionni's designs related the struggle for civil rights in the United States to Third World problems such as urban poverty and primitive agricultural methods, attempting to reveal that social unrest everywhere had similar root causes that only the American system could resolve. They made America's unfinished business seem like everybody's business and presented modernization as a universal panacea. Katherine Howard criticized the exhibit, however, for the simple reason that it did not seem to be "motivated by any good Fourth of July feeling about the U.S." Howard Cullman advised her not to get involved, warning her that James Plaut would compromise a little in the kitchen display but that he was dead set on this exhibit and opposing him would only create animosity.[13]

Leo Lionni did not follow the planning committee's advice in detail but carried out the general theme of displaying democracy as "the constant striving for ideal solutions—as the interplay of individual, community, and government." In keeping with Rostow's concept, Lionni made the race problem the primary topic of discussion, but Rostow's suggestions to emphasize foreign aid and European sources of American democratic theory were softened by the more universal themes of urban renewal and the management of natural resources.[14]

Rostow, Plaut, and Lionni—everyone involved in the exhibit—wanted to get beyond the reactionary statements emerging from the People's Capitalism campaign, which were basically rejoinders to Soviet productivity claims. The "chromium picture" created by new appliances could never efface the embarrassment of Little Rock. Indeed, one observer termed Little Rock "the biggest and newest and blackest of the black marks against us." Instead of avoiding the issue (which could not be avoided) or distracting the world with gadgets and appliances, Lionni tried to "pull a switch." Believing that a hard-sell, pro-American exhibit on segregation would be expected by the Soviet propagandists and the foreign press (and sliced to ribbons by them), Lionni created a disarming exposé that would create sympathy among Europeans who knew that economic abundance alone would not change ingrained cultural prejudices and deeply rooted social inequities.[15]

The *Unfinished Work* exhibit should probably have been kept a secret until the moment it was unveiled, or at least until after the U.S. House and Senate finished wrangling over supplementary appropriations for the American Pavilion. But the exhibit had enemies in high places (especially Katherine Howard), and perhaps that is why the *New York Times* was able to get an advance preview just before a congressional appropriations committee met to determine the final sum of money to be allotted to the U.S. Pavilion. On March 11, 1958, as the Senate was about to give approval to a supplemental appropriation of $2,054,000, the first nationally published photograph of the exhibit appeared in the *New York Times*.[16]

Southern politicians were predictably more offended by the exhibit than others. In a letter to Secretary of State John Foster Dulles, Sen. Herman E. Talmadge (D-Ga.) specified his objection:

> It is incomprehensible to me that the United States Government should be a party, either directly or indirectly, to a fawning display of its internal problems before the rest of the world. Regardless of whether one favors or opposes segregation, the question is one which, by its very nature, directs itself solely to the people of the States and regions directly affected and cannot by any stretch of the imagination be said to be one of the legitimate concerns to the citizens of other countries.[17]

Talmadge went on to say that southern taxpayers were, in effect, paying their share of this exhibit and thus deserved better representation. "I call on you, in the name of the people of Georgia . . . to repudiate the impression thereby given that the Department of State has set itself up as an arbiter of right and wrong in matters of purely internal import."[18] But he was mistaken if he believed that segregation and poverty were only southern problems or that they could be kept out of the international press. In fact, Talmadge had never seen the exhibit and did not realize how Lionni had called for progressive action, not for retribution against Talmadge's constituents.

The public nature of the debate brought out defenders from the private sector, but they had almost no clout. Rev. John B. Morris, for example, fired off this counter-response to Dulles:

> As one who was born and raised in Georgia and who still returns frequently to his beloved native State, I feel that I must suggest a contrary view to that suggested by Senator Talmadge. We of the deep South have much to be ashamed of in the developments of the last four years and, along with the rest of the nation which has its race problems, we must humbly ask the patient understanding of the Free World. While I plead with Northerners for more understanding of the complexity of the South's particular problems, I am ashamed for the tensions and hate which so many at high levels have generated in their emotional resistance to the Supreme Court.[19]

Rep. L. Mendel Rivers (R-S.C.) was another southerner offended by the exhibit. For Rivers, the whole thing appeared to be a hatchet job by Henry Luce (Lionni's employer at Time Inc.). "If Luce is permitted to construct anything which will cause the slightest reflection on our way of life—in any of its areas—you are going to hear plenty of reaction on the floor of the House. . . . It is ridiculous to think that either you or anybody in authority would countenance such colossal and unimaginable stupidity. . . . [W]e are not kidding on this matter."[20] Rivers recognized the extent to which the exhibit glorified the role of the free press at the expense of the political process. Lionni had indeed seized this opportunity to present the free press as the prime mover of democracy.

Henry Luce (and Time Inc. magazines) had long been an opponent of segregation. As his biographer, Robert E. Herzstein, explains, Luce had been born in China and reared surrounded by people of another race. His sympathy for American blacks was deepened by the fact that many blacks were, like himself, Protestants. *Life* magazine, especially, had boldly addressed the fact that segregation was "the most glaring refutation of the American fetish that all men are created free and equal." As early as 1938, *Life* had proposed that southerners adopt agricultural diversification, better public education, and industrial capitalism to "erode resistance to the advance of blacks."[21] Mendel Rivers recognized the hand of Luce in the *Unfinished Work* exhibit, which updated *Life*'s old advice with new imagery.

Some newspaper reporters exploited the commissioner general's troubles. One imaginative writer, comparing the exhibits with Soviet propaganda, called the exhibit "the weird spawn of Rostow's brainstorm. . . . It's a sure bet Soviet Russia will not have any exhibits at Brussels showing the slave workers in the mines at Vorkuta, or the miserable homes of peasants on their cooperative farms."[22] The press coverage was so bad that Katherine Howard began calling the exhibit "the outhouse," a term partly justifiable because of its ultimate location outside of the American Pavilion near the Circarama theater.[23]

A USIA official, Burke Wilkinson, investigated the exhibit shortly before it opened, in advance of a visit from Under Secretary of State Christian Herter. Wilkinson counseled Cullman to keep his staff from talking to the press, especially the *New York Times*, and to station a guard at the entrance of the exhibit until last-minute changes had been made.[24]

Wilkinson was surprised by what he found. In the original presentation to the commissioner general's staff, Lionni had said that there would not be any inflammatory pictures and that there would be only fragments of headlines to suppress controversial specifics. But Lionni had prepared the exhibit in New York and then shipped it to Brussels, where it fell into the hands of Belgian contractors. The Belgian workers were given considerable leeway with photographic blowups from the American newspapers, and had chosen images of mob violence in Cairo, Illinois, and Little Rock, Arkansas. On their own initiative they decorated the walls of the first room with enlarged, rousing headlines such as "White Pupils Jeer Negro Student," "Little Rock Policemen Drag a Demonstrator Down a Street," and "When a Negro Family Moved into Cicero, Illinois, the National Guard Had to Be Called Out to Check a Mob." Wilkinson's first priority was to get these items edited or covered so that the exhibit would be less incendiary.[25]

Regarding the second cubicle, Wilkinson asked that the photograph of children playing in a slum near the Capitol be removed, along with the image of a racially mixed college dance in which a black man appeared to be reaching out for the hand of a white woman. But he approved photographs showing black voters in the South, a black priest with an integrated congregation, integrated schools, playgrounds, and business conferences. These images were accompanied by charts and graphs showing that black college enrollment was increasing and that southern schools were moving toward integration. In the third section, Wilkinson objected strongly to the mixed group of dancing children but thought that a label might save the ring-around-a-rosy picture if it explained that "this does not represent any national objective as defined by law, but freedom of choice to play as one wishes."[26] That Wilkinson could even think this, let alone say it, probably indicated to Lionni that it would be no use arguing that the circular motif had been a crucial element in the success of the *Family of Man* exhibition of photographs—an exhibition that won acclaim for the USIA in countries all over the world. Unfortunately, once the *Unfinished Work* exhibit became identified with the crisis in Little Rock, nothing could save it.[27]

Christian Herter, arriving after the exhibit had been opened to the public, was not satisfied with the changes even though specially trained guides were escorting the public through the show, adroitly fielding questions, comparing American problems to the troubles of other nations, and reassuring visitors that all of the social problems revealed in the exhibit were under control.[28] Luckily, the local socialist paper, *Le Peuple,* came to the rescue with a sympathetic article. Whereas most of the American press treated the exhibit as if it were a freakish appendage, *Le Peuple* described *Unfinished Work* in relation to the rest of the exhibits, dealing with urban renewal and social planning, all of which were typically progressive and showed how problems could be solved through legislation and planning. The model of Philadelphia sent by the Philadelphia Commercial Museum, for instance, revealed how an area of slums and factories could be transformed into a tidy, rationally organized waterfront district with matching modern high-rises, a logical pattern of transportation routes, and parks along the river's edge. "All the town-planning heads of Belgium—those who are responsible for the development of our cities—are going to be fascinated with the Philadelphia case," stated *Le Peuple.*[29]

Le Peuple was similarly impressed by the Mobil Oil exhibit on industrial parks in which animated model buildings illustrated the new suburban and decentralized city. The paper's report compared these designs to the Belgian areas of Herstal-Rhées and Ghlin-Baudour, where socialist initiatives had resulted in similarly modern designs. *Le Peuple* added that these urban-planning exhibits appealed to both workers and industrialists, who would all benefit from the orderly cities and suburbs that had been created out of the squalor of congested, decaying city centers. Adjoining these exhibits were small screens on which the pavilion's ubiquitous loop films depicted suburbanites driving to local shopping malls with airy open courts—not unlike those of the American Pavilion itself. In one of these films, a modern General Electric plant was shown, both inside and out, its trim lawns landscaped with flowers and trees.[30] Taken together, the Mobil Oil exhibit on industrial parks, the Philadelphia urban-planning exhibit, the loop films, and *Unfinished Work* showed something of the complex changes taking place in the living and working patterns of the United States and Western Europe. But it took an energetic *Le Peuple* to ferret out this linked statement. *Unfinished Work* should have been kept inside, near other exhibits on urban planning; it was too isolated out on the terrace, as if the issues it described existed in a vacuum.

Three guides were posted inside the exhibit (one in each room). The reporter from *Le Peuple* had met with two young women (one white, one black) and at the door "a tall athletic young fellow: Kibbe Fitzpatrick, with a degree in French literature."[31] The reporter was greatly impressed by the guides, who had well-rehearsed answers to all his queries. Fitzpatrick, for example, explained how the photograph depicting the slums of Washington had already been widely reproduced in the Soviet bloc in order to denounce social conditions in the United States. But, as he pointed out, the Soviets had never paid royalties to the photographer for this privilege. Gesturing toward the more recent photographs of the city, Fitzpatrick explained that since that infamous photograph had been taken, the slums had been cleared and a modern neighborhood had taken their place. *Le Peuple* could not help but conclude that "only strong democracies are in a position to tell of both their strengths and their weaknesses."[32]

The image of dancing children in the third section was particularly appealing in the world's fair setting. This illustration of one-world harmony was very similar to the type of idealism generated by the Belgian Kingdom of Childhood, an area at the fair reserved for the visiting children of all nations. The newspaper *Le Soir* illustrated an article on the Kingdom of Childhood with an image very like the dancing children in the *Unfinished Work* exhibit—only with a Native American boy included in the integrated dance with an Asian, a Caucasian, and a black child.[33] And one of the Belgian Congo exhibits used integrated imagery, which *Le Peuple* also applauded, with only a few reservations. Although *Le Peuple* was critical of the Belgian attempt to portray the Congo as a benighted region rescued by enlightened Europeans, the paper applauded the promise to raise children of different races together so that they would overcome the ingrained prejudices of their parents. Of course, this was also one of the implicit messages conveyed by the U.S. Pavilion's Children's Creative Center.[34]

As of yet anyway, the Belgians had nothing like the Little Rock school crisis to cast a shadow over their visions of integrated schoolrooms and playgrounds. Little Rock was so embarrassing for the United States, and especially for the South, that Herter demanded the closure of the *Unfinished Work* exhibit. Privately, he acknowledged that the segregation material had caused the problems, but he asked Cullman and Plaut to tell the press that the cancellation was not because of "subject matter but because of poor craftsmanship and a failure to tell a balanced story."[35] Herter suggested that a public health exhibit replace the panels dealing with Little Rock so that *Unfinished Work* could eventually be reopened.

James Plaut, however, did not give up. Defying Herter, he had Leo Lionni flown to Brussels especially to revamp the exhibit. Late in May, it reopened for three days to test visitor reaction. Katherine Howard could only watch with shock and indignation as the guides recommenced ushering small groups through. It was her duty, as Herter's watchdog, to see that the exhibit was shut down. In a letter of protest to Plaut and Cullman, she stated, "It was my understanding after the visit of the Under Secretary of State this exhibit would be phased out and that *Fortune* would be informed that it had failed to meet expectations and the exhibit would be closed." Her anger was justifiable because Plaut had not informed her of the revisions, nor of Lionni's trip to Brussels.[36]

In the American press the exhibit was applauded by *Ebony*, whose editors supported the ideal of total integration. But as a promoter of the black middle class, *Ebony* wanted foreigners to know more about black social progress and less about segregationists, more about the Rev. Martin Luther King Jr. (whose portrait and prointegration statements did appear in the second section of the exhibit) because too often only the sensational opinions of segregationists were published abroad. *Ebony* pointed out: "At every conference table the ghost of Little Rock sits on the shoulders of American delegates."[37] With the face of the nation already clouded by shame, *Ebony*'s editors wanted to instruct Europeans in the differences between North and South, between local resistance to the Supreme Court and federal policy. Perhaps the perception of the United States among Europeans regarding this matter was indeed so antipathetic that it needed no further publicity: One black guide in the American Pavilion told an *Ebony* reporter that foreign visitors stared at her in disbelief, astonished that integration was the rule inside the pavilion. Given such adversarial conditions, the guides were proud to be ambassadors of their country, demonstrating by example that racism was not insurmountable, that there was hope for the future.

Resistance to the exhibit was represented chiefly by Rep. William H. Ayres (R-Ohio), Rep. L. Mendel Rivers (D-S.C.), and Rep. P. Preston (D-Ga.), who flew to the fair and inspected it for themselves; the addition of Preston to the corps of reactionaries was particularly damaging because he was on the Appropriations subcommittee that directly affected the USIA and the State Department. Upon their return, these self-appointed inspectors conveyed their deep dissatisfaction to George V. Allen, director of the USIA. Knowing which side his bread was buttered on, Allen sided with the congressional committee. After his own perusal, Allen told Cullman that the exhibits inside should be removed so that public health exhibits could replace the civil-rights displays.[38]

James Plaut went back to Washington to meet with Herter and Allen on July 7–9. They informed him in no uncertain terms that a public health exhibit, organized by the Department of Health, Education, and Welfare, would be arriving in Brussels on July 18 to replace the old displays.[39] Katherine Howard informed the guides with a self-satisfied memorandum, thanking them for their concern about *Unfinished Work,* reminding them that their true mission was to present a broad representation of issues, and that public health also deserved some attention.[40] But the guides were an idealistic bunch, many of whom had missed two semesters of college for this chance to serve as informal U.S. ambassadors. The guides now regarded *Unfinished Work* as their cause célèbre. The dialogue this exhibit encouraged was vital to their integrity because, like the editors of *Ebony,* they believed that it was a tragedy to give the segregationists the last word, to allow negative press coverage to go unchallenged. Angered by Howard's memo, twenty guides wrote to Sen. Theodore

F. Green (D-R.I.), chairman of the Foreign Relations Committee, begging him to intervene on their behalf.

The guides' commitment to the exhibit may have stemmed from their idealism, but it also came from the frightening anti-Americanism they were experiencing. "Without exception," their communal letter noted, "every European and Asian is familiar with the name Little Rock. But they have only heard about the violence there, which by extension appears to be happening everywhere in the Southern United States." The guides had been doing their best to diffuse negative perceptions, they explained to Senator Green, with photographs, such as one showing a black couple in a modern, upper-class kitchen in a Little Rock home. Likewise they emphasized that the photograph of the Capitol dome and adjoining slums had been placed very carefully above the scale model of a model apartment complex. However, there was no effective way completely to whitewash the racial crisis emerging in the southern United States.[41]

Unfinished Work was not the only source of information at the fair regarding race relations in the United States. Indeed, by closing the exhibit the State Department was only relinquishing what little control it had over public reception of this matter. Europeans were curious to see how Americans would address the seemingly irreconcilable differences between blacks and whites in Little Rock, and other American cities, and so looked elsewhere for news. This demand was satisfied in various ways, principally by the European press. For example, shortly after *Unfinished Work* was closed, *Le Peuple* published an article on racism in the United States written by its American correspondent, Maurice Haurez.

In the South Haurez found the expected wall of hatred separating the races, manifested by segregated drinking fountains and the Jim Crow laws. But he was surprised to hear whites pronounce that blacks also wanted this separation of the races. One white respondent told him that the accomplishments of black musicians were evidence that blacks were happy living within segregated, but culturally rich, communities. Haurez noted that these attitudes were no different from those of Belgian colonialists, arguing that the southern United States was, in all but name, a colony like the Belgian Congo. As in the Congo, blacks in the United States seemed to do most of the menial work, whereas whites reaped all the benefits. Social order was maintained both through legal devices—the poll tax—and illegal methods such as lynching. He also pointed out the connection between racism and the fear of communism, revealing that the American way of life relied on the exploitation of an ignorant lower class and the suppression of critical political views.[42]

Lionni had tried to counteract arguments such as those put forth by Haurez by creating a dialogue that provoked questions to which the guides had all the answers. However, it was the State Department's job to keep a global perspective, to measure the merits of exhibits in Brussels against events about which Lionni had little knowledge. In the summer of 1958 any exhibit touching on the relation between wealthy white Americans and poor people of color was bound to seem tactless to Herter. When he demanded that the exhibits be closed, he was, first and foremost, catering to southern reactionaries, but he was also responding to the spring riots that had greeted Nixon in Latin America. And he may have had a wary eye on nationalist movements in the Middle East and elsewhere, which tended to be critical of wealthy American developers. Herter's caution must have appeared wise, at least to some, when Arab nationalists revolted and the Marines were rushed into Lebanon on July 15, 1958.[43]

Perhaps because of the upheaval in the Middle East, *Fortune* did not publicly condemn the State Department for closing *Unfinished Work.* But in the August issue, an editorial appeared on the image of America abroad, discussing how that image had changed from the prevalent anti-Americanism of the early 1950s to the "curious admiration" of 1958, because of exhibits like *Unfinished Work.* According to *Fortune,* the attempt to woo Europeans with propaganda stressing the number of cars, model homes, and the number of televisions per American household had been a mistake. Europeans associated this materialism with spiritual vapidity, and McCarthyism had added the suspicion that mass culture was somehow totalitarian, too. *Fortune* attributed the recent improvement in attitudes toward the United States to increasing disillusionment with the Soviet Union and to the USIA's dissemination of American books (and Luce publications!), which dealt frankly with the failings of mass education, rampant conformism, and other problems of the American community. *Fortune* stated that the real success of the American Pavilion lay in its ability to uphold this new tradition of critical inquiry and reform. Instead of "chest-thumping" displays, the pavilion was "soft-spoken, self-critical, refreshing." *Fortune* proposed that this attitude would be the key to successful foreign relations in the future because nations emerging from colonialism did not want to remake themselves into a pale reflection of the United States. "If we insist on seeing the world as created in our own image, such overreaching vanity will end up in an overwhelming despair."[44]

Belgian leaders, not to mention other Europeans, were undoubtedly eyeing the civil-rights movement in the United States with some trepidation because the plight of American blacks in the South was indeed similar to that of blacks in the Belgian Congo, who had long been denied self-determination. In order to encourage public admiration for their management of the Congo, the Belgians created exhibits at the fair emphasizing the development of natural resources and improvements in public education. But the idealistic images in *Unfinished Work* suggested that even the most benign form of paternal colonialism was morally unjust, making the American exhibit frightening to Belgians living, working, and profiting from landholdings in the Congo. Herter, who had been born in France and whose life had been spent building European-American amity, did not want to create hostility at an event dedicated to furthering the aims he had struggled so long to realize.

European colonies were a heated point of contention at meetings of the United Nations. Pierre Ryckmans, honorary governor-general of the Belgian Congo and the Belgian delegate to the United Nations Trusteeship Council, was perturbed that no suitable international policy on colonialism existed during the late 1950s. Writing for the *Belgian Congo-American Survey, 1956–57,* Ryckmans claimed that the colonial problem existed wherever there were dependent populations and that it was inevitably connected with the existence of minority groups. Ryckmans believed it was hypocritical of American nations to criticize Belgium for its colonial possessions when the heirs of European conquerors were lording it over indigenous peoples themselves. Ryckman took a defensive position, maintaining that Europeans were a benevolent influence in the Congo and that their industrial development of this region was essentially no different from what the United States was doing in its own backyard.[45]

The Belgian authorities were so concerned with promoting a progressive, benign image of their activities in the Congo that they hired an American banking group, which, during the opening month of the fair, offered for sale in the United States $15 million in Belgian Congo fifteen-year external loan bonds. The proceeds were said to be "earmarked for the Belgian Congo's housing program," and the Belgian authorities hoped that this first public offering in the United States would "not only contribute toward the improvement of the housing situation but will, at the same time, call the attention of the American public to Belgium's concern with the social welfare of the Congolese population."[46] This housing program was part of an ambitious ten-year plan aimed at inducing the Congolese to settle in fixed communities and to establish a European-style culture. At the fair, this progressive image of the Congo was presented by a cluster of seven ultramodern buildings.[47] Exhibits of the Congo highlighted the Belgian administration, the Catholic missions, the financial institutions, the modern transportation routes and mining operations, and the superb flora, fauna, wildlife, and hunting. Congolese sculpture was given a place of honor because of the influence it had exerted on modern European sculpture and painting (not for its Congolese meanings). And last but not least, native Congolese performed tribal music and ceremonial dancing. This was the ideal way to divert critical comments about this wealthy colony. There was no public soul-searching, no hand-wringing, no promises to do better in the future—as in *Unfinished Work.* The Congo pavilions presented a model relationship between colony and nation: the physical abundance and spiritual vitality of the Congo invigorated the Belgians, who, in turn, offered administrative and technological experience to the colonials.

The economies of Western Europe and the United States were drawing closer by the day during the late 1950s. Men such as Jan Albert Goris, editor of the *Belgian Trade Review,* kept American businessmen apprised of the official Belgian position on the Congo, the development of the European Common Market, and the way that colonial possessions would fit into the so-called Atlantic community.

Goris, a tireless promoter of Belgian interests through the publications of the Belgian Chamber of Commerce in the United States, encouraged American dreams of a huge, unified European-African marketplace, where American-style mass-production techniques would flourish once the current trading quotas and cartels were removed. Like his Chamber of Commerce counterparts in the United States, who flew entire supermarkets to distant trade fairs, Goris believed that all good things flowed from economic development. In the publications he edited there was never any hint of culture clashes or racial disharmony. The *Belgian-American Survey, 1957–58* (which included an introduction by the U.S. secretary of commerce, Sinclair Weeks), for example, was peppered with illustrations of happy Congolese blacks in integrated schools, working at skilled occupations, and enjoying middle-class lifestyles.[48] The conservative Belgian authorities whose views Goris articulated would not have been enamored of the kind of realistic dissatisfaction that the *Unfinished Work* exhibit revealed.

The multiracial images of dancing children and integrated schoolrooms from both *Unfinished Work* and the Belgian Kingdom of Childhood projected the idea that racism could be overcome only by rearing children in an integrated environment—yet this was precisely the process that Gov. Orval Faubus of Arkansas had tried to thwart. During the fall of 1957 and the spring of 1958, Faubus and his segregationist supporters defied the federal government by denying the civil rights of black children who had chosen to attend a white school. The images of those children opposing armed troops in the name of equal opportunity were disseminated by television and still pictures throughout the United States and Europe and constituted a terrible blow to national prestige. The guides from the *Unfinished Work* exhibit said that Little Rock was the number one topic of debate. Indeed, James Plaut even positioned a young black woman from Little Rock inside the exhibit to explain that Arkansas was an isolated, atypical case.[49]

The closing of *Unfinished Work* meant that race relations in the United States would henceforth be addressed only obliquely by the appearance of black jazz musicians, movies, and by special events such as folk dancing on the Fourth of July. The jazz musicians and folk dancers demonstrated tolerance, the social benefits of diversity, and the strength of ethnic, indigenous, and black cultures. These events demonstrated to Europeans that Americans held the traditions of minorities and indigenous people in high esteem. Posters advertising the appearance of Leontyne Price, for example, emphasized her patriotism by listing the musical program inside a graphic illustration of Uncle Sam's top hat.

The performing arts and special events were politically neutralized by State Department censors, who screened for controversial content and politically suspect performers. Some films, such as *I Was a Fugitive from a Chain Gang,* were removed from the schedule even before the general public was notified that they were going to appear. But when performers were censored, it was harder to keep quiet. In the case of James Kershaw, the stage manager for the San Francisco Actors' Workshop, a particularly ugly situation was created when the State Department advised the Actors' Workshop about three weeks before opening night that if Kershaw participated in the production, in any capacity, they would cancel the show. This decision was handed down without any attempt at explanation—as if Kershaw had some sort of unspeakable disease. The managing director, Jules Irving, was shocked that the State Department could treat him in this manner after he had stripped down personnel to a minimum and raised funds by public subscription in order to help support the American effort. No explanation was ever offered, but Kershaw was probably rejected because he was a union organizer.[50]

The committees who selected the films, especially, must have realized that their choices would inevitably be compared with contemporary events in the United States. Their choices reflected this anxiety. But films being what they are—commodities that live and die in the marketplace—even the most innocuous contemporary movies were often chock-full of sensational content beneath the polite veneer of entertaining melodrama. And outside of the U.S. Pavilion, beyond the control of the State Department or the USIA, in the newspapers, at the local movie houses and film festivals, there were alternative visions of the United States that argued that the pavilion's version of American culture hardly told the whole story.

The film *South Pacific,* which was shown in the American Pavilion theater throughout May, was an effective way of showing that white Americans could overcome their provincial fear of other cultures and races. In *South Pacific,* Nellie Forbush (played by Mitzi Gaynor) from Little Rock, Arkansas, overcomes her prejudices through the guidance of the French expatriate Emile de Becque (Rossano Brazzi). De Becque has fathered children by a Polynesian woman—hardly as upsetting as a black-white romance would have been in Nellie's Little Rock—but the fear of miscegenation was strong enough to throw Nellie into a temporary hysteria. As she struggles with her conscience and eventually rises above her small-town bigotry, Nellie becomes a role model. Generally speaking, the film was an excellent way of diffusing criticism about the civil-rights crisis in Arkansas, which had reached a fever pitch just about the time the film version of *South Pacific* was released. Nellie's personal triumph over prejudice improved the image of her benighted hometown.

South Pacific was filmed with the cooperation of the U.S. Navy, which was relatively cautious when assisting Hollywood productions. The Defense Department, undoubtedly, considered this film to be excellent propaganda; but *South Pacific* must have seemed like manna from heaven to the State Department.[51] In the 1949 musical adaptation of James Michener's novel *Tales from the South Pacific,* the birthplace of Nellie Forbush was changed from the hard-to-pronounce Otolousa, to Little Rock, thus guaranteeing that Nellie's struggle to overcome her loathing of colored people would become a thinly veiled parable for real-life events a decade later. Here was a positive movie about overcoming racism just at the time Faubus had turned Little Rock into an international embarrassment. Here was a fabulous Technicolor drama that could demolish the image of Little Rock disseminated by the black-and-white still pictures cropping up in foreign newspapers. If the State Department had been able to contain the debate over segregation and civil rights to special events like *South Pacific,* the American people would have escaped from any embarrassment regarding this issue. But racism and imperialism were such pressing issues in the late 1950s that they became hot box-office commodities in films, popular entertainments, and the daily news.

The best depiction of the grim realities that had yet to be overcome in the United States was to be seen in the films appearing at the elite International Film Festival, inside the fairgrounds, which included the Orson Welles film *Touch of Evil.* Also representing the United States during the festival's American week were *The Goddess,* directed by John Cromwell; *Raintree County,* directed by Edward Dmytryk; and *The Old Man and the Sea,* directed by John Sturges. These entries, aside from their technical excellence or artistry, went considerably further than the films in the American Pavilion in their unveiling of racism and imperialism (although they were attended by far fewer people).[52] They were the type of films that the psychological novelist Georges Simenon, chairman of the film jury, could have been expected to appreciate, but their topical content made them into more than just dramas or thrillers. Far more than *South Pacific,* the American films in the International Festival were critiques of their times. *The Goddess,* for example, portrayed the drug-ridden, loveless life of a Hollywood film star; *Raintree County* featured a southern belle (Elizabeth Taylor) driven insane by her inability to reconcile northern and southern mores, and by the haunting fear that legally she might herself be a Negro. Obviously, the State Department had nothing to do with the selection of these titles, or the operation of the International Film Festival.

Orson Welles was the darling of the festival. Upon his arrival at the screening of his latest project, *Touch of Evil,* he was greeted by scores of reporters, photographers, his old friend Jean Renoir, and Georges Simenon. *Cahiers du Cinéma* commissioned a special interview for the occasion between Welles and the distinguished critic André Bazin. Welles eventually won the Best Actor prize for his characterization in *Touch of Evil* of the southern lawman Captain Hank Quinlan, an evil character pulled right out of the headlines. Welles told Bazin that Quinlan "is the incarnation of everything I struggle against, politically and morally speaking. I'm against Quinlan because he wishes to arrogate the right to judge, and that's what I detest above all, men who wish to judge by their own authority."[53] Welles had put his finger on one of the year's most controversial issues: the racism of southern politics and the relation of local authority to the greater good (or in this case international good). The North-versus-South theme of *Touch of Evil* made it into a timely parable.

Welles was eager to reveal the darkest attributes of the American dream: the B side of one-world harmony. In the initial frames of

Touch of Evil, an anonymous man winds a timer to start a bomb. Its ticking is joined by exotic conga drums that create a time-bomb theme for the entire film. The bomb is placed in the trunk of an American developer's car, and after he leaves Mexico for the United States, the car explodes. Throughout this first sequence—one of the most famous in cinema history for its length and choreography—the ticking stays in the foreground, accompanied by a wailing brass section composed by Henry Mancini and the spatially complex interweaving of pedestrians, carts, and automobiles. The Mexican hero, played by Charlton Heston, strides confidently through the shadows and menacing streets with his new bride, a beautiful American sweater girl played by Janet Leigh. By the time the car explodes, the major theme of the film has been introduced: anti-Americanism. The tall, good-looking Heston, running counter to the stereotype of the corrupt Mexican, will bring order back to the region by vanquishing the local tyrant, Hank Quinlan—the virtual incarnation of the ugly American.

The minorities represented in the film are Mexicans, not blacks, and the location is Tijuana, far from the old Confederate South—but by shooting the film in Southern California and exposing racism in terms superficially different from those in the daily news, Welles exposed the breadth and universality of Anglo-American racism. Quinlan is not the only racist in *Touch of Evil;* the real effectiveness of racism as a theme is revealed by Susan Vargas (Janet Leigh) and some of the minor characters, whose prejudices are ingrained in their every gesture. In describing this dimension of the screenplay, the critic John Stubbs has pointed out how Susan calls her husband by his Latin name (Miguel) only when she is in bed. The rest of the time she expects him to act like an Anglo. And Susan constantly stops herself in mid-sentence, unsure of things she has said in passing, worried that her husband might take them as an insult. She does not want to offend him, but, like Nellie Forbush in *South Pacific,* who laments her uncontrollable racist emotions, or Susan Drake (Elizabeth Taylor) in *Raintree County,* whose fear of mixed blood causes her eventually to lose her mind, Susan Vargas is doomed to struggle against her cultural conditioning for the rest of her life. Welles did not want to tell a story in which the slaying of a single dragon liberated the rest of the population. Everyone in *Touch of Evil* has been affected by the racist attitudes that permeated American culture.[54]

Many of the scenes take place in bordellos and cheap hotels. As portrayed by Welles, the United States was mortally threatened not only by racism but by the poverty and anger it engendered in minorities and the exploited citizens of Third World nations, symbolized here by the Grandi gang, who rule the Tijuana underground. Even more frightening were the rivers of trash, the oil rigs draining away the wealth of this Third World border town, and the returning time-bomb beat, reminding the audience that U.S. prosperity had been achieved at the expense of exploited minority groups who were no longer willing to take their place at the back of the bus.

Welles's decidedly anti-American film received only passing acknowledgment in the American press and failed in its domestic release. But if *Touch of Evil* was too bizarre or depressing to be taken seriously in the United States, the reality of the racism it depicted was reinforced by a far more popular event just outside the world's fair in Brussels—the Wild West Show, created by a private American company seeking to exploit European fantasies of the mythic American frontier. The Wild West Show was brought to Brussels by an unscrupulous entrepreneur, G. Robert Fleming, who abandoned it once the production became bogged down by bad weather, stranding some two hundred penniless cowboys and cowgirls and a band of Sioux Indians.[55] Although the show was not officially associated with the United States government, Fleming pretended that it was—to both Belgian and American supporters—creating the worst public relations disaster imaginable for the U.S. Embassy. The average fairgoer could not distinguish between publicly and privately funded American events anyway. Howard Cullman himself ignored this distinction by inviting the Wild West Show entertainers to perform on the plaza in front of the American Pavilion on July 2, 3, and 4.

People came by the busload from all over Europe to see the reenactment of scenes from cowboy films and the well-known mythical characters of western settlement. There was a rodeo, a stagecoach hold-up, Indian battles, cavalry charges, gun fights, trick riders, archery contests, and the wagon train exodus to the West.[56] Casey Tibbs, "world champion cowboy and saddle bronc rider" created a spectacle with his fringe-trimmed rhinestone coats, inlaid

Cowboys and Indians from the American Wild West Show and Rodeo are seen performing on the pavilion plaza during observance of the United States National Days, July 2, 3, and 4, at the Brussels World's Fair, 1958. National Archives.

pistols, lavender jeans, and alligator boots.[57] One member of the troupe reported that "it was such a big hit that anyone connected with the show or even wearing a western-style sombrero had open sesame to everything."[58] But when the spring rains washed out performance after performance, the huge payroll sent the company into bankruptcy.

Fleming had been living in the best hotels and spending money freely. And he was unlucky. He purchased a $60,000 inflatable tent made by U.S. Rubber to shelter the show from the incessant rain, only to watch it expire from puncture wounds shortly after its erection. He purchased and shipped specially made circus seats from the United States when a local supplier would have provided them much more cheaply. Fleming's spendthrift ways helped promote the show, but when he disappeared, local musicians were left unpaid. To complicate matters further, tickets had been sold and distributed throughout Europe in a manner that invited fraud. The U.S. Embassy was besieged by creditors and performers, who had to be interviewed on a case-by-case basis. Gene Autry, whose Rodeo Company had supplied the livestock, flew to Belgium and personally paid the passage of seventy-two cowboys back to Denver. Both Autry and Henry Fine, the Hollywood publicist who handled the show, remained convinced that the U.S. government should have been held responsible for the outrageous fraud perpetrated by Fleming.[59]

The show became a demonstration of exploitative capitalism, irresponsible management, and the mistreatment of Native Americans. Worst of all, it was aimed directly at the masses, at people who would never see a film like *Touch of Evil.* Just two weeks after closing the *Unfinished Work* exhibit, here was bitter verification that beneath the veneer of abundance in the United States there lurked tragic social inequities and greedy capitalists. When the Moscow Circus offered to put on a benefit performance for the destitute performers, the American Embassy was faced with the embarrassing task of hurrying the Indians onto a chartered airplane and settling debts as if the entire fiasco were the fault of the U.S. government. The fifty Sioux Indians eventually became charity cases in New York City until the Welfare Department sent them all home on buses.[60]

The opinions expressed by *Le Peuple*'s roving reporter Maurice Haurez revealed that presenting only the refined accomplishments of jazz musicians at this particular time in history—when Europeans, Asians, and Africans were deeply concerned with imperialism and American racism—was tantamount to siding with the segregationists. Undoubtedly that is why the guides had defended *Unfinished Work.* And that is probably also why the exhibit was not forgotten by John Slocum, a public relations officer who became the caretaker of the staff's collective memory by compiling a scrapbook of press clippings, which he reproduced and gave away as souvenirs. The scrapbook proudly credits *Unfinished Work* as the exhibit that the Europeans appreciated above all others.[61] By contrast, the official historical report presented to President Eisenhower mentions nothing about the civil-rights displays, only that the exhibit presented "sociological problems, our problems of nature and conservation, and our problems of public health and medicine."[62]

Also clipped and pasted into memory were those artists who unwittingly became the token minorities: the popular entertainer Harry Belafonte, and the jazz musicians Sarah Vaughan and Sidney Bechet, who were brought to the fair by the Newport Jazz Festival's master of ceremonies, Willis Conover. Conover, a disk jockey, was far better known in the Soviet Union than in the United States through his jazz programs broadcast over the Voice of America. His programs were subsidized by the USIA because European, and especially Soviet listeners, loved jazz, no matter what they thought about racism or political issues. By appearing on the American ticket in Brussels, Vaughan and Bechet became something like the ethnic figures on "The Land and the People" souvenir map—informal ambassadors of an American society that was racially tolerant and multicultural. In reality, racism and the lack of appreciation for jazz in the United States had encouraged Bechet to move to France. And Harry Belafonte had difficulty renting an apartment outside of the black sections of New York City, even after his extravagant stage show at the U.S. Pavilion earned universal acclaim for his country. Responding to this ironic injustice, Eleanor Roosevelt chastised her fellow New Yorkers in one of her daily newspaper columns, stating, "I can think of nothing I would enjoy more than having Mr. and Mrs. Belafonte as my neighbors. I hope they will find a home shortly where they and their enchanting little boy can grow up without feeling the evils of the segregation pattern. Discrimination does something intangible and harmful to the souls of both white and colored people."[63]

The ideal of a peaceful, culturally and commercially unified Atlantic community allied against the Soviet Union was uppermost in the minds of administrators who tried to put the nation's "best foot forward" in the U.S. Pavilion. The circular pavilion was the symbolic heart of the Western alliance; visual evidence of the "vital center" (in the words of Arthur Schlesinger Jr.), which maintained its equilibrium through realistic compromises and effective leadership.[64] In Belgium the State Department and the USIA wanted to reassure

Europeans that a moderate path could be taken toward a democratic future shared by the entire world. The People's Capitalism campaign provided the inspiration for many exhibits, notably that of the New York Stock Exchange, which demonstrated that economic opportunity was an essential component of democratic vitality. However, the authority of the People's Capitalism consensus depended on a genuine liberal polity that could be achieved only when social reforms, such as those advocated by Luce, Lionni, and Rostow were combined with the depersonalized "law" of the marketplace. It was no use pretending that the American way of life was enacted on a level playing field. Material abundance was an important tool in the democratization of the masses, but so too were education, integration, and civil rights for minority groups.

The educational, scientific, and cultural exhibitions in the U.S. Pavilion had been relatively successful in demonstrating that Americans had created a democratic culture available to rich and poor alike. The *Unfinished Work* exhibit had had the ignominious task of demonstrating that this democratic culture was available (or becoming available) to all races, as well as to all classes, but in 1958 such a demonstration was nearly impossible. Leo Lionni had been right to confront the issues directly, upsetting the moribund consensus haunting the People's Capitalism campaign; however, the race issue buried his overall presentation. Very little regarding modern agriculture or educational reform made its way into press reports. Except for *Le Peuple,* few newspapers described the exhibit as a depiction of modern, liberal ideals—as a wish list made out for the perusal of urban planners, sociologists, and economists (which it was). The exhibit was a threat to the status quo; the fact that it was created at all indicates that many people were dissatisfied with the ability of stock ticker machines and nuclear reactors to portray the ideal future. Exhibits at the next major U.S. exhibition—the 1959 American National Exhibition in Moscow—would take fewer risks and be kept under closer guard by President Eisenhower and his big-business cronies; they would see to it that commercial products, instead of radical ideals, would be the featured performers in their American-way-of-life drama.

8 Sputniks and Splitniks
Material Abundance Goes to War

After the superpowers signed a bilateral agreement on cultural exchanges in January 1958, exhibitions of art, science, technology, and culture inaugurated the new era of "mutual understanding" and "peaceful coexistence." In the spring of 1958 the Bolshoi Ballet, heavyweight wrestlers, the Moiseyev dancers, and a contingent of Soviet students toured the United States while Van Cliburn and other Americans went to Moscow. Van Cliburn won the Tchaikovsky competition and earned the title "American sputnik" for dazzling the Communists. Shortly thereafter, a protocol agreement, signed in September 1958, created the enabling legislation for a trade fair type of exhibition of culture and technology: the United States would send one to Moscow while the Soviets sent theirs to New York City. This was an occasion to celebrate for those in the United States who believed that exhibitions of commercial culture were an important method of transforming Communists into capitalists. The 1959 exhibitions also provided the opportunity for intelligence gathering: high-ranking officials of both nations would be able to look one another over before the tentative summit in Geneva.[1]

President Eisenhower assigned the project to George V. Allen shortly after Allen returned from straightening out the public relations flap at the 1958 Brussels World's Fair. Allen asked Harold C. McClellan, a Los Angeles industrialist who had once been the head of the National Association of Manufacturers and the assistant secretary of commerce, to be the general manager. McClellan had developed and managed the Office of International Trade Fairs in the mid-1950s and then returned to the private sector. McClellan remained "under the general supervision and policy guidance" of Allen at the USIA, but he was no friend of big government and ran the exhibition as if it were an advertisement for free enterprise. President Eisenhower and Christian Herter (who had replaced Dulles as secretary of state) appropriated $3,300,000 from the Mutual Security Program, and the exhibition planners were in business.[2]

McClellan had the full cooperation of President Eisenhower and some of the most experienced hands in the executive branch. Establishing a team of administrators, exhibition designers, public relations officers, and procurement specialists was therefore relatively simple. At a staff conference in the fall of 1958 in Washington, D.C., the State Department agreed to handle communications with the USSR; the Department of Commerce agreed to manage procurement services; and the USIA agreed to oversee public relations. Within this bureaucratic structure, key individuals shaped the style and content of the exhibition, especially Jack Masey, who, on loan from the USIA, was in charge of design and construction. Masey's appointment ensured the use of the explosive creativity becoming manifest within the field of industrial design. He asked Buckminster Fuller to build a geodesic dome; George Nelson, an influential modern architect and the design director at the Herman Miller Furniture Company, to supervise exhibit design; and the architect Peter Blake, then a critic working for *Architectural Forum,* to do an exhibition of modern architecture much like one he had done for the USIA a few years before at Berlin's Interbau Exhibition. After a chain of command had been established McClellan embarked for Moscow, where the particulars of the event had to be hammered out with his Soviet counterparts in the All-Union Chamber of Commerce of the USSR.

Masey understood how to get his ideas produced despite McClellan and the People's Capitalism ideologues with their trite formulas concerning the American way of life; their obsessive, almost ritualistic return to the iconic figure of Abraham Lincoln (1959 marked the sesquicentennial of Lincoln's birth); model homes; Norman Rockwell paintings; supermarket displays; automobiles and tractors. Masey had learned from years of experience on the trade fair circuit how to accommodate the conservative vision of Sinclair Weeks, Theodore Repplier, President Eisenhower, Clarence B. Randall, and Harold C. McClellan without sabotaging his own. His goal was to present the United States as a dramatic, on-going experiment . . . a flexible, even radical, system that could accommodate conflicting points of view. Innovative design was the hallmark of the Masey approach—the sort promoted and refined at the annual design conferences sponsored by Walter Paepke in Aspen, Colorado. He used contractors like Buckminster Fuller, whose defiance of tradition explained the spirit of the West in terms of elegant, hi-tech solutions to basic necessities: shelter, food, clothing. Masey pitted the design revolution in the West against the political and economic revolution of the Soviets, but modern design also comprised an implicit critique of capitalism: Buckminster Fuller, for example, would have been revolted by the notion of planned obsolescence.

Modern architecture and design kept the reformist spirit of William Morris and other nineteenth-century crusaders from fading out during the twentieth-century craze for mass-produced consumer products. This was the modernism that Walter Paepke used to blend "humanism" with commerce at his Container Corporation of America, the "enlightened commerce" championed by *Fortune* magazine, the marriage between humanists and businessmen arranged by László Moholy-Nagy and the Bauhaus émigrés. This modernism, although often incomprehensible to conservative manufacturers, was as powerful in its own way as the ideological utopianism pursued by American and Soviet politicians. Modern aesthetics, in fact, constituted a third ideology—with a socialist tint—distinct from capitalist and Communist economic solutions, both of which advocated productivity as the cure-all. This third ideology was characterized by advanced technology, creativity, and a vaguely defined humanism that cautioned against excessive consumption, political tyranny, violent confrontation. Geodesic domes and abstract paintings were icons of the modern spirit; the atomic bomb and the tail fin, their nemeses.

McClellan opened negotiations in the USSR with a request to move the American exhibit from Gorki Park, which the Soviets had proposed but which seemed a poor setting with unacceptable buildings, to Solkolniki Park, a heavily wooded, 1,550-acre traditional picnic ground in the suburbs of Moscow. The Soviets agreed to give the

Americans a triangular area toward the center of the park, a shape that suggested that a geodesic dome could be placed near the entranceway, complemented with a fan-shaped pavilion behind it, designed to span the middle of the wedge-shaped site. McClellan figured that he could afford to have exceptional buildings designed and built if he could sell them to the Soviets as permanent additions to the park. The Soviets agreed to purchase the buildings for half of their construction costs, and by early November 1958 McClellan had a signed contract to present to his architects and exhibit designers.[3]

By December 15, 1958, some 1,000 hours—by McClellan's estimation—had been devoted to theme planning and the relation between ideas, objects, and exhibition design. Representatives from the Department of State, the Department of Commerce, the USIA, and the private contractors had decided to make the geodesic dome an "information center," where visitors would get the maximum possible specific information about the United States, including the labor story, agriculture, education, science and space exploration. In the larger, fan-shaped pavilion behind the dome they decided to display a wide variety of consumer products and show how those products helped create the American way of life. In this aluminum-roofed and glass-walled pavilion there would be shelf upon shelf of pots and pans, an RCA Miracle Kitchen, a home workshop, a sewing demonstration area, and a TV studio—all the normal trade fair items and more. Behind the pavilion, filling up the widest portion of the triangle, would be those products best seen in the outdoor setting: new automobiles, farm machinery, a children's playground, restrooms, camping equipment, and, in a plastic-lined pool, fiberglass canoes and sail boats. When donations and suggestions for more product demonstration areas poured in, overwhelming the space restrictions inside the dome and the pavilion, George Nelson designed clusters of open-air shelters that were scattered around the site for a fashion show, the *Family of Man* photography exhibition, and Peter Blake's exhibition of modern architecture. A Circarama theater, a Pepsi-Cola stand, and a model home of the type seen at international trade fairs were built in the widest, rear section of the fenced-in exhibition grounds. There was a lot to see, but there was still plenty of space outside for people to enjoy fresh air, sunshine, or shade.

George Nelson's open-air shelters were made from clusters of individual plastic "parasols," like huge morning-glory flowers with thin, hollow throats tapering to a narrow base. The bottoms of the parasols were anchored in concrete foundations, where a subterranean drainage system carried away the rain, and the edges of the "petals" were fused into clusters of varying sizes to provide as much shelter as required by the different exhibits. The shelters were translucent, providing a diffuse illumination, and open at the sides. The notion of many units forming a strong unity symbolized the traditional *e pluribus unum* of American political culture, a notion that had influenced U.S. architecture since at least the time of Thomas Jefferson's Virginia state capitol building and that had been reworked most recently by Edward Durell Stone and Buckminster Fuller.[4]

Once a working plan was established, President Eisenhower suggested to McClellan that he form an advisory group from the "top-level American business and cultural" leadership. This would give the private sector a chance to participate in the exhibit and would provide whatever they needed in consumer products and supplemental funding. In May 1959 Eisenhower invited this advisory group to the White House for a presentation by McClellan and George Nelson, at which Nelson presented his plans for the interior of the glass pavilion. Nelson wanted to build "a huge modular steel shelving system" that could be constructed out of identical units made up in sections approximately ten feet square, permitting two levels for display with stairways and walkway passages on the second floor. The walls would be created out of "colorful, removable snap-in panels, and would be lighted by strip-mold wiring and plug-in fixtures." This modular, ultramodern system of shelves, platforms, and walkways—loaded with the fruits of U.S. industry—would remain light-filled and dramatically transparent within the glass walls of the pavilion. Visitors would be able to observe the exhibits above, below and on the same level at which they stood.[5]

McClellan asked his friends and colleagues in the business community for support. One automobile executive recalled, "By the time he was through with us we'd have felt downright unpatriotic if we hadn't been sending a car to Russia gratis and paying the cost of transportation besides. The next day he'd phone and say, 'By the way, Ford and GM are sending interpreters with their cars. How about you?'" It was in this manner that McClellan obtained the model home from the All-State Properties of Long Island, which was furnished by the R. H. Macy Company and General Electric.[6] President Eisenhower's cheerleading helped too: RCA executives agreed to install two kitchens and operate a complete television studio inside the glass pavilion; the Ampex Company offered to send a new video-taping device as part of the RCA color television display; General Mills volunteered items from the Betty Crocker kitchens; General Foods and the General Union Company underwrote the cake-mixing demonstrations and food displays; McGraw-Hill and Company said it would provide a book exhibit; and the Pepsi-Cola Company said it would furnish dispensing operations for its drink, including all transportation costs and the cost of the warehouse space it used in Moscow. Donald Kendall, the executive who opened Pepsi's purse, was nearly fired after spending so freely, but he was rewarded later when Nixon paused with Khrushchev at the Pepsi stand long enough to create a media sensation. Kendall eventually became the chairman of Pepsico and apparently remained a lifelong friend of Nixon's.[7]

The Moscow exhibition would have everything seen at the trade fairs and more, nearly everything that had been inside the American Pavilion at the 1958 Brussels World's Fair, with the model home and RCA Miracle Kitchens thrown in. In fact, the response to Eisenhower's call to action was so overwhelming that Nelson's supplemental outdoor shelters had to be created at the last minute with help from Albert Dietz of the Massachusetts Institute of Technology. Eisenhower hosted a second meeting at the White House for executives of the plastics industry, and these individuals were so impressed that they supplied Nelson with as much free material as he wanted. When McClellan asked for money, one executive handed him a blank check. Another company sent along a machine that fabricated plastic bowls, which were given out as souvenirs. More designers were invited to join the design office, including Peter Harnden, who helped George Nelson construct the interior of the glass pavilion.[8]

Soviet officials wanted to see American technology, "the means of production." Their exhibition in New York, set to open on June 30, 1959, would contain some ten thousand displays, occupying three floors of the New York Coliseum. The Soviet exhibition featured daily fashion shows and consumer products on the first floor, science and technology on the second, and public education, health, culture, and welfare exhibits on the third.[9] The cultural historian Karal Ann Marling has commented on the dowdy Soviet fashions and their consumer goods designed in the passé streamlined style that U.S. designers abhorred. Design and fashion did not concern the Soviet authorities, who concentrated their efforts on showing their technological superiority. This fact was dramatized by Frol R. Kozlov, first deputy chairman of the USSR Council of Ministers, who flew to New York to open the exhibition on a nonstop flight from Moscow on June 29, 1959, aboard the world's largest passenger plane (a Soviet turboprop TI-114 airliner). It was not the prettiest plane in the world—just the biggest.[10]

The Soviet exhibition catalog bragged that the USSR featured full employment, a rising standard of living for everyone, high state expenditures on social and cultural needs, paid holidays for factory and office workers, an increase in output of consumer goods, increased housing construction, and improved cultural and welfare services. The utopian vision offered by the Soviet catalog was rounded out with photographs of happy people—such as a group of workers in a ball-bearing factory, surrounded by classical busts and potted plants, painting after hours in the plant's "Palace of Culture." Culture in the USSR was integrated with daily life (at least according to the Soviet literature), but the arts were not a method of exploration or a means of acquiring psychological and spiritual freedom as had been the goal of Victor D'Amico's Creative Center. The dull happiness of the Soviet conformists fooled no one. Who in their right mind would bother to paint pictures of lathes after a hard day on the shop floor? More important than culture—in the elitist, traditional sense of the term—were the things that only vast public expenditures could obtain. Nine-tenths of the catalog was occupied with photographs and information about nuclear ice-breakers, the peaceful atom, farm machinery, radio telescopes "peering into outer space," a computing center, Moscow University, nursery schools, and *Sputnik*—the dreaded earth satellite. The exhibition featured three full-scale model sputniks along with a "cosmic rocket," which probably scared the wits out of people concerned about the space race and "the missile gap."

Sputnik itself was not too much of a threat, but the powerful booster rockets that thrust *Sputnik* into orbit indicated Soviet capacity to send "a powerful weapon at very high speeds to targets within a 4000 mile radius."[11] This was the New York of Nelson Rockefeller, after all, a man whose greatest legislative defeat in his first years as governor was his inability to "force every New Yorker to build a bomb shelter." Rockefeller asked a civil-defense seminar in March 1960, "Do you negotiate from weakness? No, you beg from weakness and creep on your hands and knees and accept surrender."[12] *Life* expressed support for Rockefeller-style preparedness by publishing a serious article about a couple from Miami who spent the first fourteen days of their honeymoon—"the crucial period of fallout danger"—in a backyard bomb shelter. The editor-in-chief, Henry R. Luce, ran this bizarre but sobering article in the same August issue that featured the 1959 American National Exhibition in Moscow.[13]

A general air of saber rattling was an inevitable part of cold war exhibitions. People knew that the vast productive capability on display in New York and Moscow represented destructive, as well as constructive capability. It really did not matter what was displayed. As the historian Stephen J. Whitfield has pointed out: "[T]he push buttons that were designed to make housework easier came from the same laboratories as the push buttons for guided missiles. . . . Chrysler, General Electric, Goodyear, and Westinghouse were also major Pentagon contractors." Those shiny chrome blenders were threatening as well as alluring.[14]

McClellan's negotiations revealed that the Soviet authorities were indeed frightened by the lavish display of U.S. consumer goods, but it was not the quantity of products on display that unnerved them so much as the emphasis on style and conspicuous consumption. On May 25, 1959, the Soviets informed McClellan that he would not be allowed to give away the makeup kits provided by Coty or the Pepsi-Cola and souvenir paper cups. McClellan argued that the 32,000 gallons of Pepsi-Cola syrup was already on the high seas; if the ship was turned back at the dock there would be negative publicity. His strategy worked and Pepsi-Cola became a hit of the exhibition. The ban on free Coty lipstick was never lifted, but cosmetics remained a fundamental part of the beauty salon, operated by Helena Rubenstein in conjunction with some hair stylists from Coiffures Americana, "where the swift hands of Carl Pace, Miss Renée and Miss Olive are an international language."[15] Fifteen Soviet volunteers were selected each day to have their hair braided, or transformed by "cold wave" permanents. The fashion models and tour guides were given make-overs at this outdoor salon while the Soviet public gawked at the "colored enamel sinks, shining equipment, pink haircurlers, adjustable hair dryers, and hair sprays," which were unfamiliar to them.[16] Philip Cortney, the president of Coty and the chairman of the U.S. Council of the International Chamber of Commerce, went to the exhibition to observe firsthand the reactions of the Russian people and reported afterward to President Eisenhower that the exhibition had been a "splendid idea."[17] At the salon and fashion show, visitors could mingle with the models, participating in the glamorous rituals of fashion like fans backstage at a rock-and-roll show. Rock and roll was, in fact, included in the fashion show, which had been designed around a number of skits.

At the Brussels World's Fair some of *Vogue*'s expensive mink coats and lavish evening ensembles had been criticized by visitors who were opposed to crass American materialism. The Women's Program in Brussels had been praised, by contrast, for showing outfits that empowered women and mirrored realistic scenarios instead of exotic fantasies. The show in Moscow used a little fantasy but kept the emphasis on middle-class lifestyles, to great effect. Only thirteen of the forty-six models were professionals. Of these forty-six, two were black, one was a Filipino, and one was a "career mother" with a set of four-year-old twins. Two families were also represented—a garment industry family and one from the suburbs. During the rock-and-roll show spiffy American teenagers danced before their enthusiastic Soviet counterparts in jeans, striped V-neck sweaters, and knee-length plaid skirts. *Life* photographers and Ed Sullivan's cameramen captured the spectacle for the folks back home.[18]

The fashion show had been organized in New York by Leonard

Hankin, the executive vice president of Bergdorf Goodman, Inc., and a group of fashion industry professionals who provided the outfits and expenses for the models. Hankin organized a preview of the fashion show in New York and prior to making his final decisions invited some 250 fashion editors to see the event. Hankin had decided to use the show as a way to promote racial integration, maybe even diffuse any criticism that might be aimed at the United States regarding this issue (an obvious American problem). McClellan had stated at a January press conference that the best way to deal with the race issue was just to present integrated situations—not talk about it—just show it in a matter-of-fact scenario, which is what the fashion committee tried to do.[19] But the fashion press in New York would have none of it. *Life* called the preview a "propaganda goof" after several fashion editors drew up a petition protesting that the runway show was not representative of the American way of life. They were specifically opposed to "an integrated barbecue, an integrated rock-and-roll party, and a civil wedding in which a black couple were attended by a white couple."[20]

Life lampooned the fashion reporters with photographs highlighting their dowdy demeanors. The petition was soon retracted. The arrow, however, had found its mark, and the show debuted in Moscow with an emphasis on family scenes; skits illustrating the ease and comfort of drip-dry nylon; and the work of individual designers such as Maximilian and Helen Rose. Even without its interracial dynamics the wedding skit was still a popular hit. One reporter suggested that because the audience was standing, rather than sitting, they became something like members of the bride and bridegroom's families. At the conclusion of the mock ceremony the crowd inevitably demanded that the bride and groom kiss, as if it were the real thing.[21]

One reporter, Tobia Frankel, observed that the U.S. models appeared unnaturally thin in comparison with "their plump Russian counterparts," so much so that the Soviet audience could not believe they were not professionals. The American women in Moscow seemed to have it all—slim figures, beauty products, convenient appliances and robotic servants, rock-and-roll plaids for daughter and ball gowns for Mom. Some twenty-eight female American guides, fluent in Russian and headed for professional careers, explained to their Soviet counterparts that the amenities and consumer products on display not only kept American women beautiful, they also helped build careers in the traditionally male business world. Helena Rubenstein herself, working in her salon exhibit, demonstrated this point admirably.[22]

Pat Nixon, the wife of the vice president, symbolized the ideal American woman. *Newsweek* editors put her wardrobe under the microscope, explaining that "millions will judge Mrs. America's wardrobe by the clothes that Pat Nixon is wearing."[23] She won the cover of *Life* in August along with Mmes. Mikoyan, Khrushchev, and Kozlov and never looked better contrasted with the grandmotherly Soviet matrons, who outweighed her by about a hundred pounds each. Mrs. Mikoyan had bags under her eyes, and Mrs. Kozlov, whose husband had just returned from opening the Soviet exhibition in New York, was caught in a profile view staring at Mrs. Nixon's trim, tightly girdled waist with a stern look of disapproval. Mrs. Nixon posed in a slim floral-print summer dress with a double strand of pearls and matching earrings. In the black-and-white photograph she looks as if she were presenting her impoverished, long-lost relatives from the old country. While her husband was wrangling with Khrushchev at the exhibition, Pat did what any upper-middle-class American lady was expected to do—she went shopping at GUM, the state department store in Moscow, and then dropped by a children's hospital, donned a volunteer's uniform, and handed out lollipops to sick kids.[24]

Elaine Tyler May's study of American families during the cold war, *Homeward Bound,* points out how the American press delighted in contrasting dowdy Soviet ladies with the stereotypical American girl-woman.[25] The fact that Soviet women were a fully integrated part of the work force never seemed to impress any American reporters. *U.S. News and World Report,* for example, tried to show that the superior work of Soviet women only proved that the Communist system was mixed-up and crazy. Two U.S. carpenters sent over by the All-State Properties Company said that a Soviet woman was the most knowledgeable, competent member of the team of electricians assigned to help set up the model house. "The women are the ones who really work," the carpenters reported. "There are a lot of Russian men who work hard, too, but the women seem to have more interest." The reporters from *U.S. News and World Report* coaxed the carpenters into describing the manual labor women performed and the lazy, shirking habits of the men, thereby offering ample evidence to the American people that the Soviets did everything backward: women received the best educations; workers painted fences from the bottom upward; men transported dirt on stretchers instead of wheelbarrows; Soviet tools were outdated; and the concrete the Soviets sold the Americans was so diluted with sand that during the exhibition shuffling feet sent up clouds of irritating dust. And they were all thieves: tools disappeared immediately if they were left unattended. *U.S. News and World Report* wanted to demonstrate the many ways in which communism perverted the individual. Gender reversal was an important aspect of this argument. Homely, overworked women were a symbol of Soviet depravity.[26]

American women were portrayed as housewives and affluent consumers, but they were important producers too. No exhibit was better at defining the productive role of American women than the food demonstration booth. Clementine Paddleford reported that "seven tons of food, the magic foods of America, the frozen products, the instants, the ready mixes, are . . . awaiting their premiere in the world's largest food demonstration." Bigger was better; American food companies wanted to demonstrate efficient, massive production! Two career women, both home economists, were asked to organize the food events. Barbara Sampson, from the Birdseye division of General Foods, and Marylee Duehring of General Mills, a supervisor in the Betty Crocker Kitchens, were assisted by five Soviet women and an American translator, Anne Anderson.[27]

The food companies wanted to demonstrate how convenience foods and time-saving appliances enabled the housewife to dress up gourmet creations. There were 110 different food items, 17,500 dishes ranging from ready-to-bake biscuits and oven-ready vegetable pies to instant coffee and Jell-O. The ladies cooked across from the supermarket exhibit inside the glass pavilion, in RCA's Miracle Kitchen of Today (the third kitchen at the exhibition!), which was open on three sides, visible from an overhead walkway and outfitted with a new gas refrigerator, oven, freezer, garbage disposer, and all the latest stove-top appliances. They cooked in shifts, eleven hours a day, seven days a week, with two demonstrations daily for the nearby closed-circuit RCA television cameras. The Soviet authorities reviewed the menu with its Oven-fried Chicken and Strawberry Dream Angel Cake and reminded the Americans that there were to be no giveaways. Barbara Sampson probably knew how to handle the censors: she had supervised food demonstrations in the U.S. pavilions at the international trade fairs in Poznań and Salonika, where things "disappeared" the instant she took her eyes off them. Things were no different in Moscow, where the Americans prevented pilfering only when they ran short of supplies. This happened quickly in the bookmobile, for example, which had to be shut down for a while until an emergency shipment of books could be flown in from New York. One of the crucial objectives of the fair, as Nixon related in *Six Crises,* was to make direct contact with the Soviet people. What better way to build mutual understanding than allowing the Soviets to steal a leg of chicken, or take home a can of Campbell soup, a packet of pink sugar, or a pocketbook edition of Philip Wylie's *Generation of Vipers*?[28]

Vice President Richard Nixon opened the Moscow exhibition on July 25, 1959. It was one of the more exciting moments in a difficult year, as he explained in *Six Crises.* Trouble for the Republican party started with the launch of *Sputnik* late in 1957, was exacerbated by an economic recession, and became chronic with internecine warfare among the Republicans themselves. In the 1958 congressional elections the Republicans suffered the worst defeat in history by a party having control of the White House. The American people had lost confidence in the Eisenhower administration; it appeared that Nixon's bid for the White House in 1960 would be hopeless if Nelson Rockefeller, who had left the administration in 1956 and become the governor of New York, jumped into the race, as many political commentators predicted. The 1959 American National Exhibition in Moscow was a golden opportunity for Nixon to show the world that he was presidential material.

It is surprising that Khrushchev and Nixon did not get along because—obvious differences excepted—they were actually very similar in temperament. Khrushchev had risen to power by promising more production of basic amenities. In 1956 he denounced Stalinism and in a new seven-year plan unveiled in January 1957 promised the Soviet people more consumer goods, an increase in the minimum wage, and eventually a shorter work week. Khrushchev believed that communism could succeed only with a practical increase in the standard of living: "You cannot put theory into your soup or Marxism into your clothes," he remarked during an interview in 1958.[29] Both Nixon and Khrushchev believed that the future would be determined by the economic system that provided the best products to the most people. Both men were relatively moderate compared with their respective right- and left-wing colleagues. However, despite the fact that there was much the two could have agreed on, they chose instead to squabble over petty differences: to trade tit for tat. This was probably because more than a hundred reporters and photographers lay in wait for the two leaders at the exhibition grounds.

Ike did not seem to have much confidence in his vice president. He said at a press conference, just before Nixon embarked for the Soviet Union, that the vice president was "not a part of the diplomatic process."[30] Far more damaging to Nixon's prestige, at least in the USSR, was the annual Captive Nations Resolution, calling for a week of prayer for the people living under Communist tyranny, passed by the U.S. Congress and signed by the White House five days before Nixon embarked. President Eisenhower waited until just hours before Nixon left for the USSR to tell him that an exchange of state visits between himself and Khrushchev had been scheduled for the upcoming year. It may have appeared to some observers, even Nixon himself, that he was being set up for a fall. However, he left the country in style aboard one of the U.S. Air Force's new 707 superjets, setting a speed record between Baltimore and Moscow (after Kozlov's splashy arrival in New York nothing else would have been acceptable). He was accompanied by Milton Eisenhower, Admiral Hyman Rickover ("father of the atomic submarine"), State Department officials, and some of the members of the president's Advisory Committee, who had provided the money and products for most of the exhibits.

After arriving in Moscow the vice president and his wife spent the afternoon and next morning on the streets of Moscow, getting acclimated but discreetly avoiding trees or bushes "large enough to conceal bugging devices." On the second day, Nixon went to the Kremlin to meet Khrushchev, who was waiting at his desk "toying with a model of Lunik," a satellite that the Soviets had recently launched into outer space. Khrushchev began a "long harangue" the moment Nixon was seated, lambasting him for the gall of arriving on the heels of the Captive Nations Resolution. Nixon explained that the president and the Congress held no ill will toward the Soviets, that the resolution simply expressed the opinion of the American people. According to Nixon, Khrushchev would not accept any excuses, and so an angry "debate" began with both politicians holding fast to their own points of view.[31]

Still arguing, the two drove across town for an impromptu tour of the exhibition grounds before the opening ceremonies later that evening. The press corps was at the park, and at least some of the staff were prepared for anything. Although few of the exhibits were ready, Nixon and Khrushchev began their quick inspection inside the glass pavilion, where the RCA technicians invited them to address the cameras. Khrushchev took the opportunity to boast that although the United States was currently the leader in the production of consumer goods, "in another seven years we will be on the same level as America. When we catch you up, in passing you by, we will wave to you."[32] Nixon replied that if Khrushchev really loved competition so much, why not allow a free exchange of ideas, too? Khrushchev indicated that competition was hardly necessary, that the Soviet Union was superior to the United States in every area. Nixon pressed the point: "You must not be afraid of ideas." Khrushchev replied, "We are telling you not to be afraid of ideas. We have no reason to be afraid. We have already broken free from such a situation."[33] The politicians bumped chests like a couple of barnyard roosters. James Reston reported later that as the initial exchange was taking place Milton Eisenhower and Llewellyn E. Thompson Jr., the U.S. ambassador to the USSR, "were standing outside wondering whatever became of diplomacy and why didn't somebody pull the plug on the whole thing."[34]

The debaters then proceeded across the exhibition grounds and entered the All-State model home. Tom Wicker, a former *New York Times* reporter, has said that William Safire, who was the public relations man for the model home (and later a junior staffer in the 1960 Nixon campaign), recognized that Nixon was treading water, and "eager to help a man he admired . . . led the official party to the kitchen" in the model home. Peter Blake also believed that Safire was one of the orchestrators of the kitchen debate but contends that photographers had been tipped off long beforehand that the model home was going to be the site of consequence. The jury is still deliberating on whether or not the kitchen debate was a carefully planned media event or just a fortuitous accident (for Nixon), but clearly the model home, as Eric Sandeen has noted, was by this point center stage in the American-way-of-life drama as it was presented at international exhibitions. The prefabricated rambler was the modern log cabin. It was everyman's castle: the preeminent symbol of the People's Capitalism campaign. And the kitchen was an important signifier of the familial norm: the "container," as Elaine May has described it, for the captive modern housewife. The illustrated home (there were pictures on the walls of a typical, white, middle-class family) was above all a symbol of Republican virtue—humble but adequate—the proper abode for those who followed the likes of "Honest Abe" Lincoln, of whom a giant bust stood on the exhibition grounds, attended by an American guide (a young black woman in one of the few existing photographs) who distributed informational pamphlets.[35]

Once the protagonists were snugly situated inside "splitnik" (the model home was divided down the center to accommodate the public), leaning on a rail that divided the kitchen from the center hallway, Nixon explained the significance of mass-produced commodities. "I think this attitude toward women is universal. What we want to do is make easier the life of our housewives. . . . Our steel workers, as you know, are on strike. But any steel worker could buy this house." Khrushchev said the house was poorly built and he did not think it would stand up very long. Nixon replied that he thought that American houses would last more than twenty years, but even so, nobody in America really wanted an old house. The dynamic U.S. economy enabled people to take advantage of "new inventions and new techniques." Without a trace of irony, Nixon maintained that planned obsolescence and constant turnover were some of the privileges enjoyed by the American citizen.[36]

After the inaugural speeches that evening Nixon escorted Khrushchev on a second tour, stopping this time at the futuristic RCA Miracle Kitchen, where they could watch the robotic maid (actually a remote-controlled floor-sweeping device operated by a hidden technician) and the home surveillance screen (a video monitor) built into the kitchen counter. Khrushchev mocked these gadgets, and at first Nixon laughed along with him but then, growing serious, noted that he hoped the Soviet premier did not miss the point: "We do not claim to astonish the Russian people. We hope to show our diversity and our right to choose. We do not wish to have decisions made at the top by government officials who say that all homes should be built in the same way." After this exchange the talk degenerated into saber rattling; but Nixon had managed to make his point: high wages and the consumer-driven economy guaranteed the highest possible standard of living for everyone; democratic freedom was best-defined as the liberty to select from among a variety of consumer products. Nixon suggested that it would be better to compete in the relative merits of washing machines than in the strength of rockets. Khrushchev quipped, "Don't you have a machine that puts food into the mouth and pushes it down?"[37]

Many Americans probably agreed with Khrushchev that there was a point at which the consumer no longer felt served by corporate innovation but instead became a hostage to it. Garishness, planned obsolescence, conspicuous consumption, tail fins, and the annual change in automobile models were criticized by U.S. cultural commentators as regularly as they were by the Soviets. John Kenneth Galbraith, attempting to dramatize the folly of squandering precious resources on novelties, wrote that the United States had become a society in which schools were old and crowded, the parks and playgrounds insufficient. The deterioration in public services appeared to be in direct proportion to the ascent of personal income and the increase in consumer products. Galbraith lamented, "The children, though without schools, subject in the playground to the affectionate interest of adults with odd tastes, and disposed to increasingly imaginative forms of delinquency, [are] admirably equipped with television sets."[38] His point was that a nation driven by profiteers and advertising would foster a weak and foolish citizenry.

Modern architects and designers also objected to the garishness of popular culture, although not from prudery. They were simply revolted by the notion that progress was usually defined in terms of the annual style change. George Nelson and Buckminster Fuller, by contrast, symbolized substantive progress: Nelson's parasols and Fuller's domes indicated a radical shift in the way architects defined their tasks. "He is a great visionary," said Edward Durell Stone of Buckminster Fuller, "a prophet." Fuller did, however, find a way to gussy up his buildings (like Stone), in this case tinting his aluminum dome a bright gold so that it "glittered like a gorgeous sunburst" at the entrance of the Moscow exhibition: Opulence was all right so long as it was not merely a veneer floated over a traditional chassis.[39]

Fuller's dome had been commissioned with the idea of making it the symbolic entranceway into the American exhibition; its gold exterior represented the sun of Western progress and the illumination of innovative technology. The *Architectural Record* ran a cartoon featuring two Soviets standing on the roadway leading to the dome, hands in pockets, one saying to the other, "When are we going to invent that?" That was precisely the intended effect. Nelson and Masey later had to install the IBM Ramac computer in the dome, which could answer predetermined questions about the United States, as it had in Brussels, along with several other exhibits trumpeting the advances of American labor, agriculture, public health and medical education, space research, peaceful atomic research, and synthetics. But they had wanted to leave the dome simple—"no glamor, no things."[40]

In the fall of 1958 George Nelson met with Charles and Ray Eames for "a few days of quiet talk." During this time they worked out the idea of transforming the dome from just an introductory exhibit into an "information machine," featuring a multiple-movie-screen presentation, "not to be treated as a series of simultaneous films but as bits of visual data."[41] The Eameses' work in film was relatively unknown at the time, evolving in conjunction with their work for IBM, beginning with the animated film *The Information Machine,* which they had created for the 1958 Brussels World's Fair. The show in Moscow was to be, in combination with Nelson's notion of the modern "atomistic" sensibility, an extension of their ideas regarding design as information. As Eric Sandeen notes, Nelson thought the relationships between things were "more important than the things themselves."[42] The geodesic dome with its expressed structure was itself a vast symbol of interrelated forces unified by theoretical relationships, and so Nelson did not want to clutter it up with objects that would only detract from its emotive power. In the final design, exhibits inside the dome were marked off by "a different color of light that reflected off the facets of the ceiling like a rainbow or a kaleidoscope." When the film presentation came on, these lights could be dimmed and the exhibits around the edge of the dome removed from the viewer's perception.[43]

Khrushchev's official evening tour of the exhibition had begun in the dome, with a viewing of the multiscreen movie by the Eameses. Peter Blake reported that Khrushchev was visibly stunned by the event. There were no negative images in the films—nothing like what had been featured in the *Unfinished Work* exhibit in Brussels. The Eameses' film was close in spirit to the *Family of Man* imagery—in which pictures were limited to a narrow band of ideological conformity. Peter Blake describes it as "a spectacular piece of highly sophisticated propaganda. Sweet, innocent, possibly naive, obviously one-sided. There were no images of crime, of poverty, of racial tension." There were pictures of spectacular mountain ranges, parking lots and suburban developments, cars speeding along highways, families gathered over supper, babies sleeping, and a final image that featured a bouquet of forget-me-nots. Some of the images were static; sometimes different imagery spread across the seven screens; at times all seven screens would erupt in sync to show cars speeding along an interstate highway, horses racing around a track, children attending schools in different parts of the United States.[44]

The Eameses and Nelson wanted there to be too many screens to comprehend individually but not so many that it became confusing. Working for IBM had taught the Eameses to focus on the importance of units of communicable information—to understand composition and content as a fractured, variable stream of information. Their film, coupled with the dome itself, was a spectacular display of the design and information revolution appearing in the West and by extension a tribute to the free-enterprise system that supported and encouraged maverick research. After viewing the introductory film, Khrushchev probably viewed the IBM Ramac computer, the heart-lung machine, and some of the other exhibits in the dome with a greater comprehension of what creativity combined with technology could accomplish.

In the glass pavilion behind the dome there were many state-fair style product demonstrations: a carpenter fabricated some of the do-it-yourself projects that could be made from patterns using the new power tools. Singer Sewing Machine had a booth in which a woman fabricated dresses. The modular-shelving system held a bewildering variety of consumer products demonstrating portability, mobility, flexibility, disposability, the decentralized kitchen: all those things that Peter Harnden and the design team in Brussels had used but with none of the surreal quackery. Interviews with visiting dignitaries—not just Nixon and Khrushchev—were filmed in the television studio, or taped and played back instantly for the crowds to see. More than just abundance was on display: objects played dramatic roles in the American way of life, where the consumer was king and products provided personal empowerment.

The art exhibition was also in the glass pavilion and, as usual, provided plenty of evidence that Americans enjoyed the freedom to express themselves, that there was no censorship in the United States. The USIA could have sent a small exhibition of realistic paintings and pleased everybody except a small coterie of avant-garde critics. But an exhibition of freedom had to demonstrate a certain amount of self-criticism, the errors that proved the rules. Knowing that controversy was sure to develop, George V. Allen selected prominent art-world professionals to be on the jury: a painter, a sculptor, an academic arts administrator, and, most important, Lloyd Goodrich, the director of the Whitney Museum of American Art.

George V. Allen wanted the jury to have complete freedom regarding specific choices but asked that they include a few paintings from the "period of Eakins, Homer, and Ryder" by way of introduction to the contemporary abstract paintings. The jury, however, did not believe it was necessary to include more than a few realistic works. Ironically, it turned out that one of these realistic paintings caused the most controversy—Jack Levine's *Welcome Home*—demonstrating that the real issue behind the debate pitting modern styles against the figural tradition was a disagreement over content, not style, over the role that art should play in a free society. To those convinced that mass appeal was the ultimate method of determining value, all perverse art, or social-protest art, or art that was incomprehensible to the masses appeared to be tainted by nondemocratic political beliefs. Under these criteria, realistic art lost out as often as did abstract expressionism. So why did the USIA allow an independent jury to send abstract and social-protest art to a popular exhibition? There were, indeed, good reasons for sending challenging pictures to Moscow, aside from the fact that avant-garde designers like George Nelson saw in the whirling rhythms of Jackson Pollock the confirmation of their own atomized sensibilities.[45]

Jack Levine's *Welcome Home* depicted a bloated general, dripping in medals, enjoying a reception in his honor. Levine's "pulled toffee" style of fun-house realism distorted the faces of everyone in the painting and plunged them into an atmosphere of old-world decadence. This was exactly the sort of thing that Soviet artists and intellectuals could never attempt to illustrate. In the USSR, a painting like *Welcome Home* was a ticket straight to the gulag. It was well known that Soviet artists wanted to see more paintings like Levine's, although they could not advertise this fact.

American artists who traveled to the Soviet Union reported that their Communist colleagues were eager to learn more about trends in the West. Rockwell Kent, for example, an American artist who was chairman of the National Council of American-Soviet Friendship, after returning from a trip to the USSR in 1958, lamented that socialist realism "has serious drawbacks—even the best of it is somewhat tainted, stigmatized by being academic." He blamed the conformity of Soviet style not on dictation from the state, however, but rather on an elaborate program of education and subsidy "so organized it acts perhaps as a restraint upon the impulse to experiment." Lloyd Goodrich and the other jury members might not have read Kent's views, but from their own experiences in dealing with censorship and the arts they would have undoubtedly applauded

Kent's concise, sensible conclusions. The best thing to do, in light of the fact that the artist was always, everywhere, threatened by the status quo, was to send a variety of styles and a range of big- and small-name talent. Let the chips fall where they may; criticism was inevitable.[46]

Kent reported that his contemporaries in the Soviet Union were sick of "the God-awful pictures of generals with medals all over."[47] This observation was confirmed by Sen. William Benton, who had also toured the USSR and in *This Is the Challenge* (1958) reported that socialist realism was just a way of turning art into propaganda."[48] The heroic portrait painting, which had begun to die out in the United States after the advent of photography, was still the bread and butter of Soviet art. Levine's gleeful antiportrait, lampooning that most tired of all clichés—the triumphal soldier—probably sent the repressed Soviet artists home in tears of rage and joy.

Rockwell Kent was not the first American artist to prowl the Soviet art scene. During the summer of 1956 Harry L. Colman, described by *Artnews* as a "midwestern Action Painter," took advantage of the thaw between the superpowers and paid a visit to the Sixth World Festival of Youth and Students in Moscow. He soon met some Russian artists who asked if he would demonstrate his method of painting in a large studio that had been set up in conjunction with the Sixth International Exhibition of Art in Gorki Park. On their first inspection of the studio, Mrs. Colman passed around a copy of *Artnews* with color reproductions of paintings by de Kooning and Pollock. The provincial Soviets did not understand the pictures, nor the explanations offered by the Colmans. When Colman set up a canvas and began to paint, however, the audience boiled with questions, accusations, opinions. The following day he was asked to paint in front of a camera crew: "I more or less stalked the canvas," said Colman. "I would lunge at it with vicious strokes; I dripped paint all over the place. At one point, in order to get some color on the wet surface, I threw paint with the brush. . . . Finally, in desperation, I picked up a handful of the paint and flung it at the canvas. The crowd roared."[49]

At a dinner later that evening Colman was asked if he would like to meet the president of the Moscow Union of Soviet Artists, the embodiment of Soviet socialist realism. Colman expected a confrontation, but it turned out to be worse than he feared: the emotional equivalent of rape. "He backed me up against the wall, held my arm firmly, and delivered a twenty minute sermon. He carried on not only about the death of abstract art, but also about the Revolution, Capitalism, and war and peace." Colman represented a serious threat to the status quo and he knew it: "There are at least two sparks in our culture which light fires wherever they land: jazz and Abstract-Expressionist art. I doubt whether Socialist Realism could long survive exposure to these two forces."[50]

Conservative critics, however, were upset by the fact that abstract art was headed for Moscow. Wheeler Williams, president of the American Artists Professional League, the largest organization of professional artists in the United States, aligned himself with the reactionary element in Congress, led by Rep. Francis E. Walter (D-Pa.), and continued the attack on the USIA that he had started during the 1958 Brussels World's Fair. Walter, chairman of the House Committee on Un-American Activities, arranged a special hearing, staged on July 1, 1959, to allow Williams to state his case. Modern art, Williams asserted, was a Communist conspiracy directed by the Kremlin, aimed at destroying the moral fiber of the United States and ripening the nation for a bloodless revolution. Williams decried the subversive imagery of Ben Shahn, Philip Evergood, and Jack Levine, and the "meaningless doodles" of Jackson Pollock in the attempt to heap scorn on all things modern. At a White House press conference shortly after the committee had adjourned, a reporter asked President Eisenhower what he thought of Levine's now infamous *Welcome Home.* Ike did not like it, but under the circumstances, he was forced to sidestep the issue by declaring that "I am not going to be the censor." Because Nixon had rubbed Khrushchev's nose in the fact that "freedom of expression" was one of the more cherished American virtues, Eisenhower could not demand that Levine's painting be removed. Ted Repplier, who had been one of the president's advisers on the Moscow show, sent Ike a letter commending his defense.[51]

The notion that modern art and material abundance posed a threat to the "moral fiber" of the nation could be advanced only because half-baked notions of social Darwinism, exacerbated by the competition between the superpowers, were common currency in public exchanges. When Nixon stood toe-to-toe with the Russian bear, poking his finger in Khrushchev's chest, he was demonstrating to the democratic coalition forming around John F. Kennedy and Lyndon Johnson, and especially the Republican coalition supporting Nelson Rockefeller, that he was fit to represent the "disciplined vigor that belied tales of the decadent and limp-wristed West."[52] The fear of losing the martial spirit that Ike had once symbolized haunted the Republican party after *Sputnik.* Kennedy's campaign would exploit the perceived weakness of the Eisenhower administration by promising more foreign aid, an increase in public sector spending and above all, an end to the "missile gap."

Intellectuals such as Walt Whitman Rostow and John Kenneth Galbraith laid the blame for Eisenhower's lame foreign policy directly at the door of the industrialists who had influenced important decisions, especially Charles E. Wilson, formerly the president of General Motors, head of the Department of Defense from 1953 to 1957, and George M. Humphrey, a former CEO with the M. A. Hanna Company, head of the Department of the Treasury during the same years as Wilson. Galbraith noted that these industrialists were convinced that production (of consumer products) was the only yardstick by which to measure the strength and success of any economy.[53] It did not matter what was produced: Conventional wisdom held that consumer choice should be the only judge of value. However, plenty of evidence showed that consumer choices were in fact determined, or at least manipulated, by the same companies that produced consumer products—mostly through advertising but also through fashionable design. David Potter and Galbraith had endeavored to illustrate that in a world where advertising and the manipulation of consumer wants had become a more powerful social force than education, the conventional wisdom of corporate leadership would lead to entropy, possibly even a Communist takeover. "Private industry did not get us atomic energy," said Galbraith. "General Motors has little interest in travel through space."[54]

In *The Affluent Society,* Galbraith pointed to Randall's *A Creed for Free Enterprise* (1952) as a preeminent example of the conventional wisdom.[55] Men like McClellan, Randall, and Nixon believed that the United States had to play a vigorous role in converting the world to capitalism, but they wanted that role firmly controlled by privately held corporations. If the Soviets grew belligerent in the meantime, a couple of well-aimed nuclear warheads could settle them down. New Marshall plans, of the sort once called for by Paul Hoffman and more recently by Rostow, the CENIS group, and Nelson Rockefeller, were unnecessary.

The architects, artists, industrialists, and designers who were usually somewhere to the left of the status quo were just as eager as their conservative business colleagues to state their case at international exhibitions. They had their own solutions to world problems. Eric Sandeen has argued that Steichen's *Family of Man,* for example, appealed to reason instead of the lust for consumer goods and was therefore a better method of diplomacy. Much the same could be said of the exhibitions created by Masey, Nelson, or Blake, who were searching for solutions to human problems through their forays into aesthetic, technological, and psychological experimentation. The real problem regarding liberal or left-wing displays, however, was that they could never replace the aid programs—such as the Marshall Plan—that had preceded them. Developing countries wanted to produce their own forms of abundance, not just buy it ready-made from the United States, Western Europe, or Japan.

As the 1950s progressed, the sentimental humanism of the one-worlders languished without more practical efforts to step up developmental aid to the world outside America's borders. Moderate Republicans like Nelson Rockefeller revealed that the private sector could indeed assist the U.S. government to carry on with the pioneering work of the Point-Four Program and the Marshall Plan. Still, it could not do so alone, and the Eisenhower administration consistently disappointed Rockefeller, along with all those who believed that the threat of nuclear holocaust would not be lifted until the entire globe enjoyed some kind of democracy and a relative, realistic chance for prosperity on the U.S. model. Those who argued for developmental aid to foreign countries were consistently ignored by fiscal conservatives, who were convinced that the U.S. government had to decrease in size and responsibilities.[56] The Kennedy and Johnson administrations would bring a new approach to foreign policy but without much more success than Eisenhower.

Individuals like Peter Blake, George Nelson, and Charles and Ray Eames worked for business leaders like Harold McClellan, Henry Luce, and Walter Paepke because these individuals captured their imagination with promises to amend the excessive materialism of the traditional capitalist enterprise. Global capitalism, with some kind of balance between the public and private sector, as Galbraith indicated, seemed like an obvious solution to most problems. Government-funded international trade fairs that advertised a worldwide unity held a natural attraction for idealistic designers and artists.

Of course not every intellectual believed that capitalism could be reformed or that a global version of the United States was necessarily a good thing. In an address to the Aspen Institute in 1958, the sociologist C. Wright Mills, calling the industrial designer "the man in the middle," warned designers to remain inner-directed, to stay with work that nourished the spirit, to hold fast to the principle that what a person is, is indeed what a person does, that labor redeems or condemns the individual, as reformers of capitalism had been saying since at least the time of William Morris. Mills stated: "The craftsman's way of livelihood determines and infuses his entire mode of living. For him there is no split of work and play, of work and culture. His work is the mainspring of his life; he does not flee from work into a separate sphere of leisure. . . . [H]e expresses himself in the very act of creating economic value."[57]

Mills cautioned the "men in the middle" not to become cynical slaves of the production—advertising—consumption wheel. He reminded his audience that the means of production were as important as the ends. But also he predicted that industrial designers would soon be devoured by capitalism, that the type of utopian design developed by, for example, Buckminster Fuller, Charles Eames, or George Nelson would be stripped of its reformist attributes and fed into the fashion machine. The designer, inevitably, would join with those of the National Association of Manufacturers and the International Chamber of Commerce, whose "God is the Big Sell." Mills asked industrial designers to reinvigorate the craft tradition. The highest human ideal, he said, was to "become a good craftsman."[58]

The Advertising Council's announcement that today "machines do the hard work" did not quite resolve the issues raised by Mills. The view of capitalism as an impersonal, devouring monster, as a system that attributes no value to work for its own sake, may have been a cliché at the time of the kitchen debate, but it still nagged the consciousness of critics, who were watching as the relentless pursuit of profits quickly transformed their world. The Soviets had not resolved this issue either. Their image of happy workers painting after hours in a ball-bearing plant certainly did not resolve the divide between labor and craft.

Nixon, and all those whom Galbraith pointed to as the status quo, believed that the vast majority of Americans already enjoyed a high standard of living, and if Khrushchev and his meddling minions would step aside and allow capitalism to spread, then the rest of the world would have prosperity too. Ironically, both Communist and capitalist leaders were steering their people toward the same utopia of material abundance. "Production," as Galbraith pointed out, was the only thing that "Republicans, Democrats, right and left, white or colored, Catholic or Protestant" could agree upon. "It is common ground for the General Secretary of the Communist Party, the Chairman of Americans for Democratic Action, the President of the United States Chamber of Commerce, and the President of the National Association of Manufacturers."[59]

Modern architects and critics such as Blake and Mills thought they could teach people to be happier with fewer (but better) things. The paintings of Jackson Pollock and the films of Charles and Ray Eames advertised an abundance of energy, emotion, and imagination that was just as, or more, compelling than the visions of prosperity offered by supermarkets and department stores. Intellectuals like Galbraith and Potter wanted better education and public services instead of faster corporate growth. As the Eisenhower years came to an end Americans looked about them and asked, "After abundance, what?"[60] Was it necessarily true, asked Potter, that "a nation with two cars in every garage" was "better equipped to fight Communism than a nation with one?"[61] The 1960s would, of course, witness a reevaluation of consumerism when it became obvious that not only was the prosperity of the U.S. economy unequally distributed but the pursuit of affluence did little to resolve domestic racism, the plight of developing nations, or the war in Vietnam.

However, there were many more festivals of abundance in the 1960s, notably the Seattle World's Fair (1962), which featured the space needle; the 1964 New York World's Fair, nurtured by Gov. Rockefeller; and the 1967 world's fair in Montreal, Expo '67, where Buckminster Fuller and Jack Masey teamed up once again to create the U.S. Pavilion. Capitalism, however, owes allegiance to no particular nation. As the power of international and transnational corporations increased, the nationalism that was an inevitable component of world's fairs no longer appealed to the civic boosters, corporate tycoons, and CEOs, who traditionally funded such events. Advances in communications and distribution technology also killed the fairs. A permanent international trade center, for example, on the model set by the Chicago Merchandise Mart, now sits in a corner of the old exhibition grounds in Brussels. Merchants can view and purchase goods from around the world at the trade center on any given business day. Why hold another world's fair? The only justification for such an event would be for advertising purposes or the need to create goodwill, and there are much better ways of doing that today. The television studio inside the remodeled 1958 American Pavilion has provided Belgian companies with far more advertising than would any modern fair.

The United States sent pavilions to international exhibitions during the 1950s first as an attempt to rally domestic and international support for a united, prosperous Europe and then later as a way of advertising, consolidating, and exporting the American way of life. Some people wanted the United States to play a more aggressive role in international development and viewed the exhibitions as an opportunity to publicize their ideals, whereas others simply saw an opportunity to expand corporate holdings. The Eisenhower administration stifled activists who believed that tax money should be used to expand the success of the Marshall Plan and help Third World nations to join the growing international economy, but it supported industrialists who wanted to spread the gospel of free enterprise through the private sector. Regardless of the means, both liberal and conservative activists agreed upon the ends, believing that only a global capitalist economy could thwart Communist expansion and eventually cause the USSR to implode.

Communism, as practiced in the now-defunct USSR, was indeed a farce, but capitalism is also a messy affair and often just a way of disguising the same elemental lust for power and accumulation among its chief exponents as was communism for the Soviet hierarchy. The kitchen debate, like some of the other set pieces of political theater from the international exhibitions during the cold war, remains memorable not because of how Nixon and Khrushchev debated the relative merits of washing machines, but because of the ongoing debate over the usefulness of the society of abundance: Will a constantly expanding capitalist economy destroy the fragile, precapitalist, unwieldy planet that serves as its host? Do we all need two cars in our garage? Is economic scarcity always such a burden? Does the consumer economy really provide spiritual or psychological abundance? The kitchen debate was an entertaining moment in this lively twentieth-century drama and will remain memorable long into the next century, because although communism has failed, there is no indication that capitalism in its mature phase will provide the world with anything more than ecological tragedy and an unstable, vastly increased, largely impoverished human population.

Notes

Introduction

1. For an introduction to the cold war see Warren I. Cohen, vol. 4 of *The Cambridge History of American Foreign Relations*, ed. Warren I. Cohen (Cambridge: Cambridge University Press, 1993), pp. 2–57. Melvyn P. Leffler, *A Preponderance of Power: National Security, the Truman Administration, and the Cold War* (Stanford: Stanford University Press, 1992), pp. 100–40.

2. George L. Ridgeway, *Merchants of Peace: The History of the International Chamber of Commerce* (Boston: Little, Brown, 1959), p. 16.

3. Kim McQuaid, *Big Business and Presidential Power: From FDR to Reagan* (New York: William Morrow, 1982), p. 109.

4. Neil Harris, *Cultural Excursions: Marketing Appetites and Cultural Tastes In Modern America* (Chicago: University of Chicago Press, 1990), p. 61.

5. Robert W. Rydell, *World of Fairs: The Century-of-Progress Expositions* (Chicago: University of Chicago Press, 1993), pp. 15–58.

6. McQuaid, *Big Business and Presidential Power*, p. 115.

7. Robert Griffith, "The Selling of America: The Advertising Council and American Politics, 1942–1960," *Business History Review* 57 (Autumn 1983), p. 393.

8. McQuaid, *Big Business and Presidential Power*, p. 151.

9. James Sloan Allen, *The Romance of Commerce and Culture: Capitalism, Modernism, and the Chicago-Aspen Crusade for Cultural Reform* (Chicago: University of Chicago Press, 1983), p. 49.

10. Ibid., p. 167.

11. Ibid., p. 168.

12. Ibid. Christopher Lasch, "The Cultural Cold War: A Short History of the Congress for Cultural Freedom," in *Towards a New Past: Dissenting Essays in American History*, ed. Barton J. Bernstein (New York: Pantheon Books, 1968), pp. 322–59.

13. Blanche Wiesen Cook, *The Declassified Eisenhower: A Divided Legacy* (New York: Doubleday, 1981), p. 83.

14. Ibid., p. 84.

15. Allen, *The Romance of Commerce and Culture,* p. 237.

16. Cook, *The Declassified Eisenhower,* p. 94.

17. Ibid., p. 295.

18. Joe Alex Morris, *Nelson Rockefeller: A Biography* (New York: Harper Brothers, 1960), p. 292.

19. Cook, *The Declassified Eisenhower,* p. 297.

20. Morris, *Nelson Rockefeller,* p. 296.

21. Ibid., pp. 262–66.

22. John Lindeman, "Economic Representation Overseas," in *The Representation of the United States Abroad* (New York: Columbia University, American Assembly Graduate School of Business, 1956), pp. 47–48.

23. Cook, *The Declassified Eisenhower,* p. 128.

24. Rydell, *World of Fairs,* p. 208.

25. Lasch, "The Cultural Cold War," pp. 350–54.

26. Ibid., p. 344. The full quote is as follows: "This propaganda, in order to be successful, demands the cooperation of writers, teachers, and artists not as paid propagandists or state-censored time-servers but as 'free' intellectuals capable of policing their own jurisdictions and of enforcing acceptable standards of responsibility within the various intellectual professions."

27. Bert Collier, "Cite 12 Apostles of U.S. Way of Life," *Chicago Daily News,* June 6, 1958, p. 46.

28. Ninkovitch, *The Diplomacy of Ideas,* p. 170.

29. Griffith, "The Selling of America," p. 407.

30. Jane Fiske Mitarachi, "Design as a Political Force," *Industrial Design* 4 (February 1957): 37–55.

31. Department of Commerce, "What's OITF?" *Fair Facts* 2 (December 1960): 1.

32. Griffith, "The Selling of America," p. 405.

33. Clarence B. Randall, *The Communist Challenge to American Business* (Boston: Little, Brown, 1959), p. 121.

1 | The Chicago Fairs of 1950

1. F. Preston Forbes, "Trade Joins Forces," *Foreign Commerce Weekly,* November 20, 1950, pp. 3–5. See also Department of State, *Foreign Relations of the United States, 1952–1954,* vol. 2, pt. 2 (Washington, D.C.: Government Printing Office, 1984), pp. 1812–13.

2. "Joint Industry-Government Program for International Trade Fairs," *Foreign Commerce Weekly*, October 25, 1954, pp. 3–4, 9.

3. For an introduction to the Crusade for Freedom see Blanche Wiesen Cook, "First Comes the Lie: C. D. Jackson and Political Warfare," *Radical History Review* 31 (December 1984): 49–50.

4. Arthur Paul, "Department's New Office of International Trade," *Foreign Commerce Weekly*, March 9, 1946, p. 3.

5. Paul Wiers, "Importance of Importing," *Foreign Commerce Weekly*, January 5, 1946, pp. 3–4, 48.

6. "World Trade Promotion: Objective of New Office," *Foreign Commerce Weekly*, April 6, 1946, p. 13. See also Charles S. Maier, "The Politics of Productivity," in *The Cold War in Europe*, ed. Charles S. Maier (New York: Markus Wiener, 1991), pp. 191–94.

7. Department of State, *Foreign Relations of the United States*, vol. 2, pt. 2, pp. 1812–13.

8. Melvyn P. Leffler, *A Preponderance of Power: National Security, the Truman Administration, and the Cold War* (Stanford: Stanford University Press, 1992), p. ix.

9. Ibid., p. 3.

10. Charles A. Thomson and Walter H. C. Laves, *Cultural Relations and U.S. Foreign Policy* (Bloomington: Indiana University Press, 1963), p. 90.

11. Leffler, *A Preponderance of Power*, p. 178.

12. Thomson and Laves, *Cultural Relations*, p. 91.

13. Leffler, *A Preponderance of Power*, p. 178.

14. Paul G. Hoffman, *Peace Can Be Won* (New York: Doubleday, 1950). See also Alan R. Raucher, *Paul G. Hoffman, Architect of Foreign Aid* (Lexington: University Press of Kentucky, 1985), pp. 64–79.

15. Hoffman, *Peace Can Be Won*, p. 16.

16. Ibid., p. 33.

17. Philip H. Coombs, *The Fourth Dimension of Foreign Policy: Educational and Cultural Affairs* (New York: Harper and Row, 1964), pp. 32–33.

18. Hoffman, *Peace Can Be Won*, p. 53.

19. Ibid., p. 87.

20. Ibid., p. 124. European Productivity Agency of the Organization for European Economic Cooperation, *Industrial Design in the United States: Project No. 278* (Paris: European Productivity Agency of the Organization for European Economic Cooperation, 1959). See also Thomas J. McCormick, "America's Half Century: United States Foreign Policy in the Cold War," in Maier, *The Cold War in Europe*, pp. 32–36.

21. Hoffman, *Peace Can Be Won*, p. 140.

22. For a synopsis of the *Life* round-table discussions and the consensus-building efforts of public-spirited intellectuals in the 1950s, see Eric Sandeen,

Picturing an Exhibition: The Family of Man *and 1950s America* (Albuquerque: University of New Mexico Press, 1995), pp. 6–10. On the Advertising Council see Robert Griffith, "The Selling of America: The Advertising Council and American Politics, 1942–1960," *Business History Review* 57 (Autumn 1983).

23. Hoffman, *Peace Can Be Won,* p. 144.

24. Ibid., p. 177.

25. Arthur M. Schlesinger Jr., *The Vital Center: The Politics of Freedom* (Boston: Houghton Mifflin, 1949), p. 234.

26. Ibid., p. 244.

27. David Riesman, "The Nylon War," in *Abundance for What and Other Essays* (Garden City, N.Y.: Doubleday, 1964), p. 71. See also David Riesman, with Nathan Glazer and Reuel Denney, *The Lonely Crowd: A Study of the Changing American Character* (New Haven, Conn.: Yale University Press, 1950).

28. Allen, *The Romance of Commerce and Culture,* pp. 107–108.

29. Robert E. Herzstein, *Henry R. Luce: A Political Portrait of the Man Who Created the American Century* (New York: Charles Scribner's Sons, 1994), p. 83.

30. Ibid., p. 179.

31. "Truman Backs Plans for Fair in Chicago," *First United States International Trade Fair* (promotional newspaper), August 7–19, 1950, p. 1.

32. "Name: Dr. Kunstenaar—Director of Foreign Affairs for U.S. Fair," *First United States International Trade Fair,* August 7–19, 1950, p. 1.

33. "Chicago a Mammoth Buying Center and Still Growing Commercially and Industrially: City Is Dynamic Market, Transportation Center of the Nation," *First United States International Trade Fair,* August 7–19, 1950, p. 2.

34. "Baedeker to the Chicago Fair," *Modern Industry* 20 (July 1950): 64.

35. Martin H. Kennelly, "Mayor Offers City's Welcome to Fair Visitors," *First United States International Trade Fair Daily,* August 7, 1950, p. 1.

36. Adlai E. Stevenson, "Exposition Leads to Market Expansion, Says Stevenson," *First United States International Trade Fair Daily,* August 7, 1950, p. 6.

37. "Baedeker to the Chicago Fair," p. 64. See also "Chicago Trade Fair Poorly Planned and Promoted," *Modern Industry* 20 (July 1950): 79–81.

38. "Facts about the Chicago Fair of 1950," F38M2, p. 1, Chicago Historical Society. See also Neil Harris, *Cultural Excursions: Marketing Appetites and Cultural Tastes in Modern America* (Chicago: University of Chicago Press, 1990), pp. 56–81, 128–31.

39. *The Chicago Fair of 1950: Official Guide Book and Program for the Pageant: "Frontiers of Freedom"* (Chicago: Chicago Fair, 1950), p. 3.

40. Ibid., p. 15.

41. Ibid.

42. Ibid., p. 12.

43. On the importance of home ownership see Elaine Tyler May, *Homeward Bound: American Families in the Cold War Era* (New York: Basic Books, 1988), pp. 16–36.

44. "News from the Chicago Fair of 1950," press release 451, April 9, 1950, F38M2, c. 1950, p. 2, Chicago Historical Society.

45. *The Chicago Fair of 1950,* p. 8.

46. Ibid., p. 9.

47. "News from the Chicago Fair of 1950," press release, July 6, 1950, p. 1, Chicago Historical Society.

2 From Union Station to Yugoslavia: International Trade Fairs and the People's Capitalism Campaign

1. "U.S. Products Now on Display at Berlin," *Foreign Commerce Weekly,* September 29, 1952, p. 19.

2. "U.S. Exhibits for International Trade Fair Shipped to Turkey," *Foreign Commerce Weekly,* August 25, 1952, p. 20.

3. "Presenting the New Foreign Commerce Weekly," *Foreign Commerce Weekly,* July 7, 1952, p. 2.

4. Department of State, *Survey of East-West Trade in 1955* (Washington, D.C.: Government Printing Office, 1956), p. 15.

5. Robert Sheehan, "Clarence Randall: Statesman from Steel," *Fortune,* January 1954, pp. 120–22. See also Clarence B. Randall, *A Foreign Economic Policy for the United States* (Chicago: University of Chicago Press, 1954).

6. "Time to Crack the Foreign Markets," *Fortune,* March 1954, pp. 81–82.

7. "Commerce Department Announces Joint Industry-Government Program for International Trade Fairs," *Foreign Commerce Weekly,* October 25, 1954, p. 3.

8. Jerome Schoenfeld, "Inside Story of U.S. Exhibits Abroad," *Sales Manager* 75 (October 1, 1955): 36.

9. Fred Wittner, "What Should Trade Missions Mean to You?" *Industrial Marketing* 44 (July 1957): 47–48.

10. Ibid.

11. Robert T. Elson, *The World of Time Inc.: The Intimate History of a Publishing Enterprise, 1941–1960* (New York: Atheneum, 1973), pp. 257–58.

12. G. Lewis Schmidt, "An Interview with Earl Wilson, October 1988," oral history, pp. 94–95, USIA Historical Collections, Washington, D.C.

13. "America Triumphs at Bangkok Fair: Balloons, Bathing Suits, and Cinerama Help the U.S. Take a First Prize at Thailand's International Fair," *Life,* January 31, 1955, p. 46.

14. Schmidt, "An Interview with Earl J. Wilson," p. 96.

15. "U.S. Employs Design for Goodwill Abroad," *Industrial Design* 2 (August 1955): 72–75.

16. Joseph A. Barry, "Proudly *House Beautiful* Shows Europe How Americans Live," *House Beautiful,* July 1955, p. 86.

17. Ibid., p. 87.

18. Ibid., p. 88.

19. Ibid.

20. Ibid., p. 94.

21. "Your Overseas Advertising Can Help in Two Ways," *Advertising Age* 25 (January 4, 1954): 38.

22. "Opportunities for Overseas Public Relations: An Address by Theodore C. Streibert before the International Advertising Association and the Export Managers' Club of New York at the Hotel Statler, New York City," March 16, 1954, James M. Lambie Jr. Papers, box 15, folder "U.S. Information Agency," pp. 5–6, Dwight D. Eisenhower Library, Abilene, Kans. (hereafter, DDE).

23. "Opportunities for Overseas Public Relations," pp. 5–6.

24. "Some Examples of Overseas Projects," press clipping, Lambie Papers, box 15, folder "U.S. Information Agency," p. 1.

25. William L. Bird Jr. "Order, Efficiency, and Control: The Evolution of the Political Soft Advertisement, 1936–1956" (Ph.D. diss., Georgetown University, 1985), pp. 55–66. See also Robert Griffith, "The Selling of America: The Advertising Council and American Politics, 1942–1960," *Business History Review* 57 (Autumn 1983): 388–412.

26. Advertising Council, *The American Round Table: A Procedure to Develop a Restatement, in Modern Terms, of the Ideals, Beliefs, and Dynamics of the American Society, Part 1, Hotel Waldorf-Astoria, New York City, January 21, 1953* (New York: Advertising Council, 1953), pp. 1–2. Advertising Council, *The American Round Table: A Procedure to Develop a Restatement, in Modern Terms, of the Ideals, Beliefs, and Dynamics of the American Society, Part 2, Hotel Waldorf-Astoria, New York City, February 25, 1953* (New York: Advertising Council, 1953), pp. 1–2.

27. Theodore Repplier, "Some Thoughts about American Propaganda," memorandum, June 28, 1955, Lambie Papers, box 17, folder "U.S. Information Agency," p. 1.

28. Ibid., p. 2.

29. Ibid., p. 4.

30. Ibid., p. 5.

31. Ibid.

32. Ibid.

33. Theodore Repplier, "They Give Us a Good Name," *Saturday Evening Post*, September 24, 1955, pp. 46–47. Theodore Repplier, "Persuasion under the Cherry Blossoms," *Saturday Review*, October 1, 1955, pp. 13, 44–45. On how the USIA used "persuasion" to create a favorable climate of opinion, see Leo Bogart, *Premises for Propaganda: The United States Information Agency's Operating Assumptions in the Cold War* (New York: Free Press, 1976), pp. 20–26.

34. Abbott Washburn to Theodore Streibert, Area Directors, Media Staffs, "American Capitalism," memorandum, October 26, 1955, Lambie Papers, box 31, folder "USIA Correspondence, 1956," p. 2.

35. "People's Capitalism—Man's Newest Way of Life," press release, February 1956, Lambie Papers, box 31, folder "People's Capitalism, 1956," p. 3.

36. Ibid., p. 2.

37. "Statement by AFL-CIO, Opening of Exhibit on People's Capitalism," February 14, 1956, Lambie Papers, box 31, folder "People's Capitalism, 1956," p. 1.

38. I. F. Stone, *The Haunted Fifties: A Nonconformist History of Our Times: 1953–1963* (Boston: Little, Brown, 1963), p. 295.

39. "Statements by Theodore C. Streibert, Director, USIA, at the Opening Ceremonies of The People's Capitalism Exhibit," Lambie Papers, box 31, folder "People's Capitalism, 1956," p. 1.

40. "Analysis of Written Comments Received from Visitors to People's Capitalism Exhibit," Lambie Papers, box 1, folder "People's Capitalism, 1956," pp. 1–8. Some 25,000 people viewed the exhibit and 750 volunteered comments.

41. Jean White, "Changes Ike Suggested to Be Made In Exhibit," press clipping, Lambie Papers, box 31, folder "People's Capitalism, 1956," p. 1.

42. *Congressional Record*, 84th Cong., 2d sess., 1956, 102, pt. 6:8515–16.

43. "Eisenhower Likened to Lincoln," *Washington Post*, February 13, 1956, p. 25.

44. U.S. Lincoln Sesquicentennial Commission, *Abraham Lincoln Sesquicentennial, 1959–1960* (Washington, D.C.: Government Printing Office, 1960), pp. 100–25.

45. "USIA CA-2510: Policy Planning Paper Sent to All USIS Posts, Annex 13," May 23, 1956, Lambie Papers, box 31, folder "People's Capitalism (1)," p. 1.

46. Edgar Kemler, "People's Capitalism," *Nation*, February 25, 1956, p. 152.

47. Eugene W. Castle, *The Great Giveaway: The Realities of Foreign Aid* (Chicago: Henry Regnery, 1957), p. 72. George V. Allen, "What the U.S. Information Agency Program Cannot Do," in *Propaganda and the Cold War: A Princeton University Symposium*, ed. John Boardman Whitton (Washington, D.C.: Public Affairs Press, 1963; reprint, Westport, Conn.: Greenwood Press, 1984), pp. 60–61 (page citations are to the reprint edition).

48. Robert C. Hickok, "Monthly Report on People's Capitalism for October–November, 1957," Lambie Papers, box 38, folder "People's Capitalism, 1957," p. 1.

49. Hickok, "Monthly Report on People's Capitalism for September, 1957," Lambie Papers, box 38, folder "People's Capitalism, 1957," pp. 3, 7.

50. "Report of the People's Capitalism Committee, Cloud Club," May 15, 1956, Lambie Papers, box 31, folder "People's Capitalism, 1956 (2)," p. 1.

51. Ibid., p. 2.

52. Repplier to Lambie, January 28, 1957, Lambie Papers, box 38, folder "People's Capitalism, 1957."

53. David M. Potter, *People of Plenty: Economic Abundance and the American Character* (Chicago: University of Chicago Press, 1954).

54. Chester J. LaRoche, foreword to *The American Round Table: Discussions on People's Capitalism: An Evaluation of Its Contribution to Our Well-Being . . . An Exploration of Our Economic Ideas and Institutions and Their Relation to Our Political and Social Ideas and Institutions, and What They May Bring to Man's Fulfillment. At Yale University, New Haven, Connecticut, November 16 and 17, 1956*, by the Advertising Council, digest report by David M. Potter (New York: Advertising Council, 1957), p. 3.

55. Bert Collier, "12 Apostles of U.S. Way of Life," *Chicago Daily News*, June 6, 1956, p. 46.

56. Jane Fiske Mitarachi, "Design as a Political Force," *Industrial Design*, February 1957, pp. 37–55.

57. Ibid., p. 50.

58. Ibid., p. 51.

59. Ibid., p. 42.

60. Ibid., p. 54.

61. Castle, *The Great Giveaway*, p. 90.

62. "Poland Samples U.S. Goods," *Business Week*, June 22, 1957, pp. 134–36. Piotr S. Wandycz, *The United States and Poland* (Cambridge: Harvard University Press, 1980), pp. 354–55.

63. "Nylon Wonderland: U.S. Exhibit in Poland's International Trade

Fair," *Time,* June 1, 1957, pp. 31–32. "The U.S. Exhibit of Freedom, a Hit in Poland," *Life,* July 24, 1957, pp. 19–26.

64. Edgar Clark, "U.S. Builder's Model House Is Biggest Hit for 500,000 Polish Fair-Goers," *House and Home,* August 1957, p. 98.

65. "S.R.O. at the Poznań Fair," *New York Times Magazine,* June 23, 1957, p. 6.

66. Lansing P. Shield, "American-Style Supermarkets Win Warm Welcome Abroad," *Exchange* 19 (September 1958): 4.

67. "Supermarket Growth Abroad Helps U.S. Food Marketers," *Printer's Ink* 262 (June 17, 1958): 60–62.

68. John M. Morahan, "U.S. Supermarket for Zagreb," *New York Herald Tribune,* July 24, 1957, p. 3.

69. "U.S. Supermarket in Yugoslavia," *New York Times Magazine,* September 22, 1957, p. 12.

70. Potter, *People of Plenty,* p. 166.

71. Shield, "American-Style Supermarkets Win Warm Welcome Abroad," p. 4.

3 | Edward Durell Stone and the American Pavilion at the 1958 Brussels World's Fair

1. Howard S. Cullman, "The United States at the Brussels Universal and International Exhibition, 1958: A Report to the President of the United States from the United States Commissioner General Howard S. Cullman," May 30, 1959, file "Exhibitions: Brussels, 1958," pp. 1–4, USIA Historical Collections.

2. "Light, Strong, and Free: Bicycle Wheel on Columns Spans 300 feet to Engineer a Crystal and Gold Pavilion for United States at Brussels," *Architectural Record* 121 (February 1957): 10.

3. "Report of Visit to Brussels," Edward Durell Stone Papers, box 866/18, folder 7, p. 1, Special Collections, University of Arkansas Libraries, Fayetteville.

4. "Memorandum on the Design of the United States Pavilion, Brussels Exposition," n.d., Stone Papers, box 866/18, folder 10, p. 1.

5. Edward Durell Stone, *Evolution of an Architect* (New York: Horizon Press, 1952), pp. 138–45. Ernest E. Jacks, telephone conversation with author, October 28, 1992. Jacks was an associate in the Stone office during the 1950s and kindly pointed out to me many of the finer points of Stone's designs.

6. See "U.S. Architecture Abroad: Modern Design at Its Best Now

Represents This Country in Foreign Lands," *Architectural Forum* 98 (March 1953): 101–15. See also "Architecture to Represent America Abroad: Regional Expressions of American Architectural Thinking Are Sought for State Department Buildings," *Architectural Record* 117 (May 1955): 186–92.

7. "Report of Visit to Brussels," p. 3.

8. Ron Robin, *Enclaves of America: The Rhetoric of American Political Architecture Abroad, 1900–1965* (Princeton, N.J.: Princeton University Press, 1992), p. 139.

9. "Citizens and Architects," *Architectural Forum* 110 (January 1959): 19.

10. "U.S. Architecture Abroad," p. 102.

11. "Architecture to Represent America Abroad," p. 187.

12. Ibid.

13. Ibid., p. 188.

14. "U.S. Embassy for New Delhi," *Architectural Forum* 102 (June 1955): 115.

15. "Group to Push Art in Lines for Home," *New York Times*, April 6, 1940, p. 20.

16. See Robin, *Enclaves of America*, p. 150.

17. "A New Public Architecture," *Architectural Forum* 110 (January 1959): 88.

18. Ibid., p. 84.

19. "U.S. Building Abroad: In Doing Its Share of a $100 Billion Postwar Job, the Building Industry Has Become a World-Wide Ambassador," *Architectural Forum* 102 (January 1955): 99.

20. Ibid., p. 104.

21. "Berlin Congress Hall," *Architectural Record* 122 (December 1957): 145.

22. "U.S. Building Abroad," p. 104.

23. "The Congress Hall Debate: Symbolizing Free Speech, the U.S. Contribution to Berlin's International Building Exhibit Has Already Provoked Some," *Architectural Forum* 108 (January 1958): 117, 170.

24. Ibid., p. 171.

25. Stone, *Evolution of an Architect*, p. 44.

26. Peter Blake, "Modern Architecture: Its Many Faces," *Architectural Forum* 108 (March 1958): 80.

27. Peter Blake, "Architecture and the Individual," *Architectural Forum* 108 (June 1958): 113, 117.

28. Frank Lloyd Wright, *A Testament* (New York: Horizon Press, 1957), p. 203.

29. James Plaut, telephone conversation with author, November 2, 1992.

30. "Saarinen Challenges the Rectangle," *Architectural Forum* 98 (January 1953): 126.

31. "Ornament Rides Again," *Architectural Forum* 108 (April 1958): 85.

32. Henry Hope Reed Jr., "The Next Step beyond Modern," *Harper's*, May 1957, p. 42.

33. "Ornament Rides Again, p. 87.

34. Jacks to author, January 26, 1993.

35. "New Building Techniques," *Architectural Design* 27 (November 1957): 404.

36. "House of the Future," *Monsanto Magazine*, Summer 1957, p. 2.

37. "Edward Durell Stone," *Architectural Record* 122 (July 1957): 134. See also Landreth M. Harrison, "Brussels Exhibition, 1958: Talk with Stone, Architect," memorandum, September 17, 1956, RG 43, lot 59D 354, box 11, folder "Stone Contracts," p. 1, National Archives, College Park, Md. (hereafter, NA).

38. Richard Lippold to President Dwight D. Eisenhower, James Plaut, John Walker, May 19, 1957, Stone Papers, box 867/19, folder 19.

39. Edward Durrell Stone to James S. Plaut, memorandum, March 11, 1958, Stone Papers, box 869/21, folder 22, p. 1.

40. Kenneth Frizzell to Edward Durrell Stone, memorandum, March 19, 1957, Stone Papers, box 869/21, folder 22, p. 1.

41. Paige Donhauser, telephone conversation with author, October 28, 1992. Donhauser was one of Stone's associates and worked on the American Pavilion.

42. James S. Plaut to Edward Durrell Stone, memorandum, January 31, 1958, Stone Papers, box 869/21, folder 20, p. 1.

43. Ibid.

44. *Congressional Record*, 85th Cong., 2d sess., 1958, 104, pt. 3:2913.

45. Ernest O. Hauser, "We'll Go on Trial at the Fair," *Saturday Evening Post*, January 25, 1958, p. 76.

4 | Exhibit Planning: The American Pavilion at the 1958 Brussels World's Fair

1. Robert W. Rydell, *World of Fairs: The Century of Progress Expositions* (Chicago: University of Chicago Press, 1993), p. 194.

2. Jon Witcomb, "Busiest Millionaire," Katherine G. Howard Papers, 1917–74, box 25, folder "Correspondence, 1957 (1)," p. 1, DDE.

3. "The Theme of the Exhibition and Its Application in 1958," Commissariat General of the Government [Belgian] Information Service, Max Frank Millikan Papers, MC 188, box 4, folder "Cambridge Study Group for the Brussels Universal and International Exhibition, 1956–58," p. 1, Massachu-

setts Institute of Technology Institute Archives and Special Collections, Cambridge (hereafter, MIT).

4. "Theme Development," November 6, 1956, Millikan Papers, pp. 1–6.

5. "Whether Hard-Sell or Soft-Sell, Good Advertising Plays Up Self-Interest," *Printer's Ink* 262 (March 28, 1958): 46–47. The soft sell is defined here as a neighborly attitude: the seller offers friendship first, then the product is introduced.

6. Brussels Fair Theme Committee, "Interview with Nelson Rockefeller and Theodore Streibert," January 9, 1957, Millikan Papers, p. 1.

7. Brussels Fair Theme Committee, "Interview with Mrs. Eugenie Anderson, Former Ambassador to Denmark," c. 1957, Millikan Papers, p. 2.

8. Brussels Fair Theme Committee, "Interview with Walter W. Rostow," January 10, 1957, Millikan Papers, pp. 1–2.

9. Brussels Fair Theme Committee, "Brussels World Fair—Advice of National Leader (Victor Reuther, AFL-CIO) Regarding Theme and Program," January 16, 1957, Millikan Papers, p. 2.

10. Brussels Fair Theme Committee, "Interview with Arthur Schlesinger, Jr.," January 2, 1957, Millikan Papers, pp. 1–2.

11. Brussels Fair Theme Committee, "Interview with Lewis Galantiere, January 8, 1957, Millikan Papers, p. 1.

12. Brussels Fair Theme Committee, "Interview with C. D. Jackson, Vice President of Time Inc.," c. 1957, Millikan Papers, p. 2.

13. USIA to John Ely Burchard, telegram, December 31, 1956, Office of the Dean, AC 20, p. 1, MIT, (hereafter, AC 20).

14. Max F. Millikan and W. W. Rostow, *A Proposal: Key to an Effective Foreign Policy* (New York: Harper and Brothers, 1957), p. vii.

15. Ibid., p. viii.

16. W. W. Rostow, *Open Skies: Eisenhower's Proposal of July 21, 1955* (Austin: University of Texas, 1982), p. 66.

17. Ibid., p. 67.

18. Ibid., p. 75. See also Rockefeller Brothers Fund, Inc., *Prospect for America: The Rockefeller Panel Reports* (New York: Doubleday, 1958).

19. Rostow, *Open Skies*, p. 72.

20. W. W. Rostow, *The Stages of Economic Growth: A Non-Communist Manifesto* (Cambridge: Cambridge University Press, 1960), p. ix.

21. W. W. Rostow, *Eisenhower, Kennedy, and Foreign Aid* (Austin: University of Texas Press, 1985), p. 127.

22. Millikan and Rostow, *A Proposal*, p. 151.

23. "Life and Work Subcommittee Report Presented at the Final Meeting of the Cambridge Study Group for the Brussels Universal and Interna-

tional Exhibition, 1958," April 28, 1957, Ithiel de Sola Pool Papers, 87-54, box 5, folder "World's Fair, Brussels, 1957," pp. 4–7, MIT. (All citations of the de Sola Pool Papers refer to this box and folder.)

24. "Idealism in Action Subcommittee Report Presented at the Final Meeting of the Cambridge Study Group for the Brussels Universal and International Exhibition, 1958," April 28, 1957, de Sola Pool Papers, p. 9.

25. "Science and Technology Subcommittee Reports Presented at the Final Meeting of the Cambridge Study Group for the Brussels Universal and International Exhibition, 1958," April 28, 1957, de Sola Pool Papers, p. 9.

26. Rydell, *World of Fairs*, p. 200.

27. "Culture Subcommittee Report Presented at the Final Meeting of the Cambridge Study Group for the B.U.I.E, 1958," April 28, 1957, de Sola Pool Papers, p. 15.

28. Gerson H. Lush, "Summary Report, BRE," March 26, 1959, RG 43, box 20, p. 17, NA. See also Office of the U.S.Commissioner General, *This Is America: Official United States Guide Book, Brussels World's Fair, 1958* (New York: Manhattan Publishing, 1958). Rydell, *World of Fairs*, pp. 203–206.

29. Lush, "Summary Report, BRE," p. 19.

30. Ibid.

31. Ibid., p. 21.

32. Ibid., p. 32.

33. Thurston J. Davies, ed., "A Report on Certain Considerations Involved in the Operation of an Exhibits Pavilion at a World's Fair," January 1959, file "Exhibits and Fairs: Brussels, 1958," p. 36, USIA Historical Collections.

5 | Victor D'Amico's Creative Center

1. Victor D'Amico, *Experiments in Creative Teaching: A Progress Report on the Department of Education, 1937–1960, Museum of Modern Art* (New York: Museum of Modern Art, 1960), p. 34.

2. Ibid.

3. Department of Commerce, *Milan Samples Fair, 1957*, pamphlet, Victor D'Amico Papers, box 17, folder "Press Releases Other than MOMA," pp. 1–4, Special Collections, Milbank Memorial Library, Teachers College, Columbia University.

4. D'Amico, *Experiments in Creative Teaching*, p. 35. See also Lois Lord and Jane Cooper Bland, "Teaching Art at the Brussels Fair," *School Arts: The Art Education Magazine* 58 (April 1959): 7.

5. D'Amico, *Experiments in Creative Teaching,* p. 39.

6. Ibid.

7. Lois Lord, interview with the author, December 4, 1992.

8. Eugene Grigsby, "Teaching Children's Art at the Brussels World's Fair," *Pacific Arts Association Bulletin,* D'Amico Papers, box 17, folder "Press Releases, Newspapers and Publicity for MOMA, and for Art Carnivals in Spain, India, and Belgium," p. 8.

9. Lord and Bland, "Teaching Art at the Brussels Fair," p. 10.

10. Jane Cooper Bland, *Art of the Young Child: 3 to 5 Years* (New York: Museum of Modern Art, 1957), p. 7.

11. Ibid., p. 32.

12. "Brussels Asks the World to Its Fair," *Life,* March 1958, pp. 23–29.

13. Lord to D'Amico, May 9, 1958, D'Amico Papers, box 8, folder "Carnival in Brussels, 1958." (All citations of the correspondence between Lord and D'Amico in 1958 refer to this box and folder of the D'Amico Papers.)

14. Hughes Vehenne, "A Visit to the U.S. Pavilion: From the Potato to the Isotope," *Le Soir,* April 23, 1958, clipping, trans. Commissioner General's Office, RG 43, lot 59D 354, box 14, folder "PA 21—Press Clippings," p. 3, NA.

15. Sloan Wilson, "It's Time to Close Our Carnival: To Revitalize America's Educational Dream We Must Stop Kowtowing to the Mediocre," *Life,* March 24, 1958, pp. 36–37.

16. William H. Whyte Jr., *Is Anybody Listening? How and Why Business Fumbles When It Talks with Human Beings* (New York: Simon and Schuster, 1952), p. 239.

17. Ibid., p. 127.

18. Daniel Bell, *Work and Its Discontents: The Cult of Efficiency in America* (Boston: Beacon Press, 1956), p. 24.

19. John Kenneth Galbraith, *The Affluent Society* (Boston: Houghton Mifflin, 1958), p. 347.

20. Riesman, Glazer, and Denney, *The Lonely Crowd,* p. 115.

21. Ibid., p. 23.

22. Vance Packard, *The Hidden Persuaders* (New York: David McKay, 1957), pp. 41–43.

23. "European Editorial Reaction to the U.S. Exhibition," Audio-Visual Records, box "Katherine Howard 87-19-1," folder "Howard 87-19-240," p. 253, DDE.

24. John Patrick Diggins, "Philosopher in the Schoolroom," *Wilson Quarterly* 13 (Autumn 1989): 79.

25. Katherine C. Mayhew and Anna C. Edwards, *The Dewey School: The*

Laboratory School of the University of Chicago, 1896–1903 (New York: D. Appleton-Century, 1936), p. 5.

26. Ibid., p. 359.

27. Diggins, "Philosopher in the Schoolroom," p. 79.

28. Ibid., p. 80.

29. Victor D'Amico, *Creative Teaching in Art* (Scranton, Pa.: International Textbook, 1953), p. vii.

30. Victor D'Amico, Frances Wilson, and Moreen Mares, *Art for the Family* (New York: Museum of Modern Art, 1954), p. 8.

31. Joseph A. Barry, "Children and Art," *House Beautiful*, September 1955, p. 124.

32. Victor D'Amico, "Changing Concepts in Art Education," November 16, 1957, D'Amico Papers, box 8, folder "Mr. D'Amico, Articles 1954–59," p. 3.

33. Helen B. Schwartzman, "Transformations: The Anthropology of Children's Play" (New York: Plenum Press, 1978), p. 9.

34. Michael Zuckerman, "Dr. Spock: The Confidence Man," in *The Family in History*, ed. Charles E. Rosenberg (Philadelphia: University of Pennsylvania Press, 1975), p. 184.

35. Spock, *The Common Sense Book of Baby and Child Care* (New York: Duell, Sloan, and Pearce, 1946), pp. 326, 329.

36. Zuckerman, "Dr. Spock," p. 194.

37. Office of the U.S. Commissioner General, "Final Report: Children's Creative Center," D'Amico Papers, box 17, folder "Other Publicity," pp. 1–5. See also Lord and Bland, "Teaching Art at the Brussels Fair," p. 12.

38. D'Amico to Lord, May 12, 1958.

39. D'Amico, *Experiments in Creative Teaching*, p. 40.

40. Ibid., p. 51.

6 | Men's Gadgets, Women's Fashions, and the American Way of Life

1. Eileen Summers, "World's Fair Is Her Forte," *Washington Post and Times Herald*, June 26, 1957, sec. C, p. 2.

2. *Current Biography Yearbook, 1953*, s.v. "Howard, Katherine G(raham)," p. 280. See also Katherine G. Howard, *With My Shoes Off* (New York: Vantage Press, 1977), pp. 165–81, 255.

3. Eleanor Roosevelt and Lorena Hickok, *Ladies of Courage* (New York: G. P. Putnam's Sons, 1954), pp. 38–43, 290. See also Howard, *With My Shoes Off*, pp. 137–55.

4. Summers, "World's Fair Is Her Forte," p. 2.

5. Randolph Wieck, *Ignorance Abroad: American Educational and Cultural Foreign Policy and the Office of Assistant Secretary of State* (New York: Praeger, 1992), pp. 21–22.

6. Christian A. Herter, *The Mutual Security Program* (Washington, D.C.: Government Printing Office, 1957), pp. 1–4.

7. "Vogue's Eye View of Going to the Brussels World's Fair," *Vogue*, April 15, 1958, p. 60. John H. Davis, *The Bouviers: Portrait of an American Family* (New York: Farrar, Straus and Giroux, 1969), p. 298.

8. Katherine G. Howard, "A Proposed Women's Program for U.S. Participation, Brussels World's Fair," March 21, 1958, RG 43, lot 59D, box 12, folder "Exhibits Specific," p. 1, NA.

9. Ibid., p. 4.

10. *Current Biography Yearbook, 1955*, s.v. "Leopold, Alice Koller," p. 360.

11. Alice K. Leopold, "Homemaker—Money Maker," *National Parent-Teacher* 52 (May 1958): 8.

12. Alice K. Leopold, "The Challenge of Tomorrow: Womanpower," *Vital Speeches of the Day* 24 (May 15, 1958): 478.

13. *Current Biography Yearbook, 1955*, s.v. "Leopold, Alice Koller," p. 360.

14. Leopold, "The Challenge of Tomorrow," p. 40.

15. Leopold to Abbott Washburn (Deputy Director, USIA), November 15, 1957, RG 86, Women's Bureau, Office of the Director, General Correspondence (1957) (hereafter, WB), box 71, folder "Federal—USIA," NA.

16. "Women Aided by USIA in Foreign Countries," *Indianapolis Star*, September 21, 1958, p. 10.

17. Leopold to Howard, April 11, 1958, RG 86, WB, box 97, folder "Foreign, Brussels," NA.

18. Howard to Leopold, April 28, 1958, RG 86, WB, box 97, folder "Foreign, Brussels," NA.

19. Ibid.

20. Leopold to Howard, May 15, 1958, RG 86, WB, box 97, folder "Foreign, Belgium," NA.

21. Ibid.

22. "Theater Program of August 12, 1958," RG 43, lot 59D, box 20, folder "Women's Program," p. 2, NA.

23. Ibid.

24. Betsy Talbot Blackwell, "Memo from the Editor," *Mademoiselle*, October 1958, p. 40.

25. "Mme. Roosevelt exalté l'experience de Bruxelles," *Le Soir*, September 5, 1958, p. 7.

26. Wilhela Cushman, "There's Something about Them," *Ladies' Home Journal*, December 1957, pp. 48–51.

27. "Vogue's Eye View of Going to the Brussels Fair," p. 57.

28. Ibid., p. 63.

29. Ibid., p. 64.

30. Ibid., p. 63.

31. "Blue Jeans in Poznań," *New York Times*, June 12, 1958, p. 30.

32. "News from the Office of the U.S. Commissioner General, Press Release 68," RG 43, lot 59D, box 13, folder "PA 201, Press Releases," p. 1, NA.

33. *Our Country*, Soviet pamphlet, Zim Collection, box 1, file "Expo '58," p. 4, National Museum of American History, Smithsonian Institution, Washington, D.C.

34. Vera Aralova, "For Women," *Soviet Union* 97 (1958): 26–27.

35. Jane Fiske McCullough, *Industrial Design* 5 (July 1958): 45.

36. Marjorie J. Harlepp, "American Styles Impress Visitors at Brussels Fair, "*New York Times*, April 19, 1958, p. 12.

37. Bernard Rudofsky, *Are Clothes Modern? An Essay on Contemporary Apparel* (Chicago: Paul Theobald, 1947), p. 230.

38. Ibid., p. 232.

39. Ibid., p. 235.

40. Richard B. McCornack, "The Diplomatic Costume Revolution," *Foreign Service Journal* 35 (May 1958): 19, 20.

41. "The Sack and a Constitution," *Life*, August 11, 1958, p. 24.

42. "The Chemise Look Bears the Paris Stamp," *Sears, Roebuck and Co., Catalogue*, Spring/Summer 1958, pp. 2–3.

43. Georgina Howell, *In Vogue: 75 Years of Style* (London: Conde Nast Books, 1992), p. 138.

44. "Sack Shows Up All Over," *Life*, April 14, 1958, p. 95.

45. "How Long Will the Chemise Last?" *Consumer Reports*, August 1958, p. 435.

46. Ibid.

47. *Congressional Record, Appendix*, 85th Cong., 2d sess., 1958, 104:A7182.

48. Caroline Rennold Milbank, *New York Fashion: The Evolution of American Style* (New York: Harry N. Abrams, 1989), p. 181.

49. Joseph Carreiro, "Interim Report on Industrial Design Exhibit at Brussels," *Industrial Design* 4 (September 1957): 53.

50. Ibid., p. 53.

51. "One Power Package Does Many Jobs," *House Beautiful*, April 1958, p. 121.

52. Jones to Plaut, January 20, 1958, Howard Papers, box 26, folder "Office Memos."

53. Howard to Cullman, Plaut, and Davies, memorandum, October 31, 1957, Howard Papers, box 25, folder "Islands for Living," p. 3.

54. Marjorie J. Harlepp, "U.S. Revises Home Show at Fair Site," *New York Times,* May 6, 1958, p. 43.

55. Marjorie J. Harlepp, "Household Show at Brussels Fair to Be Revamped," *New York Times,* April 22, 1958, p. 37.

56. Bernard Rudofsky, *Behind the Picture Window* (New York: Oxford University Press, 1955), p. 119.

57. Arthur J. Pulos, *The American Design Adventure, 1940–75* (Cambridge: MIT Press, 1990), p. 258. See also Thomas Hine, *Populuxe* (New York: Alfred A. Knopf, 1987), p. 76.

58. Sigfried Giedion, *Mechanization Takes Command: A Contribution to Anonymous History* (New York: Oxford University Press, 1948), p. 501.

59. Howard to Cullman, Plaut, and Davies, October 31, 1957, p. 1.

60. Ibid., pp. 2–3.

61. Jane Fiske Mitarachi, "Is the Kitchen Disintegrating?" *Industrial Design* 1 (August 1954): 64–81.

62. Alice B. Toklas, "A Blessed Blender in the House," *House Beautiful,* July 1955, p. 84.

63. "The American Restaurant of the United States Pavilion, Brussels World's Fair, 1958, Souvenir Menu," Edward J. Orth Collection, file "Expo '58," box 1, p. 4, National Museum of American History, Smithsonian Institution, Washington, D.C.

64. "Bold Colors and Aboveboard Cuisine for the American Restaurant at Brussels," *Interiors* 117 (May 1958): 128–29. David J. Berge, "The Brass Rail Goes to Brussels," *Restaurant Management* 84 (August 1958): 46–47.

65. Berge, "The Brass Rail Goes to Brussels," p. 51.

66. Ibid., p. 48.

67. "U.S. Frozen Foods Feed the Fair: FF Popularity Sprouts in Brussels," *Quick Frozen Foods* 20 (July 1958): 112.

68. Leslie Lieber, "The H-dog: America's Super Weapon," *Reader's Digest,* July 1958, p. 149.

69. Lieber, "The H-dog: America's Super Weapon," p. 149.

70. "The Anatomy of a Hot Dog," *Consumer Reports,* September 1958): 472.

71. "Great Britain: Insulted Banger," *Time,* May 5, 1958, p. 22.

72. "The American Restaurant of the United States Pavilion at the Brussels World's Fair, 1958, Souvenir Menu," p. 7.

73. See John F. Love, *McDonald's: Behind the Arches* (New York: Bantam Books, 1986), p. 19.

74. Maurice Haurez, "La journée de la famille Goodwyn: une famille comme il y en a 23 Millions aux USA," *Le Peuple,* July 15, 1958, p. 8.

75. Cullman, *Ninety Dozen Glasses,* p. 136.

76. Ibid., p. 167.

77. Robert Letwin, "Success in Spite of Poor Exhibits," *Sales Management* 81 (September 19, 1958): 90.

7 | The *Unfinished Work* Exhibit: Walt Whitman Rostow, Leo Lionni, and the New Liberal Consensus

1. "Exhibits Invade Stock Exchange," *Sales Management* 78 (May 3, 1957): 36. See also "Million-Dollar Exhibit to Sell People's Capitalism," *Printer's Ink* 258 (March 8, 1957): 67.

2. "Spotlight on Brussels," *Exchange* 19 (May 1958): 1.

3. See "The Ever-Broadening Ownership of U.S. Business," *General Electric Review* 60 (September 1957): 19.

4. Office of the U.S. Commissioner General, *This Is America,* pp. 40–63.

5. Charles H. Clarke, "Address to Industrial Design Institute, Detroit," January 30, 1962, p. 10. I am grateful to Clarke for showing me a copy of the address.

6. Gunnar Myrdal, *An American Dilemma: The Negro Problem and Modern Democracy* (New York: Harper and Brothers, 1944), p. 1015.

7. Sandeen, *Picturing an Exhibition,* , p. 73.

8. Rostow, *Open Skies,* p. 71.

9. John K. Jessup, "Captions for Unfinished Work," Brussels World's Fair Collection, RG 43, lot 59D, box 12, folder "Exh. 414, Unfinished Business," p. 1, NA. See also Rydell, *World of Fairs,* pp. 208–209.

10. Jessup, "Captions for Unfinished Work," p. 2.

11. Ibid.

12. Ibid., p. 4.

13. Howard to Leverett, October 21, 1957, Howard Papers, box 25, folder "Confidential, Mrs. Howard," p. 2.

14. Judith P. Murphy, "*Fortune*'s Pavilion at Brussels: What It Is, How It Came About, and Why," RG 43, lot 59D,box 12, folder "Exh. 414: Unfinished Business," p. 7, NA.

15. Ibid., pp. 7–8.

16. C. P. Trussel, "Brussels Fair Aid Raised by Senate," *New York Times*, March 11, 1958, p. 1.

17. Talmadge to Dulles, March 26, 1958, RG 43, lot 59D, box 12, folder "Exh. 414: Unfinished Business," NA.

18. Ibid., p. 2.

19. Morris to Dulles, March 28, 1958, RG 43, lot 59D, box 12, folder "Exh. 414: Unfinished Business," NA.

20. Rivers to Gerson H. Lush, April 25, 1958, RG 43, lot 59D, box 12, folder "Exh. 414: Unfinished Business," NA.

21. Robert E. Herzstein, *Henry R. Luce: A Political Portrait of the Man Who Created the American Century* (New York: Charles Scribner's Sons, 1994), p. 90.

22. Irene Corbally Kuhn, "The Way Things Are," press clipping, April 1958, RG 43, lot 59D, box 12, folder "Exh. 414: Unfinished Business," p. 1, NA.

23. Howard to Cullman, memorandum, May 30, 1958, Howard Papers, box 25, folder "Confidential Mrs. Howard," p. 1.

24. Wilkinson to Andy (Andrew Berding, Assistant Secretary of State for Public Affairs), April 28, 1958, RG 43, lot 59D, box 15, folder Exh. 414: Unfinished Business," NA.

25. Ibid.

26. Ibid.

27. Sandeen, *Picturing an Exhibition*, pp. 47–48.

28. Lush to Thurston J. Davies, May 7, 1958, RG 43, lot 59D, box 12, folder "Exh. 414: Unfinished Business," NA.

29. "Les USA exposent aussi leurs soucis: Le problème noir, les taudis, la nature . . . trois problèmes qui préoccupent les américains," *Le Peuple*, May 9, 1958, p. 2 (trans. by the author).

30. See *Philadelphia Story*, film, 18 min., RG 59, no. 205, NA Motion Picture, Sound, and Video Branch.

31. "Les USA exposent aussi leurs soucis," p. 2.

32. Ibid.

33. "Un royaume s'est ouvert," *Le Soir*, April 17, 1958, p. 11 (trans. by the author).

34. "Une demi-heure sous les tropiques: Au Congorama, un cerveau électronique ressuscite toute l'épopée coloniale avec films, bruits, musique et cartes animées," *Le Peuple*, May 8, 1958, p. 2 (trans. by the author).

35. Herter to Cullman, May 30, 1958, RG 43, lot 59D, box 12, folder "Exh. 414: Unfinished Business," NA.

36. Howard to Cullman, May 30, 1958, Howard Papers, box 25, folder "Confidential, Mrs. Howard."

37. "Unfinished Work," *Ebony,* July 1958, p. 102. See also "Brussels World's Fair: Negro Guides Help Sell Democracy at Huge Exhibition," *Ebony,* July 1958, pp. 50–51.

38. "News Conference with James C. Hagerty and George V. Allen," June 24, 1958, RG 43, lot 59D, box 6, folder "News Conferences," pp. 1–5, NA.

39. "Conversation with Mr. James Plaut," memorandum, July 10, 1958, Howard Papers, box 25, folder "Confidential, Mrs. Howard," p. 1.

40. Katherine G. Howard, "To U.S. Pavilion Guides," memorandum, July 21, 1958, Howard Papers, box 26, folder "Office Memos," p. 1.

41. *Congressional Record,* 85th Cong., 2d sess., 1958, 104, pt. 15:18879.

42. Maurice Haurez, "Une épine dans le talon des USA: Le problème noir . . . qui es d'abord un problème blanc," *Le Peuple,* July 19, 1958, p. 8.

43. See Cohen, *America in the Age of Soviet Power,* p. 114.

44. "The Image of America," *Fortune,* August 1958, p. 64.

45. Pierre Ryckmans, "Belgian 'Colonialism' and the United Nations," in *Belgian Congo-American Survey, 1956–57,* ed. Jan-Albert Goris (New York: Belgian Chamber of Commerce, 1957), p. 21.

46. "News of the Congo: U.S. Bankers Lend $15,000,000 to Improve Housing, Utilities," *Belgian Trade Review* 13 (May 1958): 30–31.

47. Commissariat Général du Gouvernment près l'Exposition Universelle et Internationale de Bruxelles, ed., *Les participations étrangères et belges* (Brussels: Etablissements Généraux l'Imprimerie, 1958), pp. 235–54. See also Robert W. Rydell, "Brussels 1958," in *The Historical Dictionary of World's Fairs and Expositions, 1851–1988,* ed. John E. Findling (New York: Harper and Row, 1963), p. 61. The colonial show at Brussels included nineteen acres of tropical gardens and seven pavilions.

48. William Ugeux, "The Belgian Congo, Ruanda-Urundi and the European Common Market," in *The Belgian-American Survey, 1957–58: A Publication Devoted to the Promotion of Trade Relations between Belgium and the U.S.A.* (New York: Belgian Chamber of Commerce in the U.S.A., 1958), pp. 78–81.

49. "Brussels World's Fair: Negro Guides Help Sell Democracy at Huge Exhibition," pp. 50–51.

50. Richard C. Sullivan, telephone conversation with author, August 27, 1993. Sullivan was the assistant to the executive director in the Cullman office at the Brussels World's Fair. See also Rydell, "Brussels 1958," p. 208.

51. Lawrence H. Suid, ed., *Film and Propaganda in America: A Documentary History,* vol. 4 (New York: Greenwood Press, 1993), p. 220.

52. Francis Koval, "Brussels' Film Festival Wasn't Helped by Brussels World's Fair," *Films in Review* 9 (August–September 1958): 353–56.

53. Terry Comito, trans., "Interview with Orson Welles [by André Bazin,

with Charles Bitsch and Jean Domarchi]," in *Touch of Evil: Orson Welles, Director,* ed. Terry Comito (New Brunswick, N.J.: Rutgers University Press, 1985), p. 206.

54. John Stubbs, "The Evolution of Orson Welles's *Touch of Evil* from Novel to Film," in Comito, *Touch of Evil: Orson Welles, Director,* p. 183.

55. "Indian Givers," *New York Times,* July 20, 1958, p. 2.

56. "Le Wild West Show and Rodeo," *Le Soir,* June 20, 1958, p. 7.

57. Joe Hyams, "U.S. Wild West Show Heading for Brussels," *New York Herald Tribune,* May 8, 1958, sec. 1, p. 1.

58. *Congressional Record—Appendix,* 85th Cong., 2d sess., 1958, 104: A6944.

59. Ibid.

60. Ibid.

61. *Scrapbook,* Howard Papers, Audio Visual Records, box 87-19-1, folder 87-19-189, p. 216.

62. Cullman, "The United States at the Brussels Universal and International Exhibition," p. 14.

63. David Elmblidge, ed., *Eleanor Roosevelt's My Day,* vol. 3 (New York: Pharos Books, 1991), p. 181.

64. See Arthur M. Schlesinger Jr., *The Vital Center: The Politics of Freedom* (Boston: Houghton Mifflin, 1962), p. xv.

8 | Sputniks and Splitniks: Material Abundance Goes to War

1. "American Sputnik," *Time,* April 28, 1958, p. 57.

2. Harold C. McClellan, *A Review of the American National Exhibition in Moscow: July 25–September 4, 1959,* Central Files, Official Files 139-0-5, box 722, folder "Moscow Trade Fair (5)," p. 1, DDE.

3. McClellan, *A Review of the American National Exhibition in Moscow,* p. 6.

4. "American National Exhibition in Moscow," *Industrial Design* 6 (April 1959): 55.

5. McClellan, *A Review of the American National Exhibition in Moscow,* p. 19.

6. A. E. Hotchner, "Mr. Mac Goes to Moscow," *This Week,* July 19, 1959, p. 5.

7. Jonathan Aitken, *Nixon: A Life* (Washington, D.C.: Regnery, 1993), p. 262.

8. McClellan, *A Review of the American National Exhibition in Moscow,* pp. 23–24.

9. "USSR Exhibition: New York 1959," souvenir program, USIA Historical Collections, pp. 1–15.

10. Karal Ann Marling, *As Seen on TV: The Visual Culture of Everyday Life in the 1950s* (Cambridge: Harvard University Press, 1994), pp. 258–59.

11. Walter LaFeber, *America, Russia, and the Cold War, 1945–1984* (New York: Alfred A. Knopf, 1985), p. 195.

12. Michael S. Kramer and Sam Roberts, *I Never Wanted to Be Vice-President of Anything: An Investigative Biography of Nelson Rockefeller* (New York: Basic Books, 1976), pp. 219–20.

13. "Modern Living," *Life,* August 10, 1959, p. 51.

14. Stephen J. Whitfield, *The Culture of the Cold War* (Baltimore: Johns Hopkins University Press, 1991), p. 74.

15. "Soviet Women Delighted by Fair's Beauty Salon," *New York Times,* July 27, 1959, p. 28.

16. Ibid.

17. Cortney to Eisenhower, August 1, 1959, Central Files, Official Files 139-B-5, box 722, folder "Moscow Trade Fair (2)," DDE.

18. "U.S. Fashion Show Baffles Russians," *New York Times,* July 27, 1959, p. 28. See also "A Barnstorming Masterpiece: The Vice President in Russia," *Life,* August 10, 1959, p. 28.

19. Sandeen, *Picturing an Exhibition,* p. 131.

20. Eleanor Graves, "Propaganda Goof over U.S. Fashions," *Life,* July 27, 1959, p. 71.

21. Tobia Frankel, "Russians Swarm through U.S. Fair," *New York Times,* July 26, 1959, sec. L, p. 28.

22. Ibid.

23. "Lady Packing for a Trip," *Newsweek,* July 27, 1959, p. 42.

24. "A Barnstorming Masterpiece," pp. 18–19.

25. Elaine Tyler May, *Homeward Bound: American Families in the Cold War* (New York: Basic Books, 1988), pp. 18–19.

26. "What Nixon Learned in Russia," *U.S. News and World Report,* August 10, 1959, p. 47.

27. Clementine Paddleford, "They're Showing Russia How America Eats," *This Week,* July 19, 1959, p. 24.

28. Richard M. Nixon, *Six Crises* (New York: Doubleday, 1962), p. 245.

29. Mark Frankland, *Khrushchev* (New York: Stein and Day, 1967), p. 149.

30. Tom Wicker, *Richard Nixon and the American Dream* (New York: Random House, 1991), p. 218.

31. Nixon, *Six Crises,* pp. 249–50.

32. "The Two Worlds: A Day-Long Debate," *New York Times,* July 25, 1959, p. 1.

33. Ibid.

34. James Reston, "A Debate of Politicians," *New York Times*, July 25, 1959, p. 3.

35. Wicker, *Nixon and the American Dream*, p. 219. Peter Blake, *No Place Like Utopia: Modern Architecture and the Company We Kept* (New York: Alfred A. Knopf, 1993), p. 244. May, *Homeward Bound*, p. 112. Sandeen, *Picturing an Exhibition*, p. 142.

36. "The Two Worlds," pp. 1, 3.

37. Ibid., p. 3.

38. Galbraith, *The Affluent Society*, p. 252.

39. Calvin Tomkins, "Architecture: Umbrella Man," *Newsweek*, July 13, 1959, p. 84.

40. "American National Exhibition in Moscow," p. 53.

41. Ibid.

42. Sandeen, *Picturing an Exhibition*, p. 134. See also John Neuhart, Marilyn Neuhart, and Ray Eames, *Eames Design* (New York: Harry N. Abrams, 1989), pp. 223–41.

43. Sandeen, *Picturing an Exhibition*, p. 136.

44. Blake, *No Place Like Utopia*, p. 242.

45. "Joint Meeting, Arts Subcommittee, Advisory Committee on Cultural Information, U.S. Information Agency and Subcommittee on USSR Exhibition Advisory Committee on the Arts, Department of State, Feb. 4, 1959," Central Files, Official Files 139-B-5, box 722, folder "Moscow Trade Fair (2)," DDE.

46. Peter Kihss, "Kent Urges Show of Russians' Art," *New York Times*, October 17, 1958, sec. L, p. 14.

47. Ibid.

48. William Benton, *This Is the Challenge* (New York: Associated College Presses, 1958), p. 61.

49. Harry L. Colman, "An American Action Painter Invades Moscow," *Artnews* 57 (December 1958): 57.

50. Ibid.

51. Marling, *As Seen on TV*, p. 270.

52. Wicker, *Nixon and the American Dream*, p. 220.

53. Galbraith, *The Affluent Society*, pp. 175–176. Rostow, *Eisenhower, Kennedy, and Foreign Aid*, p. xiii.

54. Galbraith, *The Affluent Society*, p. 354. See also Potter, *People of Plenty*, pp. 168–75.

55. Galbraith, *The Affluent Society*, p. 13.

56. Rockefeller Brothers Fund, *Prospect for America: The Rockefeller Panel*

Reports (New York: Doubleday, 1958). The panel reports express the views of a radical coalition within the Republican party, led primarily by Nelson Rockefeller but influenced by more than one hundred other advisers, including Henry Luce, Henry A. Kissinger, and Edward Teller. See also John F. Kennedy, *The Strategy of Peace,* ed. Alan Nevins (New York: Harper, 1960), pp. 33–54. Kennedy proposed that the "missile gap" and the "economic gap" were the two central issues of the 1960 campaign.

57. C. Wright Mills, "Man in the Middle: The Designer," in *Power, Politics, and People,* ed. Irving Louis Horowitz (New York: Oxford University Press, 1963), p. 385.

58. Ibid., p. 379.

59. Galbraith, *The Affluent Society,* p. 122.

60. Eric Larrabee, "After Abundance, What?" *Horizon,* July 1960, pp. 65–72.

61. Daniel Horowitz, "A Southerner Considers Affluence in the Cold War: David Potter and *The People of Plenty,*" 1995, p. 54. My thanks to Daniel Horowitz, of Smith College, for letting me read this unpublished manuscript.

Index